IMBIBE!

From Absinthe Cocktail to Whiskey Smash,
a Salute in Stories and Drinks to "Professor"
Jerry Thomas, Pioneer of the American Bar

DAVID WONDRICH

A PERIGEE BOOK

A PERIGEE BOOK
Published by the Penguin Group
Penguin Group (USA) Inc.
375 Hudson Street, New York, New York 10014, USA
Penguin Group (Canada), 90 Eglinton Avenue East, Suite 700, Toronto, Ontario M4P 2Y3, Canada (a division of Pearson Penguin Canada Inc.) • Penguin Books Ltd., 80 Strand, London WC2R 0RL, England • Penguin Group Ireland, 25 St. Stephen's Green, Dublin 2, Ireland (a division of Penguin Books Ltd.) • Penguin Group (Australia), 250 Camberwell Road, Camberwell, Victoria 3124, Australia (a division of Pearson Australia Group Pty. Ltd.) • Penguin Books India Pvt. Ltd., 11 Community Centre, Panchsheel Park, New Delhi—110 017, India • Penguin Group (NZ), 67 Apollo Drive, Rosedale, North Shore 0632, New Zealand (a division of Pearson New Zealand Ltd.) • Penguin Books (South Africa) (Pty.) Ltd., 24 Sturdee Avenue, Rosebank, Johannesburg 2196, South Africa

Penguin Books Ltd., Registered Offices: 80 Strand, London WC2R 0RL, England

While the author has made every effort to provide accurate telephone numbers and Internet addresses at the time of publication, neither the publisher nor the author assumes any responsibility for errors, or for changes that occur after publication. Further, the publisher does not have any control over and does not assume any responsibility for author or third-party websites or their content.

Parts of this book have previously appeared, in greatly altered form, in *Drinks*; in Slow Food USA's newsletter, *The Snail*; and on Esquire.com.

First edition: November 2007

Library of Congress Cataloging-in-Publication Data

Wondrich, David.
    Imbibe! : from absinthe cocktail to whiskey smash, a salute in stories and drinks to "Professor" Jerry Thomas, pioneer of the American bar / David Wondrich. — 1st ed.
        p.   cm.
    Includes bibliographical references and index.
    ISBN 978-0-399-53287-0
    1. Cocktails.   2. Drinking customs.   3. Thomas, Jerry, 1830–1885.   I. Title.
    TX951.W5663   2007
    641.8'74—dc22   2007027096

PRINTED IN THE UNITED STATES OF AMERICA

10   9   8   7   6   5   4   3   2

PUBLISHER'S NOTE: The recipes contained in this book are to be followed exactly as written. The publisher is not responsible for your specific health or allergy needs that may require medical supervision. The publisher is not responsible for any adverse reactions to the recipes contained in this book.

Most Perigee books are available at special quantity discounts for bulk purchases for sales promotions, premiums, fund-raising, or educational use. Special books, or book excerpts, can also be created to fit specific needs. For details, write: Special Markets, Penguin Group (USA) Inc., 375 Hudson Street, New York, New York 10014.

FOR MARINA

CONTENTS

C H A P T E R   1

"PROFESSOR" JERRY THOMAS: JUPITER OLYMPUS OF THE BAR

C H A P T E R   2

HOW TO MIX DRINKS, OR WHAT WOULD JERRY THOMAS DO?

CHAPTER 3

PUNCHES

CHAPTER 4

THE CHILDREN OF PUNCH: COLLINSES, FIZZES, DAISIES, SOURS, COOLERS, AND COBBLERS

CHAPTER 5

A HANDFUL OF EGG DRINKS

TODDIES, SLINGS, JULEPS, AND SUCH

COCKTAILS AND CRUSTAS

CHAPTER 8

CHANNELING THE PROFESSOR—NEW DRINKS
FROM SIXTEEN OF THE TOP MIXOLOGISTS
OF OUR TIME

CHAPTER 9

BITTERS AND SYRUPS

FOREWORD

Back in 1985, when the legendary New York restaurateur Joe Baum asked me to create a classic bar for him at the fine dining restaurant Aurora, he sent me on a search for a book that would explain what he meant by a classic bar: *How to Mix Drinks, or The Bon Vivant's Companion* by Jerry Thomas. After my initial unsuccessful attempts searching bookstores and without the Internet for quick reference, I finally discovered that Joe had neglected to mention that the book was written in 1862 and had been out of print since the Herbert Asbury edition was published in 1928. Eventually I got my hands on a copy of the later edition and started down a road that changed my thinking about bars and cocktails, and brought me to the Rainbow Room—a road that led to a revival of interest in real drinks made in a culinary style with real ingredients following original recipes, which continues to this day.

The bigger-than-life characters found in Jerry Thomas's world actually seemed familiar to me, given my deep working knowledge of numerous New York City watering holes in the late 1960s—joints where the collection of con men, politicians, sporting types, and jazz-loving foreigners was as colorful as the crowd in any Bowery music hall of the mid-nineteenth century. The bartenders at Jimmy Ryan's Club, where I practically lived back in those days, would have been right at home in one of Thomas's saloons; they could determine as you approached the bar whether you had two nickels to rub together and give you the bum's rush before you could open your mouth to order.

Colorful characters aside, what the barrel-chested and bejeweled Jerry Thomas embodied that has been lacking in the post-Prohibition bars in this country is an insatiable curiosity for the strange-sounding concoctions collected during extensive travels and adapted to his personal style—concoctions, I soon discovered, that were crafted from ingredients half of which no longer existed. But that left me undeterred in my quest to make Joe Baum's vision of a classic bar a reality.

Jerry Thomas's book taught me how to craft drinks without the aid of commercial mixers; remember, all we knew as journeymen bartenders in those years was what we had learned from other untrained bartenders who came before us. That usually comprised a shot of spirits and a good portion of sour mix or daiquiri mix and a shake. The artificial foaming agent in the mix made the drink look great; as for flavor, those who wanted it drank straight spirits. Bloody Marys were one of the few drinks we made from scratch, and not many knew how to prepare a decent Bloody Mary mix with the right balance between the hot pepper and the sweet tomato juice.

Thomas talked about sugar syrups and how to make and then use them with fresh citrus juices. He was not generous with descriptions on technique and how to assemble these drinks, but there were enough hints here and there to fill in the blanks. Those hints, and lots of trial and error, led to my first all-fresh-ingredient cocktail menu at a time when cocktail menus were as rare as hens' teeth. When I moved to the Rainbow Room with my newfound skills and the benefit of Joe's celebrity and public relations machine behind me, the idea of old-as-new-again became the cutting edge; classics revived made quite the splash in the trade and eventually in the general market.

Back then I could have used a book like David Wondrich's as a teaching tool, to take the bartenders through the logical steps of punch to sling to cocktail, allowing them to experience firsthand how the whole culture of the cocktail evolved; even tasting them through the steps.

Wondrich has provided us with the most important and authoritative book on the American cocktail to date. He pitches and swaggers his way through the eighteenth, nineteenth, and twentieth centuries, from poems to periodicals, from songs to books, becoming more intoxicated with each new find. As the pieces accumulate like an enormous jigsaw puzzle, the picture begins to make more and more sense.

Against the backdrop of Western civilization, the cocktail, like the whole American experiment, is in its infancy. But the nature of this bibulous tradition—born, as Wondrich so deftly demonstrates, in the *sporting life*—is such that even though all the drinks, stories, and recipes are less than 250 years old, there is very little left in the way of documentation.

Undeterred, Wondrich has uncovered a remarkable trail left like broken twigs on a forest path that lead the reader through the gaming rooms, saloons, gentlemen's clubs, and coffeehouses—to reveal the real story of the evolution of the American cocktail.

—Dale DeGroff, founder,
The Museum of the American Cocktail

INTRODUCTION

My introduction to Jerry Thomas wasn't nearly as dramatic as Dale's—characteristically, I read about him in a book, one or another of the various histories of American lowlife Herbert Asbury published in the 1920s and '30s. It was the early 1990s, and I was in graduate school, keeping my head down and anticipating a somewhat dull but (I hoped) pleasant life in academia. Asbury's raffish accounts of old New York, San Francisco, Chicago, and New Orleans—I read them all—and their various thugs, crooks, players, and sports were a lot more colorful than the Latin scientific poems I was studying. But work is work, so I reluctantly shelved Gallus Mag and Bill the Butcher, Bathhouse John, Belle Cora, and the bartender known as "the Professor" (who seemed to be in every book) and got back to my Manilius and Martianus Capella.

But funny things happen sometimes. Toward the end of 1999, I found myself working as an assistant professor of English at a Catholic college on Staten Island, and my place in academia fully as dull, but not nearly so pleasant, as I had pictured it. So when I got a phone call from my friend Josh Mack, then a honcho in Hearst's New Media division, asking if I might be interested in a little side project, I was pretty receptive. And when I found out that the project involved adapting the cocktail section from one of *Esquire*'s old entertaining guides for the Web, I was flat-out excited. As Josh knew, I had been writing a few little pieces on music for the *Village Voice* as a way of blowing off steam, and I liked to mix the occasional cocktail. Since this combined writing and mixing . . . Sure.

As luck would have it, *Esquire* liked the historical essays I had fitted a few of the drinks out with enough to hire me to do them for all the drinks. A new one went up on the site each week. Suddenly, I was a mixographer. Being a good academic, my first response was that I was going to need a lot more books. Well, maybe that was my second response, after kissing my wife, Karen, and mixing us up a couple of celebratory Martinis (Beefeater and Noilly Prat, seven to one, olives, as I recall). In any case, the handful of vintage drink books Karen and I had accumulated over the years—Charles H. Baker, Jr., Patrick Gavin Duffy, Harry Craddock, a couple more— were going to need some serious reinforcements. The first book I bought? "Professor" Jerry Thomas's, in the same 1928 Herbert Asbury edition Dale found (imagine my disappointment when I learned that Thomas's title was awarded not by any academic institution but by the wags of the day, who gave it to anyone who could do anything requiring superior technical knowledge, be it tickling out syncopated melodies on the piano, dealing undetectably from the bottom of the deck, or constructing a perfect Sherry Cobbler).

Having read *Straight Up or On the Rocks*, William Grimes's groundbreaking cocktail history, I knew that Thomas's book was the first of its kind, and I was a firm believer in starting at the beginning.

Over the next three years, in the service of *Esquire* and soon various other publications, I mixed literally thousands of drinks of all classes and styles. But while I often used Jerry Thomas's book as a sort of historical backstop, a place to trace a particular recipe back to, I rarely mixed any actual drinks from it. At first glance, the book's telegraphically phrased recipes seemed either uninspiringly simple or dauntingly complex; deeply weird or old hat.

But again, things happen. At the end of 2002, now an exprofessor and happy to be so, I was introduced to a couple of people from the Slow Food movement at a friend's birthday party. Since said party happened to be in a bar, I did what I do best in bars and began holding forth. Slow Food is all about preserving traditional foodways. Well, what's more traditional and American than the fine art of mixing drinks? Hell, we invented it, back in Jerry Thomas's days. In fact, somebody ought to hold a tribute to Ol' Jerry, right here in New York where he worked; the grand memorial service he never had. And so on.

The last thing I expected was that they'd take me seriously—that's not what bar talk is for. But since Shawn Kelley, Ana Jovancicevic, and Allen Katz, the people I was shooting my mouth off to, all happen to be organized, energetic, and competent, the next thing I knew the Professor was getting his tribute. And it wasn't just a couple of folks meeting up at a bar somewhere. It was at the Oak Room of the Plaza Hotel, no less, with seven of America's top mixologists and me, all making the Professor's drinks—Blue Blazers, Brandy Crustas, Tom & Jerries, a bunch more—and the great Terry Waldo playing ragtime on the piano. There was even the traditional free lunch, a spread of oysters and country ham and whatnot that wouldn't have been at all out of place when the Oak Room was the hotel's men's bar, back in the sepiatone days before Prohibition. There was even a little souvenir booklet with all the recipes we made, lovingly designed by Ted "Dr. Cocktail" Haigh, who does that sort of thing for a living. For it, I decided to write a little bio of the Professor, which meant doing a little research. You hold in your hands what happens when I start to do a little research.

Originally, this book was going to be an update of Asbury's edition—a new, more accurate biographical chapter and then all the recipes, with various historical and mixological notes attached. But the more I worked on it, and the more I learned about Thomas and the origins of his book, the more five initials kept popping up in my head. *W.W.J.T.D.: What Would Jerry Thomas Do?* Would he be content to trudge along like some electronic-age Bartleby, narrowly copying another's work and keeping his thoughts on the matter mostly to himself? Or would he have gone for it, using the occasion as an excuse to tell everything he knew? The answer was obvious. I could be true to Jerry Thomas's book, or true to Jerry Thomas. I chose the latter.

On the one hand, this means that you won't find every recipe from Jerry Thomas's book here. In fact, of the largest class of drinks in his book, the almost threescore recipes for bowls of Punch, you'll find only two. A bowl of Punch is a wonderful, even sublime thing, but it was already obsolete as a bar drink by the time his book was published, and the vast majority of the recipes were old English ones foisted on him by his publisher. Rather than swell the book by the hundred-odd pages it would take to explain them, I've reserved them for another book. I've also cut back drastically on egg drinks and the things that are made by carefully layering liqueurs in tiny glasses. On the other hand, I've used the space thus cleared to supplement the Professor's recipes with a goodly number of others from his contemporaries and immediate successors—popular, even important drinks that, I like to think, he would have included had he lived to do another edition of his book. (In all this, anyway, I'm doing no more than what he and his original publisher did: In 1876, they reprinted his book with a supplement containing new drinks, and in 1887, two years after his death, they put out a thorough update and revision, done by some unsung but expert bartender whose name has been lost to history.)

One last thing. This book took a long time to write, but what kept me going throughout was the sheer delight I got from testing the recipes. Time after time, what seemed plain on the page turned out to be subtle; what seemed baroque or fussy, rich and rewarding. But this is only proper. The average nineteenth-century drinker was accustomed to having his drinks—based not on a thin and anodyne tipple like vodka, but rather on something robust and flavorful, like cognac, rye whiskey, Holland gin, or brown sherry—made with fresh-squeezed juices, one of several different kinds of available bitters, hand-chipped ice, and a host of other touches that are today the mark of only the very best bars. In presenting the recipes I've done my best to lay bare these touches; to transmit the techniques and competencies the bartender relied on in practicing his craft; in making a few cents worth of whiskey, sugar, and frozen water into a glimpse of a better world.

CHAPTER 1

"Professor" Jerry Thomas: Jupiter Olympus of the Bar

Who Reads an American Book?

In the January 1820 issue of the *Edinburgh Review*, the noted English wit Sydney Smith closed his review of Adam Seybert's 804-page *Statistical Annals of the United States of America* with a flurry of questions calculated to let the air out of anyone whom Seybert's monument to American enterprise might inspire with admiration for the new republic's achievements. "Confining ourselves to our own country," he asks, "and to the period that has elapsed since they had an independent existence . . . Where are their Foxes, their Burkes, their Sheridans . . . their Wilberforces?"—and a good twenty-one other celebrated names to boot, covering the full spectrum of human endeavor. It's not just that the country lacks famous names, though; it's everything:

> In the four quarters of the globe, who reads an American book? or goes to an American play? or looks at an American picture or

statue? What does the world yet owe to American physicians or surgeons? What new substances have their chemists discovered? Or what old ones have they analyzed? What new constellations have been discovered by the telescopes of Americans? What have they done in mathematics? Who drinks out of American glasses? or eats from American plates? Or wears American coats or gowns? or sleeps in American blankets?

Here's the thing: Smith wasn't entirely wrong. From our perspective, two very busy—and largely American—centuries down the road, it's not easy to appreciate just how rudimentary American civilization was in its early years. Once you got more than a day's ride in from the coast, where things were maintained to a thickly provincial, mail-order version of European standard, everything was salt pork and hominy, dirt and ignorance and inebriation, all punctuated by the *splat* of expectorated tobacco juice. Or so it seemed, anyway, to the European travelers who flooded the country.

Even an impartial observer (which Smith and most of the travelers were assuredly not) would have to concede literature—although Washington Irving's 1809 *Knickerbocker's History of New York* had earned at least some amount of international notice—and drama, painting, and the plastic arts. And medicine, astronomy, and math. And manufacturing, heavy industry, light industry. Pretty much everything, in short, but raw materials, empty space and the sheer drive and feistiness needed to fill it.

But little did Sydney Smith realize that, even as he wrote, an American name was thrusting itself forward, and in an art in which Great Britain had long been preeminent. As often, this genius at first was not recognized: The earliest squint we have at him creating comes from Lieutenant the Honourable Frederick Fitzgerald De Roos, of the Royal Navy, who encountered him in 1826 and was not impressed. This was at the City Hotel, the best in New York at the time. "The entrance to the house," the fussy lieutenant writes, "is constantly obstructed by crowds of people passing to and from the bar-room, where a person presides at a buffet formed upon the plan of a cage. This individual is engaged, 'from morn to dewy eve,' in preparing and issuing forth punch and spirits to strange-looking men, who come to the house to read the newspapers and talk politics."

About that man in the cage (American hotels kept their bars right in the lobby, so they needed to be lockable when the desk clerk/barkeeper—the jobs were one and the same—was off duty, lest the guests help themselves): His name was Willard. Mr. Willard, if you were being formal. If he had a first name, nobody ever used it. If the lieutenant had been a little less stuck-up, he might have noticed that the "issuing forth" Willard was doing was something more than ladling Punch from a bowl and pouring drams. In fact, he was America's first celebrity bartender; our "Napoleon of Bar-Keepers," as he was called. As one patron recalled, "Willard was one of the first in the city to concoct fancy drinks, and he introduced the mint-julep as a bar drink," frequently mixing them up three or four at a time while simultaneously using his photographic memory to greet long-absent guests by name, supply the whereabouts of others, and answer all and sundry questions clerks and bartenders are subject to.

Indeed, as the English traveler Charles Augustus Murray observed in 1839, "by common consent" Willard, whose name was familiar to every American, and to every foreigner who has visited the States during the last thirty years," was "allowed to be the first master of [his] art in the known world." There was probably no other American in any field about whom an Englishman would admit this, but then again, Murray had tried Willard's Mint Juleps. As an Englishman, Murray knew whereof he spoke: For two hundred years, the English upper classes had maintained a reputation as the world's most discriminating consumers of alcoholic beverages. Without their educated—and insatiable—demand, Bordeaux wines, champagne, cognac, vintage port, old sherry, Scotch whisky, and liqueur rum would never have developed beyond an embryonic stage; it was the English market that nourished and shaped them. Nor was the Milords' expertise confined to straight goods alone: Punch, the nectareous and lethal concoction that for two hundred years represented the acme of the mixologist's art, was for all intents and purposes an English creation, and those men who excelled in making it were rewarded with money and celebrity. But as Murray and indeed every other traveler who visited America and was cooled by a Mint Julep on a hot day or warmed by an Apple Toddy on a cold one was forced to admit, in this one art anyway, the old order was passing and a *novus ordo potationum* was coming into being.

Now, admittedly, mixed drinks are not paintings, sculptures, novels, or poems. They are disposable and, frankly, not a little bit disreputable, standing roughly in the same relation to the culinary arts that American motor sports do to automotive engineering or hot jazz to musical composition: they smack of improvisation and cheap effects and even the most august of them lack the cachet accorded to fine wines, old whiskies, and cognac brandies. They are easily abused; they can degrade lives and even destroy them. Even if appreciated in moderation, they are appreciated in surroundings that rarely lead to detached meditation on truth and beauty (if those are not the same thing) or constructive engagement with the great moral and social questions of the age. And yet neither are they contemptible. A proper drink at the right time—one mixed with care and skill and served in a true spirit of hospitality—is better than any other made thing at giving us the illusion, at least, that we're getting what we want from life. A cat can gaze upon a king, as the proverb goes, and after a Dry Martini or a Sazerac Cocktail or two, we're all cats.

But let's leave such philosophical matters for when we meet over a drink and note that even the notorious Mrs. Trollope, who spent three and a half years in Tennessee, Virginia, and, mostly, the American "Porkopolis," Cincinnati, and recorded her frank and decidedly unvarnished impressions of the country in her 1832 *Domestic Manners of the Americans*, finally came around to admitting that here was something that Americans excelled in, and that it had merit. Indeed, she conceded in 1849, when it came to those Mint Juleps she had disingenuously held up in her book as an example of American boorishness, "it would, I truly believe, be utterly impossible for the art of man to administer anything so likely to restore them from the overwhelming effects of heat and fatigue." And these were Whiskey Juleps, mind you—if someone had managed to slip one of the more epicurean Brandy ones under her nose, who can say? She might even have given Porkopolis another chance.

Many excellent books have been written on the social history of drinking in early America. I will therefore dispense with the traditional lengthy description of the general bibulousness that prevailed; on the Slings and Juleps that, raised in honor of rosy-fingered dawn, eased men onto the proscenium of day; on the eleven-o'clock spark-quenchers of gin and the noontime whiskey drams; on the Celt and his ball of malt and the Good Old 'Nongohela of the Pennsylvanian; on Kentucky corn and Medford rum and the true purpose of the Georgia peach (like Johnny Appleseed's stock-in-trade, it was destined for the stillhouse, not the table).

Whether or not Americans ingested more absolute alcohol than their European forbears is open to debate. There's no question, though, that a much greater percentage of that alcohol was in the form of distilled spirits, and that these spirits were consumed in an unprecedented variety of mixtures. Nor can it be disputed that this facility with mixing drinks was the first legitimate American culinary art, and—along with the minstrel show, but that's another book—the first uniquely American cultural product to catch the world's imagination. In the century and a half between the American Revolution and Prohibition, this art was born, reached maturity, and spread to every corner of the globe, in the process establishing the principles, techniques, and even a surprising number of the tools and formulae that still characterize the art today.

Arts don't invent themselves. Someone had to mix the first Rum Punch, stir the first Cocktail, shake the first Sherry Cobbler, and invent the shaker to do it with. But when it comes to these early Titans of the bar, we run into the condition lamented by the Roman poet Horace, two thousand years ago:

> *There lived heroes before Agamemnon,*
> *Yet all unwept in shadow lie, for want*
> *Of poets to save their mighty deeds in song.*

Unfortunately, there was no Homer to record the names and deeds of bartenders. Other disciplines of similarly louche character found their poets—e.g., the Anglo-Irish journalist Pierce Egan's remarkable 1819 *Boxiana*, a four-volume anecdotal history of British pugilism and the culture that supported it, or its companion piece, Patrick Timony's *American Fistiana* from 1849—and there was no shortage of what was known as "convivial" or "jovial" literature, books about social drinkers and their conversation. But the nineteenth century brought forth no *American Bariana*, no chronicle of the men behind the bar, their sayings and their doings. For the most part, as far as history is concerned the great bartenders of the Heroic Age—men like Cato Alexander, a freed slave who kept a coaching inn in upper Manhattan and who, in the Federal Era, was second only to Willard in his reputation as a mixologist; or Sherwood "Shed" Sterling (alias "Napoleon II"), who presided over the grand circular bar at the Astor House; or William Pitcher, the Greek-spouting deity of the Tremont House bar in Boston—carved their deeds in ice. We might catch occasional glimpses of them in the murk, tossing drinks from cup to cup before a bewhiskered and thoroughly appreciative crowd, but beyond that they are enigmas. And they were the famous ones. Even the mighty Willard left behind no book of recipes or biographical sketch. We don't know when or where he was born or when or where he died. We don't even know his first name.

But if the vast majority of the bartenders of the period have been condemned to obscurity, there is one, anyway, who has not; one about whom a good deal has long been known and a great deal more will be revealed herein. In large part, this is because, not content to wait for a poet, he was his own Homer, telling his story to anyone who would listen and getting his deeds, his recipes between the covers of a book before anyone else. In this book, he will stand in for the countless ranks of his colleagues whom history overlooked; his character and actions for those of all bartenders. Fortunately, if there was one old-time bartender whose shoulders could support such a burden, it was Jerry Thomas.

An American, and a Sailor, Too

Oh, to have seen him as Edward Hingston saw him in 1863, presiding over the luxurious marble-and-gilt barroom of the Occidental, the newest and best hotel in San Francisco:

> He is a gentleman who is all ablaze with diamonds. There is a very large pin, formed of a cluster of diamonds, in the front of his magnificent shirt, he has diamond studs at his wrists, and gorgeous diamond rings on his fingers—diamonds being "properties" essential to the calling of a bar-tender in the United States. . . . It must be remembered, however, that he is in California, and that he is engaged as a "star."

When Hingston encountered him, Thomas was, as he noted, "one of the most distinguished, if not the chief, of American 'bar-tenders,' " his name "as familiar in the Eastern States as it now is out here in California. . . . In the manufacture of a 'cocktail,' a 'julep,' a 'smash' or an 'eye-opener,' none can beat him, though he may have successful rivals." This "Jupiter Olympus of the bar," as the preface to his book had dubbed him the year before, was thirty-three years old and he was pulling down a cool hundred dollars a week, more than the vice president of the United States.

Jerry P. Thomas—alas, we may never know what the "P." stands for—was "an American . . . and a sailor too," as he told a reporter from the *New York Sun* in 1882. He was a gold miner, a Broadway dandy, a (minor) theatrical impresario, an art collector, an artist himself (of sorts, anyway), an inventor, an author, and a gambler. A footloose type, at one time or another he tended bar in just about every place where conviviality was at high ebb, from London, England, to Virginia City, Nevada. And wherever he was, he was a man as good as any who stood before his bar, and a damned sight better than most.

Jerry Thomas was born on or around November 1, 1830. Or maybe it was 1829—things like strict chronological accuracy don't seem to have been a primary concern of his (the 1830 date comes from his death certificate and seems like the best bet). In any case, the place was Sackets Harbor, New York, a garrison town on the chilly waters of Lake Ontario not far from the Canadian border. About his parents, Jeremiah and Mary Morris Thomas, we know nothing. We know he had a younger brother, George M., because they ran saloons together, but of other siblings we also know nothing. His early childhood is a blank. We can deduce that his social class wasn't the highest, but only from his career choices. On the other hand, Richard Henry Dana and Herman Melville came from "respectable" families, and they shipped out as sailors, too, and George M. Thomas ended up as a bank director. At some point in the mid-1840s, Jerry ended up in New Haven; whether he moved there with his family or by himself is another open question.

Here's the problem: Jerry Thomas was a bartender, not a poet or a politician. Bartenders were important men in their milieu, but that milieu—discussed below—compiled its historical record by anecdote and barroom reminiscence, not systematic investigation backed by documents. That doesn't mean that we're without resources to reconstruct his life, but they tend to be catch-as-catch-can, giving us intermittent, if often vivid, glimpses of the man as he moved through his world. These don't extend to the part of his life before he learned how to mix drinks. According to the unusually accurate obituary published in his hometown paper, this occurred "at sixteen years of age, [when] he began life as a New Haven barkeeper." New Haven, which was both a seaport and a college town, would have been an excellent place to pick up the rudiments of the craft. In 1846, though, it was a craft still transmitted by long apprenticeship, and his duties in the bar would far more likely have involved sweeping, polishing, and carrying than mixing fancy drinks for customers.

In any case he didn't stick with it long: At seventeen or eighteen, as that same obituary states, "he went to Cuba as a sailor." We don't know what ship that was on, but soon enough he joined the *Ann Smith* of New Haven (William Henry Bowns, Captain) and, as he told the *Sun* in 1882, "sailed all around the world before the mast," or if not all around the world, at least to California (as he told the *New York Dramatic Mirror* writer Alan Dale around the same time). Whatever his previous sailing experience, his berth there wouldn't have been a soft one. Life before the mast was a deadly serious business, even for a lakeman like Thomas—"though an inlander . . . wild-ocean born," as Melville put it in *Moby Dick*. Not that Thomas could complain, since "whatever your feelings may be, you must make a joke of everything at sea" (so Dana). And there would have been plenty for him to joke about. Even for a boy from Sackets Harbor, who presumably knew something of knife-sharp winds, ice-glassed decks, and waves that topped the masts, rounding the Horn in Antarctic winter, as he did in 1849, must've been an ordeal: When he wasn't climbing aloft to the skyscraping top-gallants, a hundred feet and more above a pitching deck, or edging out to the ends of the yards to furl canvas stiff with ice while standing over nothing but the roiling South Atlantic, there was the constant scrubbing, scraping, and swabbing; the picking and the pounding; the stitching and the mending. And all for twelve dollars a month and rations that made prison food look wholesome.

The drinks must've helped. Now, while the Royal Navy might have had its daily rum ration, this was by no means a universal practice in the American merchant marine. Whether out of moral concern or just plain Yankee thriftiness, most ships were dry (or, more properly, like Dana's *Alert*, where "the temperance was all in the forecastle"—in other words, the officers could drink their Brandy-and-Water or Punch, while "Jack . . . can have nothing to wet his lips"). The *Ann Smith*, however, was no temperance ship. We know this because James Minor, one of the passengers on that trip around the Horn, kept a journal. A strict temperance man himself, Minor was dismayed to see his fellow passengers divide themselves into a "Temperance Party" and a "Rum Party." The latter boozed and caroused the days and nights away with Bowns not only doing nothing to rein them in, but actually joining them. If only it stopped with the captain—"many of the Rum party," Minor wrote, "have made themselves to [sic] free with the sailors by treating them, a poor policy to gain friends." Things soon reached the point that the (dry) First Mate was duking it out with drunken sailors, and the cabin boy and the captain's son were getting tanked with one of the passengers and pitching the poor ship's dog overboard. Finally, Minor concluded that "Our Captain is devoid of Order + Sobriety." (To be fair to Captain Bowns, there are other sources that recall him as a man of honor and talent.)

Minor doesn't implicate Thomas by name in any of this shipboard saturnalia. But whatever the extent of his bartending experience, one can certainly see it coming in handy on the *Ann Smith*. Herbert Asbury, in the biographical sketch he attached to his edition of Thomas's book, has him hoping that he could use the captain's "excellent grog" as a basis to "invent something which would relieve the sailor's life of much of its hardship," and the captain looking "with vigorous disapproval upon all attempts to improve the grog and drinking habits of the crew." Stripped of its circumlocution, this sounds very much like Thomas was mixing up drinks for his fellow Jack Tars above and beyond some sort of regular rum ration and the captain put a stop to it. Unfortunately, Minor's journal, which would have certainly made much of such an occasion, peters out somewhere between Rio (where there had been a lengthy layover and much booze purchased) and the Horn. In any case, this voyage, which left New Haven on March 24 bound for San Francisco, would be the last one Thomas made before the mast. When he returned east, it would be as a steamship passenger.*

IN REALMS OF GOLD

On November 4, only a few days after Thomas's nineteenth birthday, the *Ann Smith* reached San Francisco, whereupon he jumped ship and, as he put it, "ran off into the mountains after gold." Nor was he alone: The harbor in San Francisco was full of abandoned

---

* The Watertown, New York, paper makes the curious statement, seconded in a brief reminiscence of Thomas published upon his death in the *New Orleans Picayune*, that on this voyage "His adventures in Rio Janeiro, Valparaiso and other places in South America were so peculiar that his account of them has been published in book form and widely circulated." I've been unable to locate any trace of such a book, but with Jerry Thomas, you never know.

ships, their crews all having had the same approximate idea. The Gold Rush was on, and it was as great a spectacle as any human history has afforded. The San Francisco Thomas would've found when his boots hit the wharf is scarcely imaginable: a seething anthill of human greed, its streets yards-deep in mud, its sand hills poking their bald knobs over a sea of shacks, tents, tented shacks, flimsy one- or two-story frame houses, even prefab wooden huts from China—housing so temporary, so precarious, that one good blow and just about the whole city would be shaved clean off the face of California. Here and there, perhaps, a piece of the more substantial new construction that was just beginning to sprout up might be left standing, but everything else was as permanent as grass.

And the people—plow-callused Yankee farmers, pigtailed Chinese, "Kanakas" from Hawaii, Southern backwoodsmen, banker's sons from Fifth Avenue, broad-hatted Sonorans, hard-bitten "Sydney Ducks" from Australia, Illinois dirt-farmers, Chileans, Peruvians, French whores (who charged a pound or more of gold dust a trick, thank you very much), Indians, and lots and lots of just plain Americans, all burning with gold fever. They created a society like no other on Earth. University professors would be frying eggs for a living—and making more doing it that they ever did lecturing on Aristophanes. Ditchdiggers were paying an unheard-of fifty cents a drink for straight whiskey, and none of the best at that, and sending their shirts to Hawaii to be laundered. Everything was topsy-turvy and hurtling along at railroad speed.

Then there were the saloons. According to Hubert Howe Bancroft, the Gold Rush's great early historian, the Argonauts, as those who sailed after gold were jocularly called, were a bibulous bunch: "If hot, they drank to get cool, if cold, to get warm, if wet, to get dry, if dry—and some were always dry—to keep out the wet." The places they drank ranged from a tent outfitted only with a barrel of Cincinnati rectified or a few jugs of pisco to joints where three-thousand-dollar billiard tables stood on broken-up packing cases under crystal chandeliers. The city's best and most popular gambling saloon, the El Dorado on Portsmouth Square, was simply four walls and a tent roof, but "it had an orchestra of fifteen persons," as one old Forty-Niner later recalled. "It was run all night and day, with two sets of hands. It was gorgeously fitted up. What they used to stir up the sugar in the drinks cost $300. It was solid gold." If Asbury is to be believed, one of the hands wielding that golden toddy-stick was Jerry Thomas's. "The Professor," he writes, ". . . became First Assistant to the Principal Bartender of the El Dorado."

If only there were some scrap of evidence for this; the El Dorado is almost as central to the myth of the Gold Rush as Sutter's Mill or "Oh, Susannah!" and to have Jerry Thomas firmly placed behind the bar would be quite something. But not even Thomas himself claimed that he worked there, at least not in the autobiographical sketch he dictated to the *Sun*. And even if he did find a berth on Portsmouth Square, it couldn't have been for long, since the El Dorado had a distressing habit of burning down, along with much of the rest of the city. In any case, whether he stopped to tend bar or not, before long Thomas was in the mountains, trying to get rich. (Mixographer and collector of bariana extraordinaire Brian Rea believes, based on his research, that Thomas did indeed work at an El Dorado—but in Sacramento, on his way to the diggings, not San Francisco. This would make much more sense.)

Piecing together sketchy and often contradictory anecdotes, which are all we have to go on for this part of his life (a thorough combing of census records, city directories, miner's memoirs, membership rolls of Forty-Niners' societies and suchlike has turned up no trace of him whosoever), it seems that he betook himself to the goldfields along the Yuba River, in the northern range of the diggings, and set to shoveling. He didn't last long at that, either. Of all the ways to get rich in California, digging for gold was the most spectacular—one lucky stroke of the pick, and you could be set for life. But it was backbreaking, dirty work, and few of the men who did it made enough to more than cover expenses, particularly since those expenses were so very high. Pretty quickly, it seems, young Jerry gave mining up for a mug's game and went where the sure money was: collecting those expenses. He installed himself at the big saloon in nearby Downieville run by John Craycroft, ex-mate of a Mississippi riverboat, and his silent partner, a Mexican whore by the name of Chavez. One must assume that Thomas took up his proper station behind the bar and set to doling out horns of panther-sweat to the begrimed and hairy multitude. Whether it was in San Francisco, Sacramento, or Downieville (or all three), wherever Thomas tended bar in California he would have been making serious drinks. Even Hinton Helper, who was there from 1851 to 1854 and went back East full of grump and gripe at what he had seen, was compelled to admit that the raw new civilization then a-building on the Pacific coast did not stint when it came to the quality of its liquid refreshments. At one San Francisco saloon, he wrote, "We find the governor of the State seated by a table, surrounded by judges of the supreme and superior courts, sipping sherry cobblers, smoking segars, and reveling in all the delights of anticipated debauch." The two bartenders, urbane fellows, when they are not "deal[ing] out low anecdote to vulgar idlers," are mixing drinks using "the choicest liquors and artificial beverages that the world produces." Ultimately, he concludes,

I have seen purer liquors, better segars, finer tobacco, truer guns and pistols, larger dirks and bowie knives, and prettier courtezans here, than in any other place I have ever visited; and it is my unbiased opinion that California can and does furnish the best bad things that are obtainable in America.

Even Virginia, the state long considered the heartland of epicurean tippling in America, was forced to concede its place, as the *Southern Literary Messenger* acknowledged in 1852 when it noted, not without regret, that the cradle of presidents,

at one time, may have possessed a better head than most, for strong potations; but that day is long since gone by. Once, the mint julep was proverbial, but western invention has long since won far superior trophies in the cocktail, the sherry cobbler, and snake and tiger.

This is perhaps true more in the metaphorical sense than the literal one—it's hard to make a case for the Cobbler as a Western drink, and the "snake and tiger" is otherwise unknown—but it's true nonetheless.

But Jerry Thomas was a restless young man, and at some point in 1850 or 1851, "getting tired of whiskey and sixshooters" (to pinch a phrase from one of his obituarists) he downed his bartending tools and organized what he recalled in 1882 as "the first band of minstrels in California, the bills being written out by hand and posted up with pitch pine gum for want of tacks." The blacked-up, fiddle-banjo-and-percussion minstrel bands were the rock and roll bands of their day, only with the racial politics right out in the open for anyone to see. They were enormously popular in California, as one might imagine, and Thomas and his crew (although not actually the first, or anything like it) evidently made a killing touring the towns up and down the Sacramento River. But he didn't last long in that business, either. This time, though, the reason for bagging it might have been more than simple boredom or twitchy legs. If one of his obituaries is to be believed, while on the Sacramento he ran afoul of one of the great scourges of the age:

> While sailing down that river on a sloop, forty of the crew died of cholera, leaving Thomas to bury their bodies on shore and pursue his melancholy voyage to the coast. When all responsibility was over he took the cholera in a malignant form, but recovered.

Whether it was the cholera or some other reason, in early 1852, as nearly as we can determine, Thomas decided he'd had enough of El Dorado and headed back East.

This time, he could travel the easy way. Somehow or other, he had managed to amass the sum of $16,000; at least, that's what he told both the man from the *Sun* and whoever it was Asbury got his information from. Whether it was by minstrelsy, mining, which Asbury says he continued doing while bartending, or—as Brian Rea has suggested to me—by using some of his bartending money to stake other miners and taking a share of their "earnings" in return, we'll probably never know for sure. But however he got it, it was a staggering sum (equivalents are always approximate, but it's well over $300,000 in today's money). With that kind of money, Thomas could afford to take a steamboat to Panama, cross the isthmus (an arduous journey, but less so in 1852 than a couple of years earlier), and take another steamboat to New Orleans or New York. Where his journey out took him eight months of backbreaking labor, his journey back would've taken a little more than a month, during which time he could be sitting with his feet up and a steady supply of Mint Juleps from the bar.

Not that the trip was entirely without its own hazards. One of the anecdotes circulating after Thomas died maintained that

> on one occasion [he] narrowly escaped death at the hands of an infuriated congregation in Mexico. He rode into a church during service and began to light a cigar at one of the altar tapers, when the natives attacked him for his sacrilegious conduct, and he was saved from death by the intercession of the British Consul, to whom he fled for protection.

The *San Jose Mercury News*, where this was printed, gives no date or exact place for this, but the steamboats called at Acapulco on their way to Panama. There was a British Consul there, and this sounds like the behavior of a twenty-one-year-old on his way home with a medium-sized fortune in his pocket and a surfeit of Mint Julep (or mezcal) under his belt. At any rate, he seems to have made it back home without further trouble.

When Thomas got back East, he may have opened a bar in New Haven; that's what Asbury says, at least, although no Jerry Thomas appears in the New Haven City Directory at the time (there is, however, an A. J. Thomas listed in the 1852–1853 directory as a barkeeper at the City Hotel). In any case, before long he was drawn into the mad vortex of light and shadow that was New York, where he took his $16,000, as he later recalled, and "walked about with kid gloves for some time, to the great delight of myself and a select company." I won't even speculate as to what that involved or who the company was. But when the money was gone, or most of it, he quit perambulating and "started a bar with George Earle under Barnum's Museum, where the Herald building is now." While he and Earle managed to miss the New York City Directory, there's nonetheless a painting of Barnum's Museum from 1852 with a sign reading "Exchange" on the ground floor; this being one of the many synonyms for bar, we're on reasonably firm ground here. This bar appears to have been a popular one (see the note on Brandy Punch in Chapter 3). It certainly had location going for it—Barnum's Museum was one of the most popular attractions in the city, and at the time that stretch of the unregulated maelstrom of horses, wagons, carriages, and darting, weaving pedestrians that was Broadway was as busy as any stretch of road on Earth. It's hard to imagine he wasn't making money there. No matter. Within months, Thomas was pulling up stakes again.

Let's not worry too much about the next four or five years. Almost all we know about how he spent them can be summarized in a brief sentence he dictated to the man from the *Sun*: "In '53 [I] went as bartender to the Mills House in Charleston; followed that up by similar professional efforts in Chicago, St. Louis, and along the Mississippi." One of his obituaries has him briefly running a saloon in the busted-flush boomtown of Keokuk, Iowa. The preface to his book adds that he was "proprietor of one of the most *recherche* saloons in New Orleans" and that the stint in St. Louis was as "presiding deity" over the bar at the Planter's House hotel, generally regarded at the time as the best in all the West. Beyond that, there's nothing. Not a single document, directory entry, reminiscence, nothing. But itinerant young bartenders are hard to track even in the Internet age, at least until they become stars and get located—which is precisely what happened to Jerry Thomas in 1858, when a job brought him back to New York. It was a good one: principal bartender at the large and very fashionable Metropolitan Hotel, perched at the corner of Prince Street and Broadway, in the heart of the city's shopping district.

THE SPORTING FRATERNITY

Before telling the rest of Jerry Thomas's story, it's worth pausing for a moment to discuss the so-called sporting fraternity, as the loose association of individuals whose avocation was the life of sports and games was known. It didn't look at sports the way you or I might. While it might maintain a general, conversational sort of interest in all species of contests of man against man, man against beast, beast against beast or anything against the clock, when it came right down to it there were only two sports that really counted, and you didn't actually play either one of them. You watched them from a safe distance, limiting your participation to the realm of speculative finance. The Turf and the Ring. Now, if the extent of Thomas's interest in the Sport of Kings is unknown (although at one point he did have a racing book operating out of his saloon), by his own testimony his acquaintance with the squared circle was more than a passing one: As he told the *Sun* in 1882, he had been present at

The Yankee bartender, date unknown—but certainly before bartenders had to wear uniforms. (Author's collection)

twenty-nine bare-knuckle prizefights, including the epic 1860 battle between the American John Carmel Heenan and the Englishman Tom Sayers for the first heavyweight championship of the world.

But to be a member of the sporting fraternity involved far more than merely taking an interest in sports. In the nineteenth century, there were really two Americas; two kinds of Americans. There were the ones to whom the freedom upon which the country was founded meant something like, "If I work hard, avoid temptation and play by the rules, I will be unmolested in my enjoyment of the fruits of my labors," and the ones to whom it meant "Nobody can tell me what to do." The Victorians, and the sporting fraternity. Where the first group tried to lead a measured life, centered on work and the home with a weekly detour through church, the Sports (who came from all degrees of society) hung around in saloons and gambling halls, avoiding their civic duty to act all responsible and work long, sober hours for peanuts to increase the profits of other men. If they had hearths to go home to, you wouldn't know it. If they belonged to a church, you wouldn't know that, either. And as for money, when they had it they had it and when they didn't you wouldn't know it by looking at them—the sporting life was all about maintaining a "front," and a true sport would spend his last fifty cents on a cognac Cocktail and having his coat brushed, with a ten-cent tip for the boy who brushed it. You were rich, you were broke, you were rich again—sometimes all on the same day. For the Victorians, money was an object; for the Sports, it was a process.

Some parts of America were more congenial to the fraternity than others. Small towns were bad, big cities were good, and some—New York, New Orleans, Chicago—were exceptionally good. New England was lukewarm at best; California, Nevada, and anywhere along the Mississippi were very good. Some professions were sportier than others, too. Some of them were even legal: actor, musician, newspaperman, politician. And, of course, saloonkeeper. In fact, as Mark Twain wrote in *Roughing It*, "I am not sure but that the saloonkeeper held a shade higher rank than any other member of society. . . . Youthful ambition hardly inspired so much to the honors of the law, or the army and navy as to the dignity of proprietorship in a saloon. To be a saloon-keeper . . . was to be illustrious." He was talking specifically about Nevada, but his words could have applied equally well to anywhere the fraternity congregated.

If his chosen profession or the prizefights, or the towns he tended to gravitate to, or the fact that he always seemed to have a book running out of his bar (if it wasn't horse, it was riflery contests, elections, or any other damn thing you could put money on), or the Parisian gold watch he always wore with the golden seal, sovereign, and "dog's head" on the other end of its heavy gold chain, or his close involvement with the theater and its folk aren't enough to mark Jerry Thomas as a member of the sporting fraternity, that bit with the $16,000, the kid gloves, and the select company should be a dead giveaway. Considering that room and board at the Astor House, New York's best hotel, went for two dollars a night and dinner with rare wines at Delmonico's might conceivably cost as much as five, for Thomas to blow such a sum in the few months between his return from California and his employment at the Mills House speaks to a serious dedication to amusement. Either that or sports betting.

MIXING EXCELLENT DRINKS

One thing Mark Twain was wrong about: He considered keeping a saloon to be "the cheapest and easiest way to become an influential man and be looked up to." Tell that to the New York barkeeper George Augustus Sala described in an 1853 article in Dickens's popular journal, *Household Words*:

> The bar keeper is a scholar and a gentleman, as well as an accomplished artist, captain of a fire company, and, I believe, a man of considerable property, and unapproachable skill in compounding and arranging these beverages, and making them not only exquisite to the taste, but delightful to the view. His drinks are pictures. [Here I've omitted a very long and thirst-provoking paean to one of this paragon's "Fiscal Agents," a once-popular drink for which no formula has been recovered; for what it's worth, it appears to be a fancy Julep.] The barkeeper

and his assistants possess the agility of acrobats and the prestidigitative skill of magicians. They are all bottle conjurors.— They toss the drinks about; they throw brimful glasses over their heads; they shake the saccharine, glacial and alcoholic ingredients in their long tin tubes; they scourge eggs and cream into froth; they send bumpers shooting down the bar from one end to the other without spilling a drop; they give change, talk politics, tell quaint anecdotes, swear strange oaths, smoke, chew and expectorate with astonishing celerity and dexerity. I should like to be a barkeeper, if I were clever enough.

Admittedly, Sala might be laying it on a bit thick, but only a bit (and knowing Sala, who always displayed a detailed curiosity in the American mixological arts, he was only half kidding about wanting to be a barkeeper). If the efforts of Willard and Cato and Shed Sterling had established the basic techniques and procedures of mixing individual drinks *a la minute*, the mixologists of the 1850s lit the afterburners. Clearly, to preside over a bar like this—although the *Brooklyn Eagle* identified it as the St. Nicholas, the description could apply just as well to the Metropolitan—one needed formidable skills. But one also had to be a sporting character of wide experience and infinite jest; as the *Chicago Tribune* noted in 1870, a good barkeeper

becomes part and parcel of a saloon, knows all the customers, is on familiar terms with them, learns to call them Tom, Dick and Harry, knows their weaknesses for a particular tipple, and mixes it to suit their tastes. . . . Sporting news is his delight. He is learned on the base ball nines, pretends to forecast the result of the coming prize fight, talks wisely of the last "chicken dispute," and criticizes actors and actresses with a happy confidence in his own opinions. He is a two-legged sporting journal with a dramatic column . . .

Jerry Thomas was just that. For the next eighteen years, all those skills and the jest that went with them would keep him in the limelight as America's most famous bartender.

His run at the top started off auspiciously enough when, after a couple years at the Metropolitan and a quick sporting jaunt to London (the Heenan-Sayers fight; according to what he told Alan Dale, this was only the first of many visits), the thirty-year-old Thomas opened his own place, just a couple of blocks up from the Metropolitan at 622 Broadway. This elaborate establishment was in the same building as Laura Keene's New Theater and probably, as was customary, attached to it. Certainly La Keene (the most popular actress of her day, and the only one to run her own theater company) displayed no conspicuous Temperance proclivities that would have prevented the usual connection being made. In which case Thomas might have noticed, one night in 1861, an intense, dreamy-eyed man on the edge of middle age pop in for a quick Gin Cocktail or Santa Cruz Sour. Some old friends of Stephen Foster's were in town from Pittsburgh and had managed to extricate the songwriter, then just beginning his final slide into destitution and death, from the East Side liquor groceries where he was killing himself on adulterate rum. After dinner at the St. Nicholas, they treated him to a play at Laura Keene's. I can't imagine Foster handling the second half without a bracer.

Foster wasn't the only celebrity to come within the Professor's orbit at 622. In October 1860, Queen Victoria's son Edward, the Prince of Wales, visited New York. The reception he received was overwhelming—for a free people, Americans of the day were shocking royalists. Poor Edward's hotel, the Fifth Avenue at Twenty-third and Fifth, was so besieged by crowds that he was essentially trapped there.

In 1902, however, an old newshound by the name of George Forrester Williams published an interesting story to the effect that one night during the prince's visit, he and Mortimer Thomson, a fellow scribe who had achieved a fair degree of fame for the dialect humor he wrote under the pseudonym "Doesticks," managed to achieve a private audience with His Royal Highness. Upon perceiving how miserable the man was to be trapped in his hotel, they suggested sneaking him out the back way for a quick tour of the neighborhood. He immediately assented (for more on the prince, see the Prince of Wales's Cocktail, in Chapter 7). Since the crowd was watching the front—royalty doesn't use the back door—things went off without a hitch. The trio stalked briskly down Twenty-third Street toward Sixth Avenue, a street of saloons, gambling-houses, minstrel theaters, dance halls, and oyster houses. Real New York. As they turned up Sixth, Doesticks posed the question: "Have you ever drunk a mint julep, sir?"

No, the prince had not. Yes, he would. And here's the kicker: "Thomson led the prince into a famous barroom presided over by the no less famous Jerry Thomas, one of the greatest artists in his line or time." His Royal Highness watched the "elaborate and pic-turesque style of manufacture practiced by the mixers of elixirs in those antebellum days with profound curiosity and admiration," took a sip, said, "Why, it's only a lemonade, after all," revised his opinion as the Julep-glow suffused him, and pronounced it "very, very nice." End of anecdote. Now, if there were ever two people who should have met, they were the Prince of Wales and Jerry Thomas; they had much in common, from a deep curiosity into the composi-tion of drinks to an interest in the operation of the rules of proba-bility to an unshakable personal dignity leavened with humor. But the details, the details. What was Thomas doing up there on Sixth Avenue when his bar down Broadway was open? And why is there no other record of this bar? And, most of all, what the hell was he doing putting lemon in his Julep? Other than that, the story is pos-sible. But Williams might not have told the whole of it (and, for the record, there are plenty of lemon Juleps to be found in the litera-ture).

But according to one Richard Doolittle, a New York business-man, the outing was rather wilder than Williams, who has things ending quickly and sedately, let on. As Doolittle recalled in 1892, the prince and his party ended up downtown, rather worse for the wear, and—as happens in these situations—got separated. "The heir to Britain's throne wandered, unattended, into a . . . resort and proceeded to make things pretty lively," whereupon "the bartender started in to squelch him, and would have done so effectually had I not taken charge of the roisterer and piloted him back to his party."

Jerry Thomas's bar was downtown, it should be noted, and I doubt he was disposed to take any guff from splificated customers, heirs to the throne or not.

It was while he was at 622 Broadway that Thomas did something no American bartender had ever done before and put the unruly mass of formulae that every skilled mixologist carried around in his head down on paper. Barkeepers tended to regard their recipes as trade secrets, not to be exposed to the *vulgus profanum*. For whatever reason, though, Jerry Thomas broke the mold. (Rather than clog things up here with a detailed discussion of his book, its genesis and its fortunes, I've put all that in Appendix I.) The book certainly didn't hurt his star power, anyway, on the strength of which he was able to go to the Occidental in San Francisco in 1863, as we have seen. Why he would want to leave a thriving bar of his own to do so is another question. Perhaps the Leland brothers, who ran both that hotel and the Metropolitan and hence knew his work well, simply made him an offer he couldn't refuse.

But I suspect that there was more to it: In the summer of 1863, as the Civil War was raging, the draft came to New York, and Jerry Thomas was highly eligible. The sporting milieu he was a part of looked unkindly on the war to begin with, and a bolt-hole in San Francisco must have seemed pretty attractive. Even more attractive, however, was the vast and vulgar spectacle that was unfolding two hundred miles to the east in Virginia City, Nevada, where a city of thirty thousand had sprung up overnight on top of the massive mountain of silver known as the Comstock Lode. By 1864, Thomas was there, either (as local legend has it) at the famous Delta Saloon or at the Spalding Saloon on C Street, where the City Directory found him—or, of course, at both. Wherever he wielded his shaker, he would've known local newspaperman Samuel Clemens, who was then just beginning his literary career and didn't think a Whiskey Cocktail would bite, much. Unfortunately, the *Territorial Enterprise*, Twain's paper, burned in one of Virginia City's frequent fires, and all its archives and most of its back issues with it.

In 1865, as soon as the shooting stopped, Jerry Thomas was back in New York, operating a saloon with his brother, George, at the very fashionable address of Fifth Avenue and Twenty-second Street, just south of Madison Square. The space, at 937 Broadway, was "a narrow strip about 15 feet wide and 150 feet deep," as the *New York Times* described it, that ran through the block and had a second entrance on Fifth. "It was a great place," the Professor recalled in 1882.

> After two years our bar receipts ran $400 a day, and the way people used to drop in to look at Mr. Thomas Nast's pictures was a pleasing thing to us, who stood ready to serve them with what they wished to drink when they were done. You remember the Hogarth prints, the full set, without mercy—the fine illustration on steel of Mr. and Mrs. Gyges that—what's his name?— the father of history—Herodotus—tells about, and the oysters and rarebits, cooked special, to say nothing of the chops, and the fat and lean looking glasses (for the first time), and the tables that ran along all in a row, as cosy as chickens on a roost and not near so crowded.

Between the art and the drinks and the free lunch and the steaks and chops and the funhouse mirrors, for a few years there the Thomas brothers ran what was probably the most famous free-standing bar in America. According to an 1871 article in *Appleton's Magazine*, it was a "favorite resort of the American *jeunesse dorée*" and, after the bar at the nearby Fifth Avenue Hotel, "probably the most frequented place after dark" in the city.

Things were so good that for once the Professor stayed put. In fact, in 1867 he even got married. Henrietta Bergh Waites, a New York City native, was a widow some five years younger than her husband with a teenage daughter, also named Henrietta. Before long, she had another child to take care of: Milton, or Minturn— records differ—was born the next year. A daughter, Louise, followed some three years after that. For a time, anyway, Jerry Thomas was a family man and successful businessman—a proper Victorian. He even took to joining things—he turned up as a member of the stuffy Wine & Spirit Traders' Society and the rather less tony Fat Men's

Association (at a portly but still mobile 205 pounds, he was one of the lightest members).

As the Professor's reminiscences suggest, he had more than a passing interest in the contemporary equivalent of pop art—indeed, his place was "a museum as well as a bar," to quote *Appleton's*, containing "all, or nearly all, the caricatures of celebrities, painted by Nast for the *bal d'opéra* a few years ago; to these a good many additions have been made, so that Jerry Thomas's comic gallery is as well visited and appreciated as the exhibitions of the National Academy." And well it might be—the walls of his saloon displayed caricatures of all the political and theatrical figures of the day, drawn by the most popular artists. Nast, though, was the star; the most celebrated and controversial caricaturist of his day, through his platform in *Harper's* magazine he was a political and cultural force to be reckoned with. When he did your caricature, you'd best make sure you saw it, and many of his subjects—e.g., Ulysses S. Grant—did just that.

It couldn't have hurt Thomas's collecting that he was an artist himself. When Hingston encountered him at the Occidental, he noted that Thomas "is clever also with his pencil . . . and behind his bar are specimens of his skill as a draughtsman." Indeed, according to Thomas his work, "Jerry Thomas's 'Original Dream,' which is a vision of all the famous men and women of America sitting together in three tiers, . . . tickled P. T. Barnum so much that he came and asked me to make him one like it, only having him, of course, asleep in the big, crimson-cushioned, central arm-chair, instead of me." It's one of my fondest hopes that this book spurs some talented researcher in American art to track down one or both of these *Dreams*—and, while he or she is at it, the series of pictures where Nast, according to a contemporary newspaper, "delineated the head-barkeeper [i.e., Thomas] in nine tippling postures colossally."

In 1872, faced with the kind of massive rent increases that are an eternal characteristic of the New York real estate market, the Thomas brothers moved their operation uptown to 1239 Broadway, near West Thirtieth Street. This was in the heart of the rip-roaring Tenderloin, where New York came to unwind (either within the bounds of the law or without). Apparently, it was business as usual: Thomas was surrounded by his pictures, and the place was, as one history of the New York stage notes, "popular with Wall Street men and members of the theatrical profession"—key constituencies for building a clientele. Finance and celebrities.

In fact, Thomas's bar was popular enough to become proverbial, the name you would reach for when you were looking for an example of a New York saloon. It appears as such, anyway, in two of the popular dialect humor books by "Eli Perkins" (alias New York journalist Melville D. Landon), and in 1875, it even made it into poetry, when George Augustus Baker, Jr. included a stanza in his "Les Enfants Perdus," a bittersweet ode to New York's gilded youth, wherein the "juvenile Comuses" all drink champagne and are "known at Jerry Thomas's." But suddenly, thronged as his place was, Thomas was done, broke, and had to sell his store to John Morrissey. That was in 1876, when he was pulling in at least $200 a day, at a time when a bar could turn a profit on $50 a week. (Alas, not even his artistic skills could help him: the patent he was awarded on February 1, 1876, for a kind of signboard "intended to represent a book suspended by the head-band or upper end as is very commonly done with directories or other books for public reference" failed to pull him out of the hole.) His obituaries blamed the closing on financial problems caused by buying stocks on margin. Knowing the Professor's clientele, and knowing his sporting proclivities, I have little reason to doubt them. Thus ended Jerry Thomas's run as a star.

EPILOGUE

With the closing of this, his last high-profile bar, Jerry Thomas was relegated to keeping establishments in out-of-the way corners of the city, first at 3 Barclay Street, across the street from the faded glory that was the old Astor House hotel, and then—after a last, Hail-Mary fling at easy money in Denver and Leadville, where gold fever was again running high—on Sixth Avenue and West Tenth Street, under the Elevated tracks across from the Jefferson Market Police Court. In both of these, apparently, he was without his

The Professor's (enigmatic) card, 1882. (Courtesy John C. Burton)

brother, George, who wisely retired from the saloon trade sometime around then and went into banking, although he still appeared as a member of Thomas's enigmatic Gourd Club.*

In March 1882, the Professor had to sell out for good. This time the pictures had to go, too—auctioned off to various fellow-bartenders and Sarony, the famous portrait photographer. The highest price paid at his auction was a paltry $26, for a caricature of the editor of one of New York's second-tier newspapers. All the Hogarths together brought a mere $49.50.

Although the reporter from the *Sun* had found the Professor full of big plans for reopening on Broadway, he never owned a saloon again. For a time after this, by one account he briefly tended bar in New Rochelle (his wife and children lived in nearby Mamaroneck; I don't know if he lived with them), and then for a good stretch at the quaint old Central Park Hotel, a wooden structure at the corner of Seventh Avenue and West Fifty-ninth Street (while there, he gave a testimonial to the makers of St. Jacobs Oil, a patent medicine, who used it in their advertising; ostensibly it had

* This organization, ostensibly a bunch of gourd-growing fanatics, met in the Barclay Street saloon for a while in 1878 and left their fetish-objects festooning the bar. According to the *Times*, Thomas was their leader, and had various grandiose plans for exhibitions, thrones made out of the things, and so on and so forth. The whole business seems fishy to me, but I can't put my finger on the exact angle being worked, and in any case by 1879 we hear of it no more.

cured him of his neuralgia). This is where Alan Dale of the *Dramatic Mirror* found him, tending bar one Sunday afternoon in blatant disregard of the city's blue laws. "He was a stout, thick, good-tempered-looking, greasy little man, of about fifty-five years of age," he recalled. While that "greasy little man" hurts (I must confess), it's true that the Professor was sick and broke, and that never presents you at your best. Nonetheless, "his forehead was bulging, as became a master-mind" and "his aspect was severely respectable" and when he introduced himself, giving Dale the full "Jeremiah P. Thomas," he expected to be recognized—as well he should have.

He was still full of plans. This time, he was going to go over to London to set up a bar that would straighten out their garbled notions of American drinks:

> Then I'll teach the Britishers what's what. Then there'll be no need to brew bogus Yankee drinks. No, sir, for I'll give them the full benefit of my inventions, and they shall see what kind of a boy a New York bartender is. I'll revolutionize the bar in England when I go over, you bet your boots!

Instead of London, he went to Brighton. The Hotel Brighton, that is—a rather seedy, gambler-infested joint at Broadway and Forty-second Street, whose "café" (for which read "bar") he began managing at the end of 1884, supposedly with the intention of turning it into a real attraction. But on December 14, 1885, he left work right after noon, went back to his house at Ninth Avenue and West Sixty-third Street, and dropped dead. His death certificate lists "Vascular Disease of the Heart" as the cause. He was fifty-five years old. His grave, near the northeast corner of the "Poplar" plot in Woodlawn Cemetery in the Bronx, is marked by a stone that reads simply "J P. Thomas"—punctuated exactly like that.

The *New York Times*, the *New York World*, the *New York Post*, and a bevy of other papers, from one end of the country to the other, all printed substantial obituaries of Jerry Thomas, all of them chockablock with inaccuracies, all of them crediting him with drinks he didn't invent. His real epitaph, though, came a few months before he died, in an editorial from the *Brooklyn Eagle*:

> A man does not need to be very old to remember a time when the average barkeeper was a very different sort of person from what he is at present. During the war and some years after it when money was flush and times booming the average bar-keeper, with his pomade plastered hair, his alleged diamonds, his loud oaths and his general aspect of bravado, was a sort of a cross between a dandy and a highwayman. . . . This old type of bar keeper has disappeared from the earth as completely as the mammoth and the present age knows him no more. Anything constructed on his lines turned into a modern bar-room would convert it into a solitary desert in a couple of weeks. The modern American will not submit to the same kind of treatment which his free born fathers endured; he looks for civility and he declines to go where rowdy instincts are rampant.

When the *Sun* interviewed Jerry Thomas in 1882, the reporter couldn't help but note that, "two white rats that were pretty enough to be guinea pigs, and that would be taken for such except for their long and unmistakable tails, cut capers upon his shoulders, caressed him at the corners of his moustache, and mounted occasionally to the top of his Derby hat, whence he removed them with a patient persistency that had no effect upon them whatsoever." Yeah.

CHAPTER 2

How to Mix Drinks, or What Would Jerry Thomas Do?

Jerry Thomas would have laughed at the very idea that you could learn how to mix drinks from a book. Sure, you could pick up a few recipes, a few proportions in which to combine the standard ingredients, but turning them into a liquid work of art and making a bar full of skeptical, sporty gents give props as you do it? That's like learning to box, or play Hamlet, from a book. The only way to master such things is to glue your eyes on the people who know how to do it and then practice, practice, practice. Accordingly, his recipes are essentially devoid of the helpful hints that one finds in modern essays in the genre. Indeed, not until the 1880s, when the profession was losing its ties to the sporting fraternity and started admitting miscellaneous clerks, waiters, and immigrants, did you find mixographers giving tips on technique, and even then they rarely tackled anything so basic as how to hold a shaker or what kind of strainer to use.

I can see their point. Thirty seconds spent watching Dale De-Groff effortlessly waltz the ice around in his mixing glass as he stirs a Martini will teach you more about the proper use of the barspoon than thirty pages of dense prose on the topic. In other words, this book can't teach you how to mix drinks like Jerry Thomas; no book can. The Professor's art came from constant practice and the knowledge that what he was doing was important to his customers and they'd think badly of him, who was as good a man as any of 'em, if he screwed it up. All I can do is explain how they used to do it, supply modern equivalents for things that no longer exist, and pass along a few hard-earned pointers from my experience with making these drinks. Fortunately, while that might not have you tossing drinks over your head in liquid rainbows as white rats frolic on your shoulders, it'll at least have you turning out some pretty damn tasty drinks.

I. HOW THEY USED TO DO IT

If literature and painting can have their ages and eras, so then can mixology. In fact, considered from the perspective of the man behind the bar, the 140-odd years between the end of the Revolution and the imposition of Prohibition can be carved up into three Ages: the Archaic, the Baroque, and the Classic (in most arts, of course, the Classic precedes the Baroque; but what do you want from history that happens in a bar?). Fittingly enough, Jerry Thomas was born on the cusp of the second and died on the cusp of the third.

Fashion Beer Goblets.

THE ARCHAIC AGE (1783–1830)

In the formative years of American mixology, the tools were few, the recipes simple, the ingredients robust, and the mixology rough and ready. Sure, the more sophisticated towns maintained a handful of establishments where a tavern-keeper might have to invest in a few silver Punch ladles and lemon-strainers, a set of good china Punch bowls, and a barrel or two

By the mid-1870s, bartenders had taken to using beer mugs like this as mixing glasses, a practice that did not survive Prohibition. (Author's collection)

of imported arrack to fill them with (the best kind came all the way from Indonesia and fetched four or five times the price good Jamaica rum did). But all the average barkeeper needed was a knife with which to cut lemons and what-have-you, perhaps a reamer to help juice them and a strainer to catch the seeds, a nutmeg grater, and one or two pieces of equipment peculiar to the craft.

The most important of these was the toddy-stick, a five- to ten-inch hardwood or silver (or whatever a sharp Yankee peddler could pass as silver) pestle with a rounded handle on one end and a flattened knob on the other. This, a somewhat more graceful version of the modern muddler, was the general mixing tool of the age, used to crush lumps of sugar and mix them into the drink. Since ice—in whose presence sugar dissolves poorly—was rare in drinks and boiling water common, this was entirely adequate, and its characteristic raps and taps against the side of the glass aroused much the same Pavlovian response in the topers of the day that the rattle of ice in the shaker does now.

Beyond that he might need a "loggerhead" or "flip-dog" for hot drinks (this was nothing more than an iron poker that would be heated and plunged into drinks, making them hiss and steam) and perhaps an Egg Nog stirrer, made by passing a splint of wood sideways through the end of a stick, which would then be twirled between the palms, thus whipping up the eggs. Some basic glassware—large tumblers, small tumblers, stemmed wineglasses and mugs for hot drinks—and a cruet for bitters, with a goose-quill forced through the cork as a dasher-spout (this actually worked quite well, but before long it was replaced by the purpose-made metal-and-cork "dasher top"), and the bar was equipped, at least in terms of dry goods.

The wet goods were equally simple and robust. While Madeiras and sherries excited the merchant class and the swells drank champagne as always, for everyone else

No. D 82. Patent Combination Shaker.
Price......90c

Combination Shaker. (Author's collection)

rum loomed large, particularly in the earlier part of the period. The good stuff came up from Jamaica and St. Croix in the Virgin Islands, the less good from Boston and Providence and the towns thereabouts. In fact, when, a bit later in the century, Maine-born dialect humorist Artemus Ward opined that New England rum was "wuss nor the korn whisky of Injianny, which eats threw stone jugs & will turn the stummuck of the most shiftless Hog," he was reflecting the consensus of public opinion. (The great exception here was Daniel Lawrence & Sons' Old Medford rum, a byword for quality from 1824 to 1905, when the company fell into the hands of a Lawrence who happened to be a Methodist bishop and promptly closed it.) But speaking of whiskey, barkeepers mixed drinks with that, too, although not necessarily the ones fortunate enough to work in the established cities of the East. There, the epicures preferred imported French brandy or Dutch gin—"Hollands," as it was known—or the aged domestic brandy distilled from peaches and their pits. In the backcountry, it was whiskey (and generally unaged whiskey at that) all the way down, interrupted only by the occasional tot of applejack or other rough fruit distillate.

But that's the way things went in the backcountry. In the city, loaf sugar—a relatively refined off-white affair that came in hard, conical loaves (barkeepers had to cut pieces off with snips)—prevailed among the discriminate, such as the two black chimney sweeps satirized (gently, for once) in 1825 in the pages of the *New York Literary Gazette* for having palates so delicate that they would always insist on "white sugar" in their Slings. The indiscriminate or underfunded used a darker, more raw form of sugar (also produced in loaves), or molasses, or whatever the country provided in the way of maple sugar or honey or what-have-you. In the city, lemons and limes were common; in the country, they were scarce. On the other hand, country topers could count on fresh milk and eggs and clean water whereas their city brethren found all of those problematic.

The 1810s and '20s saw considerable development in the barkeeper's art, as pioneers such as Willard of the City Hotel and Cato Alexander made their influence felt and new drinks—the individual Punch, the iced Mint Julep, the Cocktail—achieved near-universal popularity. Things were happening in the boonies as well, particularly as rum began its long decline from its perch as America's spirit of choice and Pennsylvania's old Monongahela rye and old Bourbon from Kentucky began to come into their own.

THE BAROQUE AGE (1830–1885)

In the fifteen-odd years between Jerry Thomas's birth and his apprenticeship behind the bar, the profession of barkeeper changed utterly. Not everywhere, of course. The land was still infested with a vast profusion of low doggerys where the man behind the stick was required to do nothing more complicated in the way of serving liquors than put them in a glass, if that—for most of the century, it was customary to put the bottle and a glass in front of the man ordering straight goods and allow him to help himself (those who took advantage could expect to face the barkeeper's ridicule).

But in the best places, the barkeeper at work was, as we have seen, a marvel of the age. It was ice that did the trick; that turned him from a host and server, albeit an unusually busy one, into a juggler, a conjuror, and an artist. Iced drinks had always been available for the few, but in the 1830s, with the burgeoning trade in fresh, clean New England ice, delivered by horse-drawn carts from insulated central warehouses even in the hottest months of the year, ordinary people started getting used to the stuff, expecting it, calling for it in their drinks. Suddenly, the bartending game was entirely transformed. Ice, combined with the American drinking public's ever-increasing preference for individual drinks made to order over things drunk communally out of bowls, meant that the barkeeper had to add a whole set of tools to his kit. Once the blocks—in New York, at least, they were cubes twenty-two inches per side—reached the bar, they had to be butchered, as it were; cut into useable pieces. This meant ice-tongs and ice-picks (both single- and multipronged), ice-shavers, ice-breakers, ice-axes, ice-scoops, ice-bags, ice-mallets—a whole world of new tools to master. It also meant straws: the state of nineteenth-century dentistry dictated that if at all possible the stuff be kept away from direct contact with people's teeth.

And it also meant the eclipse of the venerable toddy-stick. Once bartenders started mixing their drinks with ice, its days were numbered as the primary mixing tool due to the awkwardness of fitting both it and the ice in the same glass (its sugar-breaking function was obviated by switching to syrup). By the 1860s, after ice had found its way into just about any drink that wasn't made with actual boiling water, old-timers were reduced to fond memories of how "the ring of the tumblers, as [the toddy-stick] hit the sides in mixing, had its peculiar music, with which nearly every one was familiar." Bartenders would still keep one around, to be sure, but its uses were very limited.

For stirring, bartenders replaced the toddy-stick with a long-handled spoon with a twisted stem, whose design appeared to have remained pretty much unchanged until Prohibition.

. No. D 44. Ice Pick.
Hardwood Handle.......................90c

No. D 53.   Best Steel Needle Ice Pick.
Price............15c each.

No. D 300 ICE SHAVE

Will fit any glass. Can be taken in the hand and carried to the ice box, filled with shaved ice and used without wetting the hands or soiling them in any way.
Price........................35c each

No. D 55, Ice Shaver. Best Steel........ 20c each.

The nineteenth-century bartender needed a whole armory of tools to reduce the large blocks of ice he was supplied with to usable size. The "No. D300 Ice Shave" is designed to shave ice right into the mixing glass. (Author's collection)

Far more interesting, though, was the new method of mixing iced drinks delineated by Charles Astor Bristead in his 1852 novel *The Upper Ten Thousand*, when one of his characters prepares a Sherry Cobbler:

He took up one of the spare glasses, covered with it the mouth of the tumbler which contained the magic compound, and shook the cobbler back and forwards from one glass to the other a dozen times without spilling a drop.

No. D 84.
Miller Patent Shaker
and Strainer
Planished tin. . 50c
Nickle plated....90c

No. D 83.–Seamless Shaker.
Silver plated inside, nickle outside.
Small 5 in. high, 3¼ in. wide..45c
Med. 6 in. " 3¾ in. " ..55c
Large 7 in. " 4 in. " ..65c

The 1840s-vintage shaker (right) was too simple and effective a device to escape the American need to improve things. The hermaphrodite shaker-strainer on the left, patented in 1882, is one of the more benign results. (Author's collection)

This way, the ice itself did the mixing. Neat enough, and effective (I've done it myself countless times in hotel rooms). It wasn't long, though, before the knights of the bar figured out that this is much more fun if you don't keep the glasses jammed together. Case in point, this description (from Mayne Reid's 1856 novel *Quadroon*) of a Mississippi riverboat bartender making a Julep:

> He lifted the glasses one in each hand, and poured the contents from one to the other, so rapidly that ice, brandy, lemons, and all, seemed to be constantly suspended in the air, and oscillating between the glasses. The tumblers themselves at no time approached nearer than two feet from each other! This adroitness, peculiar to his craft, and only obtained after long practice, was evidently a source of professional pride.

I shouldn't wonder. Ten or twelve tosses and the drink was mixed, and all without spilling a drop—or rather, as one barfly of the day observed, at least without seeming to.

Although spectacular, this method did have its drawbacks. For one thing, as can be readily ascertained by a few minutes spent with a couple of Old-Fashioned glasses and some ice water, it was damned difficult to do well, and damned messy to do poorly. It was also too gentle to work with every kind of drink: eggs and fruit need to be hit with some kinetic energy before they'll blend properly, and it was inadvisable to toss the drinks too hard. Writing in 1848, pioneering lowlife reporter George Foster provided the first record of the bartenders' solution, and the next major addition to their kit, when he described a man behind the busy bar of a New York oyster cellar who, "with his shirt-sleeves rolled up and his face in a fiery glow, seems to be pulling long ribbons of julep out of a tin cup." This cup—it could be made of cupronickel, brass, or tin (plated or unplated) or even of solid silver (stainless steel didn't appear on the scene until the eve of Prohibition)—would be just big enough to fit over the mouth of the mixing glass, allowing it to be jammed onto it. With the ice cooling the air trapped inside, a vacuum is formed, in theory keeping the hybrid contraption from leaking without the need for any mechanical assistance and allowing the contents to be shaken with considerable violence (not that you'd know that by the way most bartenders use it today).

This "shaker," as it came to be known, went by several names. Bartending as a profession has never had a governing authority, and it's in rather trivial matters like this that the lack is most keenly felt. In 1862, Jerry Thomas noted that "every well ordered bar has a tin egg-nogg 'shaker,' which is a great aid in mixing this beverage." In 1868, though, we find George Augustus Sala writing about "a young officer in the Blues" who owned "a pair of 'cocktail-shakers,'" which he defined as "a brace of tall silver mugs in which the ingredients of the beverage known as a 'cocktail' . . . are mixed, shaken together, and then scientifically discharged." But here, it seems, the British were going their own way, both in the use of two metal cups and in what they were being called: In America, the metal shaker appears to have always been used singly, in conjunction with the mixing glass, and it wasn't until the twentieth century that it had "Cocktail" spliced onto its name, never to be torn asunder. By then, the Brits were calling their two-cup apparatus, with rather more justification, a "Cobbler shaker" (Cobblers contain slices of citrus that need the extra mixing force; Cocktails do not) or, for reasons that have entirely eluded my or anyone else's research, a "Boston shaker." Bartenders being a perverse race, this last is of course the name that has stuck, although now it refers to the American-style metal-and-glass version, rather than the British all-metal one. It's all enough to make you want to take the pledge—in which case, you'll have to call it a "lemonade shaker," another name that was often attached to the apparatus.

Whatever it was called, bartenders took to using this classic bit of American improvisation more and more, not just when they needed that extra oomph: It was simple, it didn't leak (much), it was cheap, and the parts were infinitely interchangeable. It was often used in conjunction with another piece of gear that came into use roughly at the same time. In the early days of iced drinks, the practice was to leave the ice in the drink and give the drinker a straw (another marvel of the age as far as European travelers were concerned). Not every tippler liked that, particularly if he was going to throw back his portion and get on with his business. Accordingly, as we see in some of Jerry Thomas's 1862 Cocktail recipes, barkeepers began straining the drinks off the ice. (This must have been a fairly recent innovation, as iced Cocktails had only caught on the decade before.)

As with the shaker, here the bartender improvised. One method for holding back the ice, still in use, was to break the seal between the mixing glass and the shaker, hold the apparatus sideways over the glass and let the liquid trickle out. But this only worked if you were using the shaker, and many bartenders persisted in the two-glass method for Cocktails. For this, some bright spark whose name is lost to history made the discovery that a piece of silverware known as a "caster spoon" or "sugar sifter"—a spoon with a wide, scalloped bowl with little holes punched in it, used to sift sugar over a bowl of berries—could also be used to hold the ice in the mixing glass while letting the liquid trickle out. By the 1860s, special bar versions were being made, with handles bent just so to fit them into the glass. This came to be called a "Julep strainer," not because you strain a Julep, but because for a time in the 1860s and '70s some bars would put them in the drink itself and the customer would drink through them (they were even manufactured in sizes small enough to fit into a whiskey glass). Eventually, the old, scalloped models were replaced by one with a larger, oval bowl, which fit the glass better but didn't look nearly as nice.

The earliest mention of anyone chilling the glass the drink is strained into—necessary if you're not shaking it in the glass in which it will be served—comes in 1883 from a Kansas City bartender, who described a procedure involving "putting out a whiskey glass full of ice water, setting an empty glass on top of it, and then turning the water from one to the other." For what it's worth, ten years later a Brooklyn bartender could still describe chilling the glass as one of the arcana of the bartender's art, practiced only by thirty-third-degree adepts.

It wasn't just the tools and the techniques that got more elaborate; the drinks themselves did, too. Fancy garnishes of berries and artfully cut pieces of fruit; imported French syrups and Dutch and Italian liqueurs for sweetening; various kinds of bitters (in the early days, there was just one in general use); aristocratic wines and long-aged spirits—the colors on the barkeeper's palette multiplied exponentially. The language even created a term for those who could master all of this: "mixologist." In France, it takes an academy of intellectuals to modify the language. In America, all it takes is a guy with an idea. The term first appeared in the *Knickerbocker Magazine* in 1856, in a humor piece by Charles G. Leland—see the Philadelphia Fish-House Punch in Chapter 3—whose narrator overhears a Sport in the hotel-room next door referring to the bartender as a "mixologist of tipulars" and "tipicular fixings"; Leland's coinage caught on, first humorously and then, *faute de mieux*, as a way of referring to a bartender who was, as the *Washington Post* later phrased it, "especially proficient at putting odds and ends of firewater together." (Other terms that were floated and sank include Chicago's "cocktail architect" and "drinkist.") By the 1870s, saloon-keepers were using it in their advertising, with only a hint of a smile.

THE CLASSIC AGE (1885–1920)

The artistic mixologists of the Golden Fifties and Bloody Sixties were working at a pitch that couldn't last. As the nation grew in size, population, wealth, and industrial heft, the sporting milieu that produced men like Jerry Thomas and nurtured them in their craft began sliding into decline. Ironically, this served to liberate the Cocktail from some of its louche connotations, as the kind of upper-crust gents who would previously have confined themselves to wine learned to drink Manhattans and such—a new, lighter, and simpler breed of Cocktail. The theatrics that characterized Baroque Age mixology came to seem embarrassingly gaudy. Rather than display maximum effort and enjoyment in their work, the new-school bartenders of the Gay Nineties cultivated economy of gesture, deploying the spoon rather than the shaker wherever possible.

At the same time, the elegantly simple shaker-glass-strainer combination fell victim to the American thirst for progress. Sure, it worked fine, if subject to the occasional glitch (with heavy use, the mixing-tins tended to erode or crack at the place where they met the glass and get gunky with verdigris, and the strainers didn't always fit the glass perfectly). But from the 1870s on, there were numerous attempts to improve things. The first one to stick was patented in 1884 by one Edward Hauck, of Brooklyn, New York. This is, more or less, the same three-piece shaker we know today, with a mixing tin, a metal cap with a strainer in the middle of it, and another cap on top of that. (A Chicago man had patented a similar three-piece shaker in 1877, but it had a complicated air vent and didn't catch on; then as now, for bar gear simpler is better.) It's uncertain how many actual bartenders used these "combination shakers." The parts were harder to keep track of in a busy bar, and ice tended to block up the strainer and slow the straining process. But some did, anyway, particularly in Britain.

The strainer, too, got an upgrade, although not until 1889: That's when a Connecticut man by the name of Lindley came up with the bright idea of threading a spring around the edge of the thing, thus enabling it to fit into any size glass. This received its current name, the "Hawthorne strainer," three years later, when the Manning-Bowman company of Connecticut put out a slightly improved version, which had a row of little holes around the edge forming the word "Hawthorne". (It took another fifteen years for the device to sprout ears to hold it over the top of the mixing tin, thus assuming its present-day form.)

There were other technical innovations—fancy new lemon-squeezers, metal jiggers to replace the sherry-glasses that had been previously used to measure out drinks (the standard nip-waisted double cone was patented in 1892 by Cornelius Dungan of Chicago), bartop hot-water dispensers, champagne-taps that screwed right through the cork, thus allowing the stuff to be dispensed one squirt at a time, and so forth. All of these worked to simplify and stream-line the mixologist's art (when, that is, they worked at all); to open it up to general participation.

The one area the Classic Age surpassed the Baroque in elabo-rateness is in the profusion of glassware. As the nineteenth century wore on and the mixologist's art gained in complexity, he required more and more types of glasses into which to deposit his creations. Willard at the City Hotel probably made do with only four or five different kinds of glasses—small tumblers, large tumblers, small and large wineglasses, perhaps a few cordial glasses, and something for hot drinks. By the end of the century, that would have been woefully inadequate. In 1884, New York's G. Winter Brewing Co. published a little bartender's guide, containing a list of the glass-ware required for a first-rate saloon:

Champagne, Claret, Port, Sherry and Rhine Wine Glasses, Cocktail Glasses for Champagne and also for Whiskey, etc., Julep and Cobbler Glasses, Absinthe, Whiskey, Pony Brandy, Hot Water, John Collins and Mineral-Water glasses, as well as large Bar Glasses for mixing purposes and for ornamentation, together with all sizes of Beer, Ale and Porter glasses. There should also be a great variety of Fancy Glassware, to be used in decorating the shelves behind the counter.

This list is actually fairly conservative: it omits the so-called small bar-glass, glosses over the knotty issue of the absinthe glass (there were two kinds available, each adapted to a different way of serving the verdant elixir; a first-class bar would have both), and skimps on the small goods required for the various cordials and Pousse-Cafés in style at the time. Of course, only a few bars would carry such a freight of glass. If, on the one hand (as the *New York Tribune* opined in 1908), "the array of gleaming, highly-polished glassware displayed and used in the hotels and cafés in Manhattan is unexcelled anywhere in the world," it's equally true that there were plenty of joints on that very same island that had no problem making do with beer mugs and whiskey glasses and would treat the order of a Pousse-Café as an invitation to physical violence.*

It wasn't just the tools that changed; the spirits did, too. With a savage yank from a pesky insect known as phylloxera, brandy was dragged out of the spotlight, which it had so long occupied as the premiere mixing and sipping spirit, to be replaced by American whiskey in the mixing glass and Scotch whisky in the clubroom. At the same time, dry gin drove out the lightly sweet styles that had previously prevailed, just as the dry Bacardi rum from Cuba chased out the heavier rums from St. Croix and Jamaica. Imported liqueurs multiplied behind the bar, and even such exotica as Russian vodka began popping up in the occasional mixture (mezcal and tequila, however, although drunk in some quantity in the Southwest, don't appear to have cracked the mixologist's armamentarium until the 1920s). Even the mixers changed: vermouth, known (if not savored) in the United States since the 1830s, suddenly appeared in a dizzying variety of Cocktails, mixed with every spirit known to commerce. The definition of a Cocktail stretched to include ingredients like lemon juice, orange juice, pineapple juice, and the faddish and pink-making grenadine. By 1920, just about

---

* The canonical long-stemmed, conical Martini glass does not appear on the scene until the 1920s, although the engravings of Cruikshank are full of Victorian Londoners drinking gin and punch from short-stemmed, flaring affairs that bear some similarity, and the 1902 Albert Pick Company catalogue displays a conical Cocktail glass that gives one pause. For what it's worth, Hollywood seemed at first to consider the iconic, streamlined version we use today to be a champagne glass—that's how it appears, anyway, in Lewis Milestone's 1928 *The Racket* and Buster Keaton's 1929 *Spite Marriage*—in the latter, in a scene where people are also drinking Cocktails, out of the standard coupes. Both films were made by different studios, so we know it's not some brain-bent set dresser's mistake.

every technique and major ingredient known to modern mixology was in play (okay, there wasn't a lot of flavored vodka, but they made up for it by selling artificial sour mix and cellulose cocktail cherries). Only now, with the introduction of so-called molecular mixology, with its foams, gels, infusions and vapors, are we beginning to break new ground. But that's (thankfully) beyond the scope of this book.

II. How to Do It Now

As you've no doubt gathered by this point, accurately reproducing pre-Prohibition drinks is a tricky business. It only gets worse when you start digging into the actual recipes, which are far more inconsistent than my thumbnail history of mixology suggests. Even when everyone else is shaking their drinks, you can always find some crossgrained son of toil who will grumble that they're all doing it wrong and you really have to stir it. Bartenders are an individualistic lot, and always have been.

Happily, reproducing these drinks deliciously isn't nearly so hard, and while bull's-eye accuracy is elusive, you can at least get the vast majority of 'em into the black, and often enough a good deal closer than that. What follows are some general suggestions and observations for making them work as smoothly and easily as possible; I'll discuss exceptions and other specifics under the individual drinks.

BAR GEAR

Let's begin with the basic tools and how to use them. You can haunt eBay for Julep strainers and old-style barspoons and such if you're so inclined, but they're certainly not necessary for making the drinks in this book come out well. One of the defining characteristics of American mixology is its inherent resistance to change, and the modern bartender's kit isn't all that different from what his predecessor would have been using a hundred years ago.

If you want to go Baroque and "toss the foaming Cocktail" (as they used to say) from glass to glass, please let me know if you fig-

Cocktail Essentials, circa 1900: Cocktail glass, bar-spoon, and Lindley-type strainer. (Author's collection)

ure out how it's done; after considerable practice, I've come to the conclusion that there's some kind of trick involved, and I don't know what that trick is. One thing's for sure: The guys who knew how to do it weren't about to let it get into print; while spectators' accounts of it abound, I have yet to find one penned by a practitioner. Otherwise, it's the mixing glass and shaker, both of which are readily available and easy to use.

To shake a drink, simply combine all the ingredients in the glass (that way you can see if you're missing anything), bung in the ice—I'll discuss that below—and cover it with the shaker. Then give the upturned bottom of the shaker a tap with your fist to seat it and shake it vigorously up and down like a piston with the metal part on the bottom so that if—heaven forfend!—the seal should break, the mess will end up on you rather than your guests. To break the seal, hold the shaker in your weak hand, with your fingers overlapping the join between the parts. Then take your other hand, point your fingers up to the ceiling, and with the heel of your hand sharply tap the spot on the mixing tin where the rim of the glass touches it inside. If the seal doesn't break, rotate the glass a quarter-turn and try again. Repeat as necessary. Since the drink will be left in the mixing tin, you'll have to strain it out with a Hawthorne strainer, which is designed to fit over the tin.

To stir a drink (or "mix" it, as some mixologists called it), proceed as before except rather than fitting a shaker over the mix-

Ice Spoon. Plated, 4/6

This is better known as the "Julep strainer." (Author's collection)

ing glass you'll be sliding a spoon into it and whirling it around. The key here is to expend as little energy as possible, and at all costs avoid vigorously thrashing everything about. (Very unbartenderly.) This is much easier if you use fine ice, discussed below. In any case, you'll want to stir a good ten or fifteen seconds and then strain the drink out with the spoon-shaped Julep strainer, which is sized (or should be, anyway) to fit right into the mixing glass. To be authentic, leave the barspoon in the glass while you strain.

When to shake and when to stir? Modern orthodoxy dictates that one should shake any drink with fruit juices, dairy products, or eggs and stir ones that contain only spirits, wines, and the like. This is based partly on the fact that these last ingredients are harder to mix and partly on the fact that shaking clouds up liquids by beating thousands of tiny bubbles into them. If you don't mind your Martinis, Manhattans, and Improved Brandy Cocktails cloudy, go ahead and shake them; many an old-time mixologist did. Conversely, though, I don't recommend stirring a Ramos Gin Fizz; no amount of agitating with a spoon will make it come out right. You can probably stir a Whiskey Sour or a Daiquiri though, should you feel strongly about it, without causing permanent injury to its recipient.

If you're making drinks from the toddy-stick era, simply use its modern descendent, the muddler—which is nothing more than a thick hardwood dowel with a flat knob on one end and a rounded bit to serve as a handle on the other. Like Americans themselves, this might be a little stouter than its ancestors, but it still works pretty much the same.

Sugar

This brings us to the question of ingredients in general, and in specific sugar, which was, with a handful of exceptions (see the Apple Toddy, the Crushed Raspberry Fizz, and the Clover Club), the only thing the toddy-stick or muddler was used to crush. While a visit to any tony grocer's shop will turn up a surprising array of sugars for sale, none of them are a precise equivalent for what was available in the nineteenth century, particularly in the earlier years. Our loaf sugar comes in crumbly little cubes, rather than the dense, resistant loaves that it once did, and our white sugar is too dazzling white, relying on production methods not known to the ancients of mixology. On the other hand, our raw sugar, the nearest step down the scale, is too brown. Given a choice, I'll use the raw sugar—either a Demerara or a turbinado, such as the supermarket-friendly Sugar in the Raw brand. To make this easily soluble, though, it must first be pulverized in a food processor. If that's too much trouble, superfine sugar will work just fine, although it will convey a little less depth of flavor.

Whichever sugar you use, if you're making an iced drink you'll have to melt the sugar first in a little water, since both ice and alcohol impede its dissolution. Simply begin building the drink by putting the quantity indicated into your glass, add an equal quantity of water and give it a quick stir, then proceed with the rest of the recipe. Of course, you can also replace the sugar with gum syrup or simple syrup, as many period bartenders did (see Chapter 9). If you're using a thick, 2:1 syrup, you can usually use a quantity equal to the amount specified of powdered sugar and the drink will come out fine. My general preference is to use what I call "rich simple syrup," which is a 2:1 syrup made with Demerara sugar. Be warned, though: It's dark enough to throw the color off of some of the more delicate tipples. Myself, I'll take a little dinginess in return for the rich, sugarcane flavor it adds. And if you want to make your syrup with gum arabic, that will also add an amazingly smooth mouthfeel to liquor-heavy drinks like the Sazerac and the Improved Cocktail.

Twists

Modern practice is to twist a swatch of lemon or orange peel over the top of the drink at the very end, to get a little sheen of aromatic oil on the surface of the drink. With his usual care for consistency, Thomas suggests doing it this way for some plain Cocktails and squeezing it into the drink before stirring for others. That being the case, I prefer to follow the modern practice: cutting a 1½- × ½-inch strip of peel with a paring knife (including as little as possible of the white pith) and twisting it over the drink after mixing. Some nineteenth-century mixologists suggested that, its work being done, the spent peel should then be discarded. Others dropped it into the drink by way of garnish. As usual, Thomas goes both ways, with a preference for throwing it in. In that he is my guide.

Cherries and Olives

The end of the nineteenth century saw a revolution in the art of the garnish. The admittedly fussy—but fresh and healthy—berries and fruits Jerry Thomas called for began falling by the wayside, to be replaced by an assortment of pickled or macerated items that could linger behind the bar for a while without going off. Some—pickled French hazelnuts, pickled walnuts—are no longer seen. Others—olives, "pimolas" (pimiento-stuffed olives)—are very much with us. Yet others fall into the realm of the undead. Here I am referring specifically to the maraschino cherry. In the 1890s, a maraschino cherry was nothing more than a sour cherry that had been macerated in maraschino liqueur. You can still buy these, made by the Luxardo company (who make the best maraschino). By the time Prohibition rolled around, this expensive, imported item had gone through the American production mill and emerged as either a blob of artificially colored cellulose or, hardly better, the product we know today, in all its zombielike glory.

I should also note that it wasn't until the early twentieth century that bartenders figured out that cherries belong in sweet drinks and olives (or pickled nuts) in dry ones. Before that, you'd find either in either.

Eggs

Nineteenth-century eggs were much smaller than the extra-super-jumbo ones we get today. Use the smallest ones you can find. When making drinks with egg white, you can get away with using one (modern) white for every two drinks.

Ice

Before we get into the spirits, a word about H_2O in its solid form. Because barkeepers carved their ice from large blocks, they could make it any size they wanted. This, too, became a part of the art, knowing which type of ice went into which type of drink. The 1887 rewrite of Thomas's book added a note on the subject that neatly sums up the prevailing wisdom:

> In preparing cold drinks great discrimination should be observed in the use of ice. As a general rule, shaved ice should be used when spirits form the principal ingredient of the drink, and no water is employed. When eggs, milk, wine, vermouth, seltzer or other mineral waters are used in preparing a drink, it is better to use small lumps of ice, and these should always be removed from the glass before serving to the customer.

This is in general still sound, although vermouth drinks should be moved into the shaved ice category. Citrus drinks can go either way; I generally use shaved ice or its equivalent when I'm going to strain the drink, and lump ice when I'm not. Whenever a recipe calls for "shaved," "fine," or "cracked" ice, in the absence of a large block of ice and a shaver, simply take dry, cold ice, put it in a canvas sack and quickly whale the tar out of it with a mallet (this apparatus is known these days as a "Lewis bag," after the modern manufacturer who revived it; you can also simply wrap the ice in a large, clean dish towel). Whatever type of ice you use, you can be a little more generous with it than Thomas and his peers were. It's cheaper now and we're more used to extreme coldness in drinks, so go ahead and fill the glass at least two-thirds with the stuff. (A note to the daring and the dexterous: for drinks that are shaken—i.e., tossed back and forth—Thomas specifies that the ice be "fine," and indeed using cracked ice will theoretically make for a thick, supercooled slurry that shouldn't splash about quite so much when you're rainbowing it over your head. In theory.)

Glassware
Happily, for the purposes of accurately reproducing the recipes contained in these pages, your glassware needs will be closer to Willard's than the array listed in the G. Winter book. Here are the main glasses called for, with their capacities.

Labels in illustration:
Small Bar Glass, Medium Sized Glass, Tall Stem Glass, Claret Glass, Sherry Glass, Fancy Bar Glass, Thick Bar Glass, Fizz Glass, Lemonade Glass, Pony Glass, Thin Goblet, Goblet, Whiskey Glass, Wine Glass, Cocktail Glass, Stem Punch Glass, Tall Thin Highball Glass

Fancy glassware, circa 1905. (Author's collection)

LARGE BAR OR MIXING GLASS. This held 12 ounces but for most uses can be admirably represented by the modern mixing glass, which holds 14 ounces.

SMALL BAR OR MIXING GLASS. This was rather more variable in size, running between 5 and 8 ounces. Usually, it took the form of a short, flared glass with a heavy bottom. At the end of the century, however, many mixologists preferred to use an 8-ounce, straight-sided stemmed beer goblet of heavy construction. A regular (not double) Old-Fashioned glass will do admirably, if you can find one. For most mixing purposes, though, it's easier to simply use the large glass.

COCKTAIL GLASS. A stemmed glass, more rounded than V-shaped, holding no more than 3 ounces. Cocktail glasses this shape and,

Cocktail Glass.

No. 2549. Pressed Cocktail.
The only correct shape glass for cocktails. This style which has a pressed bowl and imitation cut stem is exceedingly popular everywhere. Although of pressed glass it is of the kind made for bar use and much thinner than the glassware commonly called pressed which is quite heavy and clumsy.
The size, 4-ounce, is just right for cocktails and at the price offers very good value.

Price, per dozen................... 75 cents

Cocktail glass, 1902—a short step to the modern Martini glass. (Author's collection)

especially, size are not easy to come by these days, but the small (4- to 5-ounce) Cocktail glass you do come across will do fine as long as you're willing to accept a little airspace above your drink.

EARTHENWARE MUG. Preferably without Garfield or Dilbert on it.

Optional

COLLINS GLASS. A tall glass in the 14- to 16-ounce range.

TUMBLER. A rather robust 8-ounce glass, taller and narrower than the small bar glass.

FIZZ GLASS. A slender 6- to 8-ounce glass of delicate construction, often slightly flared.

RED WINE GLASS. A glass for red wine, not a wineglass that is red (although they had those, too). Also called a "Claret glass." Capacity: 4 ounces.

SHERRY GLASS. A narrow, stemmed 2-ounce glass.

PONY GLASS. The pony was a small, narrow stemmed glass holding 1 ounce or a little more.

III. SPIRITS

Lemons are lemons, more or less, and sugar is sugar. There might be some differences in incidentals between what was available along those lines before Prohibition and what we can get now, but they won't be decisive. Spirits, however, are entirely products of art, and though art is long and life is short, it's still subject to the game of telegraph that is the transmission of information over time. I have taken the liberty, therefore, of suggesting some brands that in my experience work well in historical drinks; that, to the best of my knowledge, are reasonably close to what would have been available in Jerry Thomas's day and immediately after.

Whatever spirits you use, they should ideally be at what would have been considered "proof" at the time, which translates to around 116 degrees in the system we use now. Unfortunately, genever (aka Dutch gin) and brandy are rarely marketed at this strength, so to compensate you'll have to cut the water back.

ABSINTHE

There is no substitute for real absinthe. The best modern ones are made by Ted Breaux and are available, at great expense, from abroad. (The fact that they are not legal in America does not help to lessen that expense. Go to www.bestabsinthe.com; I like the Edouard version.) But a bottle will go a very long way if used in dashes. Failing that, there is Lucid, a new, U.S.-legal absinthe also created by Breaux. Although somewhat lower in proof and less pungent than his others, it will certainly do. Of the legal substitutes, Absente is closest in proof and Versinthe closest in flavor.

APPLEJACK

Before prohibition, the "Jersey Lightning" used in the better bars would not have been blended. For genuine American applejack, there's only one player left standing: Laird's, of New Jersey—in fact, it's probably the oldest brand of liquor in the country. Unfortunately, the regular Laird's applejack one sees around is a blended product, and is hence mostly neutral spirits and water. If you can't find their (pure) bonded version or their old apple brandy—and odds are you won't be able to—better to use a VS-grade Calvados from France (and, while you're at it, drop Laird's a line encouraging them to goose up their distribution of the bonded stuff).

BRANDY

Cognacs and brandies were sold at rather higher proof than they generally are now. Unfortunately, there's no way to adjust for this other than to reduce any quantity of water that might be in the drink. In general, for the best drinks you'll want to use a VSOP-grade cognac or better. This is pricey, but it's one place where you'll just have to grin and be a sport. It's worth it.

CHAMPAGNE

The champagnes popular in Jerry Thomas's day were much sweeter than those we prefer today. The brut champagnes we favor did not become popular in America until the 1890s. That said, I still prefer my drinks with brut.

CURAÇAO (AKA CURAÇOA)

This orange-flavored liqueur was one of the essentials of the bar. Early versions were based on young brandies or rums, rather than the neutral spirits used today. For me, the best substitute is therefore the cognac-based Grand Marnier, which was originally sold as "Curaçao Marnier." The Marie Brizard Orange Curaçao is also acceptable.

GIN

This one's a real problem. In the 1862 edition of Jerry Thomas's book, fourteen of the fifteen gin-drink recipes don't specify what kind or style, and the fifteenth calls merely for "old gin," without indicating its origin. Given this lack of detail, most modern readers and mixologists have assumed that Thomas's Gin Cocktail, Gin Julep, Gin Smash, and all the rest were based on English-style gins, either the lightly sweetened Old Tom or the unsweetened London dry. In the course of researching this book, it has become increasingly clear to me that the gin Thomas had in mind was in fact Hollands; a Dutch genever or an American approximation of it (this would explain that "old gin" in his book; despite its name, Old Tom gin was not aged any longer than the time it took to ship the barrels to their destination, whereas Dutch gins were often aged).

For one thing, there's no evidence that English-style unsweetened gin was available in America in any quantity until the 1890s. Even Old Tom gin, although sold in America since at least the late

1850s, had very limited distribution until the early 1880s: Before that it was known and occasionally called for, but it was still a relative rarity. On the other hand, import figures show Dutch gin coming into America in large quantities at least through the 1870s, and Dutch brands such as Meder's Swan (one of the most popular brands of spirits in America for much of the nineteenth century) and Olive Tree were frequently advertised. What's more, if distiller's handbooks are to be believed, domestic American gins were modeled on the heavier, maltier Dutch style rather than the lighter, cleaner English style.

In the 1876 second edition of his book, Jerry Thomas added a further six gin drinks but still did not specify which kind; again, one must assume either that he meant genever or that he considered genever and Old Tom close enough in style that it made no difference which was used (both were in fact sweetened). The only mention of unsweetened gin in America I've been able to find prior to the 1890s recommends its virtues as a fabric cleaner.

Eventually, with the introduction of dry vermouth as a mixing agent and the American public's turn to lighter cocktails in the 1880s, Old Tom and then London dry gin (as well as the also-unsweetened Plymouth gin) began to displace the richer Dutch style. Finally, in the anonymous 1887 revision of Thomas's book, we find gin styles specified. Eight of the drinks call for Old Tom gin, including the Martinez. But there are still twelve drinks calling explicitly for "Holland" gin. It was only with the rise of the Dry Martini, in the 1890s, that Dutch gin began disappearing from the bartender's armory. Unfortunately, it mixes poorly with dry vermouth, and that would prove to be the death of it as a dominant spirit in America. From then until Prohibition, unsweetened gins—Plymouth and London Dry—are the cutting edge, although one still finds plenty of Cocktails and other drinks calling for Old Tom and even Holland gin.

Now comes the problem. Old Tom is completely unavailable; about the best thing to do is take a good, fragrant London Dry and sweeten it. Tanqueray used to make an Old Tom, so why not start there? A half-ounce of gum per bottle should do. As for Hollands. Its import status right now is in flux. I have hopes, though, that it will come back into the American market. What you want is either a *korenwijn* (also spelled *corenwyn*) or an *oude genever*, both of them thick, malty, and divine; the former, in particular, shows the spirit's surprisingly close kinship with whiskey. Alas, the lighter and more common *jonge genever* is an artifact of World War I, and hence not technically accurate, although it still makes a far richer and tastier plain Cocktail than the lighter English gins.

If, as is unfortunately likely, you have difficulty securing a steady supply of Hollands, the only substitute I know—and it's not a particularly adequate one—is to mix 8 ounces of John Power & Son or Jameson Irish whiskey with 10 ounces of Plymouth gin and then tip in ½-ounce of rich simple syrup. This works tolerably well in Punches and the like, but less so in Cocktails.

MARASCHINO LIQUEUR
The Luxardo brand is the gold standard here and always has been.

RUM
Alas, the old style of Jamaica rum, pot-stilled, strong, and redolent of funk, is no longer made in Jamaica (unless, that is, you count Wray & Nephew's White Overproof, the most popular rum on the island; but this is unaged, and the ones Jerry Thomas called for had some barrel age). The best substitute I know is the Inner Circle, from Australia: it's a pot-stilled rum of the old school, and it's glorious. Look for the version sold at 115-proof; the "Green Dot." Otherwise, Pusser's Navy Rum is acceptable, as is Gosling's Black Seal; better than both is an equal-parts mixture of the two.

Santa Cruz rum is more difficult to substitute for because it's more difficult to pin down exactly what the hell it was. It's clear that it was lighter than the Jamaican style, but not by how much. In general, I use something like Cruzan Estate Diamond, Mount Gay Eclipse, or Angostura 1919 for this, but I make no claims as to their accuracy. They do make for tasty drinks, though.

WHISKEY

This one's easy. While the distillation of bourbon and rye has changed a good deal in terms of scale and a certain amount in terms of technique since the late 1800s, the way the resulting product is aged has changed very little indeed, and experienced whiskeymakers tell me that aging accounts for some 70 to 80 percent of the finished whiskey's flavor. Good enough. In short, any bourbon or rye aged between four and fifteen years and bottled at 90 proof or above will work just fine (anything at lower proof would have generated adverse comment and, most likely, shooting). For the very earliest drinks here, though, you'll have to lay out a little more money and pick up a bottle of Old Potrero, which is a wonderfully archaic pot-stilled rye whiskey (in fact, there are two kinds, one aged in uncharred barrels in the eighteenth-century style and one in nineteenth-century-style charred barrels).

For Scotch whisky, you'll want something strong and smoky and single-malty. The Laphroaig cask-strength and the Talisker both fit the bill. For drinks from the very end of the nineteenth century and the beginning of the twentieth, though, you'll want a blended Scotch. I like White Horse or Johnnie Walker.

For Irish whiskey, it's all about the pot-still, which makes the Redbreast your man.

Finally, whiskey geeks might be interested to know that the convention by which American and Irish varieties of the stuff are spelled with an *e* and Scotch and Canadian without is entirely a modern invention.

IV. QUANTITIES

The quantities prescribed in Jerry Thomas's book and those of his contemporaries and immediate successors are not only inconsistent between the various books, but within them as well. Mixologists tended to pick up recipes from all over and few bothered to straighten out little differences in recipe-writing styles.

There are some small-scale measures that were never fully

standardized. The "wineglass"—the standard dose of spirits in Jerry Thomas's book—has been treated as one of them, but it was in fact a standard measure, representing two ounces (although there is the occasional puzzling reference to a "small wineglass" and a "large wineglass"; these will be dealt with on a case-by-case basis). The teaspoon, on the other hand, is variously quoted as $\frac{1}{4}$ ounce and $\frac{1}{6}$ ounce (the modern teaspoon). Since the things measured in teaspoons are usually sweet, using the modern measure may lead to some drinks being more austere than they need be. In other words, if interpreting the recipes yourself use your judgment.

If there are two possible teaspoons to choose from, that's nothing compared to the dash. Then, as now, no measure is more variable. If, in 1867, Charles B. Campbell could note that "four or five dashes of syrup" equaled 1 teaspoon of sugar, to apply this prescription to the drinks of his contemporaries would yield many a thin Cocktail and tooth-strippingly sour Punch. On the other hand, the "half-teaspoon" given as a dash in the 1871 *Gentleman's Table Guide*, an English work written with the cooperation of an American professor ("whose unsurpassed manipulation was the pride successively of the St. Nicholas, the Metropolitan and Fifth Avenue Hotels"), if applied to the same formulae might render them sticky. So whenever a recipe is sweetened by dashes, I've tried to suggest a more measurable quantity, but be aware that there is more than a dash of arbitrariness in my suggestions. The only exception is when it comes to bitters. There, a dash is whatever squirts out of the top of the bottle.

TABLE OF MEASUREMENTS

1 Quart (Imperial) = 40 ounces

1 Quart (Wine) = 32 ounces

1 Bottle = circa 24 ounces; French champagne was imported in liter and half-liter bottles, which were called "quarts" and "pints"

1 Pint (Imperial) = 20 ounces

1 Pint (Wine) = 16 ounces

½ Pint (Imperial) = 10 ounces

½ Pint (Wine) = 8 ounces

1 Gill (Imperial) = 5 ounces

1 Wineglass = 2 ounces

1 Jigger = 1 Wineglass; later, also 1½ ounces or, in the bars around Wall Street, 1¼ ounces

1 Pony = ½ Wineglass or Jigger, or 1 ounce

1 tablespoon = ½ ounce

1 teaspoon = ⅓ or ½ tablespoon (see above)

1 dash = 1 dash (see above)

A NOTE ON THE RECIPES

The next five chapters are full of old recipes, which I've presented as close to verbatim as possible. Jerry Thomas and his peers have left little or nothing to posterity beyond these formulae, making the ways that they are phrased and organized the only traces we have left of their individuality; in effect, their fingerprints. Accordingly, all I've done with them is expand an abbreviation here and there, and occasionally consolidate several almost-identical recipes into one (e.g., the Gin Fix, the Brandy Fix, and the Whiskey Fix). Where this has caused me to alter anything, I've indicated that with brackets. Where it's caused me to omit anything, I've deployed a line of dots. Where the original recipe uses an obsolete or imprecise unit of measurement or calls for a quantity of something that, according to my experience and testing (usually checked against other contemporary recipes), needs adjustment, I've taken the liberty of adding my own suggested quantity, in brackets. Note that this won't always jibe with the table of measurements in Chapter 2, but you're of course always free to make it the way the original recipe says.

There are passages in the chapters that follow, I should also note, where the grain of the historical detail gets rather fine. Many of these drinks are entangled in tenacious (and widely publicized) webs of myth, falsehood, and incomplete information, and I can think of no other way to extricate them than to lay out the facts in all their minute, even trivial detail. I've done my best to keep this within reasonable bounds—you should see what I left out—but where I've failed, I ask your indulgence. At least the anecdotes and citations that convey the detail are for the most part newly excavated from the archives and thus, I hope, will have the force of novelty.

CHAPTER 3

PUNCHES

For nearly two hundred years, from the 1670s to the 1850s, the Kingdom of Mixed Drinks was ruled by the Bowl of Punch, a large-bore mixture of spirits, citrus, sugar, water, and spice that bears the same relation to the anemic concoctions that pass under its name today that gladiatorial combat does to a sorority pillow fight. This isn't the place to go into its origins or its early history; those deserve a book of their own, and God willing they'll get one. Suffice it to say that it appears to be a version of the English drink detailed by George Gascoine in 1576 in his *Delicate Diet for Daintie Mouthde Droonkardes*, consisting of wine with "Sugar, Limons and sundry sortes of Spices . . . drowned therein," made by English travelers in India with local ingredients—various strong spirits and lots more citrus—and spread by sailors to the mother country, her colonies and neighbors, and eventually the world.

At its peak, the ritual of the Punch bowl was a secular communion, welding a group of good fellows together into a temporary sodality whose values superseded all others—or, in plain English, a group of men gathered around a bowl of Punch could be pretty much counted on to see it to the end, come what may. This was all in good fun, but it required its participants to have a large block of uncommitted time on their hands. As the eighteenth century wore into the nineteenth, this was less and less likely to be the case. Industrialization, improved communications, and the rise of the bourgeoisie all made claims on the individual that militated against partaking of the Flowing Bowl. Not that the Victorians were exactly sober, by our standards, but neither could they be as wet as their forefathers. In 1853, *Household Words*, the magazine edited by Charles Dickens, printed a nostalgic little piece titled "A Bowl of Punch," prompted by the author—the article was unsigned, but it well may have been Dickens himself—going into the Cock Tavern in Fleet Street and finding that the familiar old china Punch bowls that had occupied a shelf in the barroom, all ranked in a row ready for use, had been stacked up in a corner "as if no longer asked for." This was in fact the case. As Robert Chambers put it in 1864, "Advanced ideas on the question of temperance have doubtless . . . had their influence in rendering obsolete, in a great measure, this beverage."

The same fate befell the bowl of Punch in America, only two generations sooner. It's not that Americans suddenly stopped liking Punch. But they were busy, or at least thought it a virtue to seem that way. To sit around at a tavern ladling libations out of a capacious bowl was as much as to confess that you didn't have anywhere to be for the next few hours, and America was a go-ahead country, as everyone was always saying. (Americans were in no way averse to daytime drinking, I hasten to add; but it had to be quick.) From a workhorse of daily drinking, the bowl of Punch got promoted into a job that was largely ceremonial. It became a thing to be trotted out at club banquets and on holidays.

Its size and potency aren't the only things that sidelined the bowl of Punch. Improvements in distilling and, above all, aging of liquors meant that they required less intervention to make them palatable. The maturation of the global economy made for greater choice of potables and a more fragmented culture of drink. To some degree, central heating dimmed the charms of hot Punch. Ideas of democracy and individualism extended to men's behavior in the barroom, where they were less likely to all settle for the same thing or let someone else choose what they were to drink. In short, like all long-running social institutions the Bowl of Punch was subject to a plethora of subtle and incremental strains. By the time Jerry Thomas set pen to paper, it was already old-fashioned, and though his book contained recipes for fifty-nine Punch-bowl drinks, it's safe to say that most of them were foisted on him by his publishers and were essentially obsolete. The 1887 edition of his book finally acknowledged this by bumping the section on Punch from the front of the book to the back and replacing it with the one on Cocktails. (In the bartending guides of the late nineteenth and early twentieth centuries, the section devoted to bowls of Punch is truly vestigial, generally offering something like a dozen formulae and no more.) I have followed this tradition and reserved all but three recipes for Punch by the Bowl for their own book; those three, native American concoctions of great potency and charm, will be found after the section on Punches by the Glass.

Of course we didn't stop drinking Punch; it was too delectable and cooling a drink for that. We just figured out a way of having it quick and on the spot—as a people, we hate to hear the word *no*, and like nothing better than having it both ways. And we're willing to pay for it. Where there's someone willing to pay, there's usually someone willing to take that money. When Captain Fitzgerald saw Willard at the City Hotel, you'll recall, he was "preparing and issuing forth punch and spirits to strange-looking men." This suggests a much higher level of activity than the landlord's leisurely mixing of a bowl of Punch; it's likely that Willard was making them to order, one glass at a time. That's certainly how he was doing them later, and that's also how, before long, everybody else was taking them. The American plan has always been "I want mine now," and why shouldn't that apply to Punch as well? In fact, Willard wasn't even the first: According to the memoirs of the rowdy rambler Big Bill Otter, by 1806 plenty of New York bars were selling Punch by the glass, both large and small. In this chapter, we'll tackle the

Greater Punches, as it were, the ones generally made long and strong.

I. A LARGE GLASS OF PUNCH

By Jerry Thomas's day, there were a great many formulae for one-shot Punches in circulation (sadly, though, the formula for Willard's famous Extra Extra Peach Brandy Punch appears to have died with its creator). I present here a generous selection of the most important and, of course, tastiest.

BRANDY PUNCH

The first drink in Jerry Thomas's book—and indeed quite possibly his first acknowledgment as a bartender: On February 7, 1853, page four of the *Brooklyn Daily Eagle* carried a set of verses on a newspaper P. T. Barnum had launched, including these lines, satirizing Barnum's support of Prohibition (which

BRANDY PUNCH.

Brandy Punch. From *The Bon Vivant's Companion*, 1862. Note cigars, right. (Author's collection)

had been enacted in Maine in 1851, with the lax and arbitrary enforcement that usually accompanies such schemes):

In Yankee land, the papers say,
Barnum talks "Maine Law" all day,
But beneath his monster show,
Brandy punch is all the go.

If Thomas and George Earle were still running the Exchange under Barnum's Museum and Thomas was making the Punch the same way at age twenty-three as he was at age thirty-two when his book came out, small wonder it was all the go. In Thomas's hands, the individual Brandy Punch is the very epitome of the Fancy Drink; indeed, he felt so strongly about it that one of the book's few illustrations was devoted to it.

The popularity of Brandy Punch peaked before the Civil War, with the popularity of brandy itself. Postwar, many of the gents who drank it—the ones who survived the shooting, that is—seem to have switched their attention to the Sour, for which see below. A cautionary note, though: Like many of the Professor's drinks, this one's not for the novice tippler. It's a potent drink for long, slow sipping.

(USE LARGE BAR-GLASS.)

1 TABLE-SPOONFUL RASPBERRY SYRUP

2 TABLE-SPOONFULS [2 TSP] WHITE SUGAR

1 WINE-GLASS [2 OZ] WATER

1½ WINE-GLASS [3 OZ] BRANDY

½ SMALL-SIZED LEMON

2 SLICES OF ORANGE

1 PIECE OF PINE-APPLE

Fill the tumbler with shaved ice, shake well, and dress the top with berries in season; sip through a straw.

SOURCE: JERRY THOMAS, 1862

NOTES ON INGREDIENTS: The sugar should be superfine, the brandy cognac, and the berries whatever strikes your fancy. The illustration in Thomas's book appears to show a raspberry and a strawberry.

Thomas provides three close variations for this: To make this into **Curaçoa Punch**, substitute that liqueur for the raspberry syrup, replace 1 ounce of the brandy with Jamaica rum and "sip the nectar through a straw." For **West Indian Punch**, "add a clove or two of preserved ginger, and a little of the syrup." For **Barbadoes Punch** (as Thomas spells it), "add a table-spoonful of guava jelly." Both are very fine drinks, particularly if you drop the raspberry syrup and increase the sugar to ½-ounce. These two should also be made with 2 ounces of brandy and 1 ounce of rum, with Mount Gay or Cockburn's in the Barbadoes Punch and pretty much any rum you like in the West Indian. From Charles W. Campbell's 1867 *American Barkeeper*, we collect another West Indian variation, the **Tamarind Punch**. Make as the Brandy Punch, cutting the brandy back to 2 ounces, substituting 1 tablespoon of tamarind jelly for the lemon juice and dashing a fragrant Jamaica rum liberally on top at the end.

NOTES ON EXECUTION: Begin by squeezing the lemon into the glass. Add the sugar and the water and stir. Then pour in the syrup and the brandy. The orange slices and the pineapple are a matter of taste and conjecture. The engraving accompanying the recipe shows them as a mere garnish, but there's every possibility that that was mere artistic license and everything, berries included, was all shaken up together; that's what the 1869 *Steward & Barkeeper's Manual* states, anyway, and very clearly at that. If done in a Boston shaker with plenty of ice, the result would be a gooey mess. But rolled back and forth with shaved ice, which lacks the kinetic energy to break up fruits, it would be rather more attractive. In short, I'll use the fruits as garnish if all I've got is bar ice; if I've got shaved or finely cracked ice, I'll give everything a gentle shake, reserving a couple of berries for the top.

The jellies in Barbadoes Punch and Tamarind Punch take special handling, since they will not readily dissolve in cold water. Put the jelly in the glass first and add a splash of hot water (½ to ¾ of an ounce), stirring well before adding the rest of the ingredients (the water should be reduced accordingly). If making a bunch of these, you can do this in advance, preparing a sort of syrup with equal parts water and jelly.

VANILLA PUNCH

One more quick Brandy Punch variation from Professor Thomas. Clearly it was a specialty of his, and I'll respect that. This one is simple and very tasty. The 1869 *Steward & Barkeeper's Manual* published by Haney & Co. in New York calls this a "Scadeva Punch" and notes that "this drink is seldom called for at a bar, and is known to only a few prominent bartenders" (the name is either a typo or a mangling of something intelligible or it's the Italian word for "it fell off," which is hard to explain unless the recipe fell off the back of a dray-wagon).

(USE LARGE BAR-GLASS.)

1 TABLE-SPOONFUL [2 TSP] OF SUGAR

1 WINE-GLASS [2 OZ] OF BRANDY

THE JUICE OF ¼ LEMON

Fill the tumbler with shaved ice, shake well, ornament with one or two slices of lemon, and flavor with a few drops of vanilla extract.

This is a delicious drink, and should be imbibed through a glass tube or straw.

SOURCE: JERRY THOMAS, 1862

NOTES ON INGREDIENTS: If at all possible, use a good vanilla extract, such as the one made by Charles H. Baldwin & Co of

Stockbridge, Massachusetts, an old Yankee brand if ever there was one.

PISCO PUNCH

"You should have had a snort of Mrs. Sykes' Pisco Punch. . . . It was said New York had not before ever seen or heard of the insidious concoction which in its time had caused the unseating of South American governments and women to set world's records in various and interesting fields of activity. In early San Francisco, where the punch first made its North American appearance in 1856, the police allowed but one drink per person in twenty-four hours, it's that propulsive. But Mrs. Sykes served them up like *pain, à discrétion*, as the signs used to say in front of the little restaurants in Paris, meaning you could have all the bread you wanted. As a consequence, discretion vanished."

In 1950, when A. J. Liebling's pal James A. MacDonald, alias Col. John R. Stingo, was recalling these events (which transpired when a party of San Francisco con artists came to New York), Pisco Punch was the mixological equivalent to a lost Mozart symphony. Before Prohibition, this particular twist on the old Brandy Punch had been San Francisco's secret weapon, a drink so smooth, delightful, and potent that, well, as the Colonel says . . . Though, as Harold Ross of the New Yorker later recalled, "All San Francisco bars used to serve them, and one or two served nothing else," it was universally acknowledged that the one true and authentic recipe—complete with secret ingredient—was in the sole possession of a closemouthed old Scot by the name of Duncan Nicol, proprietor of the historic Bank Exchange saloon; he died in 1926, his secret seemingly intact. Five or six years later, the historian Herbert Asbury scoured the town "industriously, even desperately" for a bottle of pisco, the clear South American brandy upon which the drink was based; he found none. Nor did the situation improve much after Repeal: there was a short-lived attempt to sell a bottled Pisco Punch, and San Francisco maintained a "House of Pisco" for a while in the mid-1940s, but by 1950 both Punch and pisco had effectively vanished from the American pharmacopoeia. While I cannot in good conscience call this a tragedy, it is certainly a shame. For the seventy-odd years leading up to Prohibition, San Francisco had witnessed the finest flowering of the American sporting life—that created by the "gentleman of elegant leisure," as one early San Franciscan defined his occupation, and the soiled doves with which he associated—and Pisco Punch was its Oil of Anointment. That life is beyond recovery, but thankfully the Punch is not. Although a few recipes were published in the 1900s and 1910s, this one, from Nicol's bar manager, has the greatest claim to authenticity.

1. Take a fresh pineapple. Cut it in squares about ½ by 1½ inches. Put these squares of fresh pineapple in a bowl of gum syrup to soak overnight. That serves the double purpose of flavoring the gum syrup with the pineapple and soaking the pineapple, both of which are used afterwards in the Pisco Punch.

2. In the morning mix in a big bowl the following:

> **½ PINT (8 OZ) OF THE GUM SYRUP, PINEAPPLE FLAVORED AS ABOVE**
>
> **1 PINT (16 OZ) DISTILLED WATER**
>
> **¾ PINT (10 OZ [SIC]) LEMON JUICE**
>
> **1 BOTTLE (24 OZ) PERUVIAN PISCO BRANDY**

Serve very cold but be careful not to keep the ice in too long because of dilution. Use 3 or 4 oz punch glasses. Put one of these above squares of pineapple in each glass. Lemon juice or gum syrup may be added to taste.

SOURCE: WILLIAM BRONSON, "SECRETS OF PISCO PUNCH REVEALED," *CALIFORNIA HISTORICAL QUARTERLY*, 1973

NOTES ON INGREDIENTS: If possible the pisco should be of the varietal known as Italia (Barsol and Don Cesar are two particularly good brands). One of the early recipes claims that lime juice can also be used. It can. It has been suggested to me that Nicol's secret ingredient was cocaine, at least until it was outlawed. I don't recommend it.

NOTES ON EXECUTION: Nicol had his own procedure for preparing this, which included compounding part of it in secrecy in the basement every morning. Pauline Jacobson, a color writer for the *San Francisco Bulletin* who did a piece about the Bank Exchange in 1912, watched Nicol assemble the drink and recorded one of the regulars' commentary on the process:

> "See . . . he is squeezing a f-r-e-s-h lemon. In the bar uptown they have the lemon juice already prepared, which leaves a bitter taste after drinking. And Duncan n-e-v-e-r uses any of them effervescent waters. . . . He always uses distilled water."

This, combined with Jacobson's description of Nicol, "intent upon his work, with hands trembling with the years, yet measuring with the nicety of an apothecary," prompts me to suggest the following procedure:

First, prepare the pineapple syrup, as above. Mix this with the pisco, with three parts pisco to one part syrup and bottle it (this will keep in the refrigerator for at least a couple of weeks, and longer if you strain out the sediment that it will throw off). To assemble the drink, combine in a cocktail shaker 2 ounces of the pisco-syrup mix, 3/4 ounce distilled water (or bottled water, or tap water if yours is good), squeeze the juice of half a (small) lemon or lime into this, add ice, shake, and strain into a small bar-glass; add a chunk of syrup-soaked pineapple and serve.

COLD WHISKEY PUNCH

While the early mixographers pretty much ignored American whiskey Punches, their nonliterary peers and their customers didn't. "An iced monongahela punch," as a correspondent in New Orleans informed the readers of the *Brooklyn Eagle* in 1852, "is not at all bad to take . . . it forms a most admirable thirst-quenching and exhilarating drink. The liquor should have age to render it excellent."

(USE LARGE BAR-GLASS.)

TAKE ONE TEASPOONFUL OF POWDERED WHITE SUGAR, DISSOLVED IN A LITTLE WATER

JUICE OF HALF A LEMON OR ONE LIME

ONE AND A HALF WINE-GLASSESFUL [3 OZ] OF RED TOP RYE

FILL GLASS WITH SHAVED ICE

ADD TWO DASHES [1 TSP] OF RUM

Shake well and strain into cool stem punch glass. Add two thin slices of lemon and any other seasonable fruit. Serve with a straw.

SOURCE: ANON., *RED TOP RYE GUIDE* (CA. 1905)

NOTES ON INGREDIENTS: Red Top is no more, but any good straight rye or, for that matter, bourbon will make a tasty Punch like this. The rum should be a Jamaica style.

HOT WHISKEY PUNCH

For this Caledonian staple, see the Whisky Skin, in the section on Hot Toddy.

GIN PUNCH

By far the most common form of single-serving Gin Punch was the John Collins, which you'll find immediately below. But that didn't reach the height of its popularity in America until the 1870s. Before that, we had this—and very tasty it is, too.

(USE LARGE BAR-GLASS.)

1 TABLE-SPOONFUL OF RASPBERRY SYRUP

2 TABLE-SPOONFULS [2 TSP] OF POWDERED WHITE SUGAR

1 WINE-GLASS [2 OZ] OF WATER

1½ WINE-GLASS [3 OZ] OF HOLLAND GIN

[JUICE OF] ½ SMALL-SIZED LEMON

2 SLICES OF ORANGE

1 PIECE OF PINEAPPLE

Fill the tumbler with shaved ice.

Shake well, and ornament the top with berries in season. Sip through a glass tube or straw.

SOURCE: JERRY THOMAS, 1862

NOTES ON INGREDIENTS: There's enough going on here that you can substitute Plymouth gin, or even a London dry gin, for the Hollands and still enjoy complete satisfaction. The anonymous 1887 version of Jerry Thomas's book adds "1 or 2 dashes of Maraschino," which is a good idea, and a "slice of lime," which is neither good nor bad.

NOTES ON EXECUTION: Begin by dissolving the sugar in the water.

JOHN COLLINS (AKA TOM COLLINS)

One dull and rainy morning around 1830 (give or take a few years), two of the grandsons of Richard Brinsley Sheridan, the wittiest of Anglo-Irish playwrights, got to versifying to kill the time. Charles and Frank might not have been sparklers of their grandfather's stature, but judging from what I've seen of their work that day neither were they the Adam Sandlers of their age. Unfortunately, I've never seen a complete version of it; when and if the whole thing was ever printed, I don't know. But it circulated in manuscript and memory for many years and later antiquarians and nostalgic old men quoted a few stanzas in passing. One stanza, however, and only one made it into the public sphere (there are several variations on the last line):

My name is John Collins, head-waiter at Limmer's,
The corner of Conduit Street, Hanover Square;
My chief occupation is filling of brimmers,
To solace young gentlemen laden with care.

In the rest of the verses, which were meant to be sung to the then-popular Welsh tune "Jenny Jones," Collins—who was described by those who knew him as a "little, round, rosy-gilled body" with a good deal of bustle and a colorful turn of phrase—goes on to dissect Limmer's Hotel's other staff and, more important, many of its frightfully aristocratic, fast, and sporty guests and frequenters. Along the way, the brothers Sheridan allow their narrator to express a little pride in his barkeeping:

My ale-cup's the best that ever you tasted,
Mr. Frank always drinks my gin-punch when he smokes;

I'm old but I'm hearty; I'm grey, but I'm merry;
I don't wish to go, and few wish me gone;

Shall I bring you a pint, or a bottle of sherry,
To drink the good health, and long life of Old John?

But as we all know, it wasn't sherry or pints of champagne that would ensure Old John's long life; it was that "gin-punch" that Frank Sheridan liked so much. I don't know how the formula for what Old John was serving at Limmer's (usually as an eye-opener or corpse reviver) compares to what was later circulating under his name, since I've been unable to unearth a detailed description of the hotel's Punch. But judging from that drink, the Punch was quite close to the Gin Punch served at the time by London's Garrick Club, which combined gin, lemon juice, maraschino liqueur, and chilled soda water.

No matter; authentic Limmer's recipe or not, *a* Gin Punch, anyway, got Collins's name welded onto it and before you knew it "England's morning 'John Collins' [was] following the sun and circling the world" (thus Webster). The *New York World* believed that the vector for transmission was officers of the British army, which is entirely plausible, the upper reaches of the army and Limmer's drawing from the same social class. According to the *World*, the drink made it to New York in the late 1850s, when "a very eminent officer of the Royal Artillery" taught it to the boys behind the bar at the Clarendon Hotel, his New York head-quarters. By 1865, anyway, it's being mentioned in print, and before too many years have passed it's become one of the indispensable summer drinks.

But America's a big country, and things echo strangely in all that space. That happened to the John Collins in the 1870s. When it turns up in the new edition of Jerry Thomas's book in 1876, it's somehow turned into a *Tom* Collins. What gives?

It's that echo. In 1874, you see, an annoying bit of tomfoolery began crisscrossing the country. It couldn't be simpler: Turn to the guy standing next to you at the bar and say that you heard Tom Collins was going around badmouthing him, and that you just saw said Mr. Collins around the corner, down the street, across town, wherever. It sounds moronic, but judging from newspaper accounts of the hijinx that ensued—only a few of them fatal—it worked. At any rate, for people who had never heard of Limmer's or Old John, "Tom Collins" must have made more sense as a drink name—particularly since the thing was generally made with Old Tom gin, one of the growth spirits of the time. Before long, the drink was a Tom Collins, and the name *John Collins* was reserved for offshoots and variations.

It's likely that Old John was spared news of this travesty. Having put in his forty-odd years at Limmer's and seen a great deal of life in the process, he retired in the late 1850s to a cottage outside London, where Dickens once visited him (Boz was a Gin Punch man from way back). I don't know when he died, but it can't have been all that much later.

(USE LARGE BAR-GLASS.)

TEASPOONFUL OF POWDERED SUGAR

THE JUICE OF HALF A LEMON

A WINE GLASS OF OLD TOM GIN

A BOTTLE OF PLAIN SODA

Shake up, or stir up with ice. Add a slice of lemon peel to finish.

SOURCE: *STEWARD & BARKEEPER'S MANUAL,* 1869

NOTES ON INGREDIENTS: Actually, many in fact preferred the softer, maltier Hollands in this drink. That bottle of soda would be the small kind, which held 6 ounces. As for variations: In 1876, Jerry Thomas (who was of the Tom gin school) listed whiskey and brandy versions alongside the gin one. The formulae were otherwise the same.

NOTES ON EXECUTION: There are few arguments in the world of bartending more perennial than the distinction between Collinses and Fizzes. They both have essentially the same ingredients and both are tall, so it ultimately comes down to what you do with the ice: Do you leave it in or take it out? Considered historically, the way is a little clearer than many make it out to be.

The glasses of Gin Punch Old John would have been handing around would have been made with chilled soda water, but would not have had ice in them. In America, however, there was more ice and tall Punches were generally made with it in the glass, and this was a tall Punch (although the influential formula the *New York World* printed in 1877 left the matter up to individual taste). America's bartenders were also used to shaking drinks and straining them. This is how Jerry Thomas made his, adding the cold soda at the end. But this is also how he made his Gin "Fiz"—in fact, the only difference between the two is that the Collins uses more of everything and goes into a bigger glass. The Fizz is, essentially, a short drink: It's meant to be drunk down with dispatch. The Collins, however, is too big for that. This distinction is what bartenders seized on. Because it had some staying power in the glass, the Collins also had the potential to get warm. The answer to this is to put ice in the glass, and once you're doing that there's no point to shaking and straining. This, then, became the classic distinction between the drinks: a Fizz is shaken and strained, a Collins built in the glass over large, slow-melting cubes—and the larger the glass, the better. Eventually, the Tom Collins would have its own glass, a big, long 16-ouncer (bars were stocking special "John Collins" glasses as early as 1884).

The *World* had one stir the sugar in at the end, which will make the drink foam in a pleasing manner.

CLARET PUNCH

"You never see the perspiring laborer, with brawny arms bared to the elbow, and a brow beaded with huge drops of honest sweat, step up to a bar in a hot Summer's day, and call for a claret punch!" No, for him it will be "Bourbon, rather than the delicious claret punch. . . . But your fine snob, or your cultured gentleman, will wipe his brow with his perfumed handkerchief, while he sips his punch, and insinuate that it's 'very hot, by Jove, you know.' "

Well, that's the way the *Brooklyn Eagle* saw things in 1873, anyway. The *Eagle* says nothing about the **Sauterne Punch** that Thomas included in his book (simply substitute a cheap Sauternes for the claret), but if Claret Punch is a dude's drink, that's got to be one, too.

(USE LARGE BAR-GLASS.)

1½ TABLE-SPOONFUL [2 TSP] OF SUGAR

1 SLICE OF LEMON

2 OR 3 SLICES OF ORANGE

Fill the tumbler with shaved ice, and then pour in your claret, shake well, and ornament with berries in season. Place a straw in the glass.

SOURCE: JERRY THOMAS, 1862

NOTES ON INGREDIENTS: The wine doesn't strictly have to be a Bordeaux; any full-bodied, dry red will do just fine.

NOTES ON EXECUTION: Dissolve the sugar in a little water first (or just use an equal quantity of gum syrup). Add the wine, the citrus, and the ice, and shake vigorously. Pour unstrained into a tall glass and finish as directed.

MILK PUNCH

As a Punch bowl drink, Milk Punch goes back to the late 1600s or early 1700s (at the time, its invention was attributed to Aphra Behn, wit, actress, courtesan, and the first woman ever to earn her living solely by writing). But Milk Punch in a glass and Milk Punch in a bowl or bottle are two entirely different drinks. In the latter, the cream is deliberately made to curdle and then strained out. This makes for a drink that's stable and undeniably smooth, but not necessarily lush. But in the former, where stability isn't a concern since it only has to sit around long enough for the sport who ordered it to pick it up and insert it into his head, it's all about the cream. And, in the case of the Professor's formula, the alcohol. Not that he was alone in this regard: as the *Brooklyn Eagle* noted in 1873, speaking no doubt from experience, Milk Punch is "the surest thing in the world to get drunk on, and so fearfully drunk, that you won't know whether you are a cow, yourself, or some other foolish thing."

(USE LARGE BAR-GLASS.)

1 TABLE-SPOONFUL [2 TSP] OF FINE WHITE SUGAR

2 TABLE-SPOONFULS [2 TSP] OF WATER

1 WINE-GLASS [2 OZ] OF COGNAC BRANDY

½ WINE-GLASS [1 OZ] OF SANTA CRUZ RUM

⅓ TUMBLERFUL OF SHAVED ICE

Fill with milk, shake the ingredients well together, and grate a little nutmeg on top

SOURCE: JERRY THOMAS, 1862

NOTES ON INGREDIENTS: This drink will not lose its appeal should you follow the path of discretion and cut back by half the brandy (use a good cognac) and the rum (which should be smooth, rich, and well-aged). For the variation known as **Egg Milk Punch**, see Egg Nogg, which is the same thing.

NOTES ON EXECUTION: Begin by dissolving the sugar in the water; shake with extreme prejudice (and if using an egg, with even more violence than that). Serve with a straw.

MISSISSIPPI PUNCH

I don't know if Jerry Thomas picked this up when he was at the Planter's House in St. Louis or in New Orleans, Keokuk, or somewhere else during his days "along the Mississippi," as he put it. Wherever it's from, it testifies to the capacity and taste of our forbears.

Cut all the boozes in half and you have the **El Dorado Punch**, which was included in the section of new drinks tacked on to the end of the 1876 second edition of Thomas's book. Was this a liquid reminiscence of his forty-niner days? The fact that it wasn't included in the first edition somewhat militates against that, but maybe he just forgot and took the opportunity to correct his error.

(USE LARGE BAR-GLASS.)

1 WINE-GLASS [2 OZ] OF BRANDY

½ WINE-GLASS [1 OZ] OF JAMAICA RUM

½ WINE-GLASS [1 OZ] OF BOURBON WHISKEY

1½ TABLE-SPOONFUL [1 TBSP] OF POWDERED WHITE SUGAR

¼ [½] OF A LARGE LEMON

Fill a tumbler with shaved ice.

The above must be well shaken, and to those who like their draughts "like linked sweetness long drawn out," let them use a glass tube or straw to sip the nectar through. The top of this punch should be ornamented with small pieces of orange, and berries in season.

SOURCE: JERRY THOMAS, 1862

NOTES ON INGREDIENTS: Major Unett, of Her Majesty's 3rd Light Dragoons, included a Mississippi Punch in the list of "American summer drinks" he published in the *Illustrated London News* in the late 1850s; his version relied on "one glass [i.e., 2 oz] of Outard [sic] brandy, half ditto of Jamaica rum [and] a tablespoonful of arrack" for its motive power. This is delightful, if you can get your hands on the arrack (what you want here is the Indonesian kind, as aged and bottled in Northwest Europe, rather than the anise-flavored Middle Eastern kind).

NOTES ON EXECUTION: Squeeze the lemon into the mixing glass, add the sugar, and stir to dissolve it. Then add the spirits and the ice and shake well. Serve unstrained.

ST. CHARLES PUNCH

The St. Charles Hotel was one of New Orleans's two finest. Where the St. Louis (which stood on the site now occupied by the Royal Orleans) served the French Quarter, the St. Charles was on the avenue of the same name, across Canal in the American part of town. There's no shortage of lore about the St. Charles, which before the Civil War was for a time considered one of the two or three best hotels in America, but the stories will have to await another venue. Suffice it to say that its Punch, which Thomas must've picked up in New Orleans, speaks for it eloquently.

(USE LARGE BAR-GLASS.)

1 TABLE-SPOONFUL [1 TSP] OF SUGAR

1 WINE-GLASS [2 OZ] OF PORT WINE

1 PONY-GLASS [1 OZ] OF BRANDY

THE JUICE OF ¼ OF A LEMON

Fill the tumbler with shaved ice, shake well, ornament with fruits in season, and serve with a straw.

SOURCE: JERRY THOMAS, 1862

NOTES ON INGREDIENTS: The port should be a decent ruby, the brandy cognac, the ice cracked, and the fruits berries. With a few simple changes, this becomes pioneer San Francisco mixologist Charles B. Campbell's aptly named **Enchantress**, which is found in his 1867 *American Barkeeper*: simply double the brandy, replace the sugar with two teaspoonfuls of orange curaçao, shake with ice (although Campbell's is in fact un-iced), and strain the whole thing into a "small wine goblet"—I like to use a champagne flute. Then smile.

NOTES ON EXECUTION: Begin by dissolving the sugar in the lemon juice.

NATIONAL GUARD 7TH REGIMENT PUNCH

The Seventh Regiment was *the* National Guard—before that title was applied to all the states' militias, it was applied to New York State's, and before that only the Seventh was entitled to it. If there's such a thing as a white-shoe regiment, the Seventh was it—or rather, a "Silk Stocking Regiment," as it was known. With a roster that was virtually cut and pasted from the Social Register, it was the toniest of outfits. And if the only fighting it saw as a unit during the Civil War was in quelling the New York City Draft Riots, for which it was called back while on its way to Gettysburg, the Seventh made up for it by taking on the Hindenburg Line in World War I.

(USE LARGE BAR-GLASS.)

> 1 TABLE-SPOONFUL [2 TSP] **OF SUGAR**
>
> THE JUICE OF ¼ [½ OZ] **OF A LEMON**
>
> 1 WINE-GLASS [2 OZ] **OF BRANDY**
>
> 1 WINE-GLASS [2 OZ] **OF CATAWBA WINE**
>
> FLAVOR WITH [1 TSP] **RASPBERRY SYRUP**

Fill the glass with shaved ice. Shake and mix thoroughly, then ornament with slices of orange, pineapple, and berries in season, and dash with Jamaica rum. This delicious beverage should be imbibed through a straw.

SOURCE: JERRY THOMAS, 1862

NOTES ON INGREDIENTS: The brandy should, of course, be cognac. For the Catawba, see the Chatham Artillery Punch (page 94). In 1887, though, the revised edition of Thomas's book calls for sherry instead; the results are not bad (use an oloroso).

NOTES ON EXECUTION: Begin by dissolving the sugar in the lemon juice.

69TH REGIMENT PUNCH

Where the Seventh was Fifth Avenue, the Fighting Sixty-Ninth (a nickname given to it by Robert E. Lee) was the old East Side. Irish, Catholic, rough and tumble, Democratic, it was everything its rival wasn't, and vice versa. It fought just as hard, though, if not harder. Repeatedly cut to pieces at Fredericksburg, Chancellorsville, and Gettysburg, it nonetheless fought through until Appomattox. The unit is still around and still fighting hard, having lost nineteen members to date in Iraq.

The Sixty-Ninth's Punch, homely but stalwart, stands in the same relation to the Seventh's that the Fighting Irish did to the National Guard.

The Punch combines Scotch and Irish whiskies, which is rather puzzling, what with the Scots being largely Protestant—not entirely, though, and if you use a malt from the Western Highlands, which are still in part Catholic, you might just be able to squeak by.

(I N   E A R T H E N   M U G .)

> ½ WINE-GLASS [1 OZ] OF IRISH WHISKEY
>
> ½ WINE-GLASS [1 OZ] OF SCOTCH WHISKY
>
> 1 TEA-SPOONFUL OF SUGAR
>
> 1 PIECE OF LEMON
>
> 2 WINE-GLASSES [4 OZ] OF HOT WATER

This is a capital punch for a cold night.

SOURCE: JERRY THOMAS, 1862

N O T E S   O N   I N G R E D I E N T S : Both whiskies should be pot-still, if at all possible; see the Whisky Skin (page 144). The sugar should be Demerara or turbinado. The lemon—use a half-wheel—can be reduced to a long strip of peel.

N O T E S   O N   E X E C U T I O N : See the Hot Toddy (page 137).

HOT MILK PUNCH

The nineteenth century may have lacked Ambien, but it had this.

(U S E   L A R G E   B A R - G L A S S .)

> 1 TABLE-SPOONFUL OF FINE WHITE SUGAR
>
> . . . .
>
> 1 WINE-GLASS [2 OZ] OF COGNAC BRANDY
>
> ½ WINE-GLASS [1 OZ] OF SANTA CRUZ RUM
>
> . . . .

Fill with [hot] milk, [stir] the ingredients well together, and grate a little nutmeg on top.

SOURCE: JERRY THOMAS, 1862 (COMPOSITE)

NOTES ON INGREDIENTS: Again, the spirits can be safely reduced here without affecting the drink's epicurean qualities.

NOTES ON EXECUTION: As the reviser of Jerry Thomas's book reminds us, "in preparing any kind of a hot drink, the glass should always be first rinsed rapidly with hot water; if this is not done the drink cannot be served sufficiently hot to suit a fastidious customer."

II. THREE BOWLS OF AMERICAN PUNCH

In general, the Bowl of Punch was a transatlantic institution, with—give or take a little smuggled French brandy or native New England rum—pretty much the same things going into the bowl in Britain and America, so that, for instance, George IV's favorite tipple, Regent's Punch, turns up as a specialty of Albany, New York (I will not speculate why). Here, though, are three characteristically American formulae for charging the Punch bowl.

PHILADELPHIA FISH-HOUSE PUNCH

Fish-House Punch is thrice blessed. Its name is memorable and strangely alluring, its history is august and eccentric, and its formula is delicious and deadly. The greatest of all American Punches, it deserves to be protected by law, taught in the schools, and made a mandatory part of every Fourth of July celebration, with dilute portions given to those not yet of legal age, so that they may be accustomed to the taste.

The eighteenth-century Englishman was an extremely clubbable fellow. He formed regular social associations at the drop of a tricorn hat. Many were rather informal affairs, a few friends meeting at a set time and place to push the port around a bit and drain a bowl or two of Punch, preferably with a roast to keep body and soul together. Others were a little more eccentric. Take the Colony of Schuylkill, a rod and gun club founded by thirty of William Penn's followers on the banks of the Schuylkill in 1732, when Americans were still English. First off, they claimed that their little acre of land was an independent colony of its own, complete with governor, secretary of state, assembly, code of laws, coroner, and sheriff. After the War of Independence, they changed their name—along with everyone else—from colony to state. As the State *in* Schuylkill (exactly why they changed "of" to "in" I've never quite been able to grasp), they persisted through thick and thin, moving their simple wooden fishing-house (the "Castle") once or twice when civilization encroached, giving up the hunting when the woods got too crowded to have bullets flying through them and the fishing when the refuse from the gas-works upstream killed the river. But no matter; every other Wednesday from May to October, year in and year out for more than two hundred years the twenty-five "citizens" and five "apprentices," or citizens-in-training, would gather to execute the club's business. For all I know, they may be there still.

That "business"? Eating and drinking and precious little else. But what set the State in Schuylkill apart from other rich-people's clubs is that its "citizens" traditionally did all the work. There was no staff to do the marketing, sweep out the Castle, gut the fish (the Coroner did that), build the fire, plank the shad, truss the pig, grill the steaks, or brew the Punch. All pitched in, each according to his abilities, the citizens instructing the apprentices. And when guests came (each member was allowed one), they pitched in, too. In 1825, Marquis de Lafayette turned steaks on the grill. I don't know what they had George Washington doing when he visited in 1787, but rumor has it that in 1882 Chester Arthur—the only other sitting president to be a guest—donned an apron and shelled peas.

The club's world-renowned "Fish-House Punch" was traditionally made in a large bowl that did double duty as a baptismal font for the citizens' infant sons; "its ample space . . .

would indeed admit of total immersion," as one citizen noted. I doubt that there was Punch in it at the time—it was far too precious for such usage, and far too potent. The earliest recipe I have for it comes from Jerry Thomas, who evidently got it in turn from an issue of Frederick S. Cozzens's *Wine Press*, who got it from Charles Godfrey Leland, a Philadelphia lawyer who was primarily known for his literary endeavors. Since he was also a citizen of the State in Schuylkill, his formula for the stuff—"as delicious as [the famous Punch] of London civic banquets," as he recalled in his memoirs—must be considered authentic, although alas it can no longer be executed as written. But even in its modern, fallen state, Fish-House Punch lives up to the old verses:

There's a little place just out of town,
Where, if you go to lunch,
They'll make you forget your mother-in-law
With a drink called Fish-House Punch.

[FOR QUANTITIES, SEE NOTES ON INGREDIENTS.]

(FROM A RECIPE IN THE POSSESSION OF CHARLES G. LELAND, ESQ.)

⅓ PINT OF LEMON JUICE

¾ POUND OF WHITE SUGAR

1 PINT OF MIXTURE*

2½ PINTS OF COLD WATER

THE ABOVE IS GENERALLY SUFFICIENT FOR ONE PERSON.

* TO MAKE THIS MIXTURE, TAKE ¼ PINT OF PEACH BRANDY, ½ PINT OF COGNAC BRANDY, AND ¼ PINT OF JAMAICA RUM.

SOURCE: JERRY THOMAS, 1862

NOTES ON INGREDIENTS: There's too much sugar in this, but that's the least of our problems here. The thing that's so high we can't get over it, so deep we can't get under it, is the complete disappearance of real peach brandy. With other great archeological ingredients like Batavia arrack, Holland gin and absinthe, at least we have some recourse—they're still made *somewhere* in the world, after all, and with a little persistence, ingenuity, and cash they can be secured or imitated. With peach brandy, we're screwed. A dry eau-de-vie that was distilled from peaches and their pits and then aged in oak barrels, often for many years, real peach brandy never really came back after Prohibition. Maybe it's because the Southern states that specialized in it caught the Baptist anti-booze flu early; maybe it was just too pungent or too expensive. Fortunately, the State in Schuylkill outlived it and made its own adjustments. These work out to adding 1 ounce of the modern, sweet peach brandy to 9 ounces of brandy and 6 of rum (there are some good recipes that reverse the proportion of cognac and rum; if that's what you like, go ahead).

You will note Leland's statement on quantity. He may not be kidding. For the modern partygoer, though, free from having to plank shad and shell peas in the great outdoors before stuffing himself to the bursting point with fish and pig and beef, it may be a bit much. The best solution, I find, is to triple the recipe—1 pint of lemon juice, 1 pound or a little more of Demerara sugar, 3 ounces of peach brandy (use a good brand like Marie Brizard, if you can), 27 ounces of cognac, 18 ounces of rum, and 3 quarts of water—and try to serve twelve to fifteen with it.

NOTES ON EXECUTION: Before juicing the lemons, peel three of them with a swivel-bladed vegetable peeler, doing your best to avoid including the pith. In a large bowl, muddle the peels in with the sugar until as much as possible of the lemon oil has been extracted (this was known to the old adepts at making Punch as "preparing the oleo-saccharum"). Heat 1 pint of the water to boiling and add it to the bowl, stirring until the sugar has dissolved. Fish out the lemon peels, add the lemon juice, the liquor, and the rest of the water. Let this cool in the refrigerator for 1 to 2 hours, add a large block of ice (this can be made by freezing a gallon bowl of water overnight) and serve.

ROCKY MOUNTAIN PUNCH

If the Major James Foster, whom Thomas credits for this famous recipe, is the same as the Colonel James Foster of St. Joseph, Missouri, who came home from the Idaho diggings in 1864 bearing suspiciously accurate tales of vigilante justice—highwaymen hung, banditti bearded in their lairs by concerned citizens, posses winkling desperados out of their lairs with "mounted howitzers"—it adds extra savor to this already plenty savory Punch.

To look at the recipe for Rocky Mountain Punch is to assume that the name is merely honorific, assigned from the comfort of a club chair two thousand miles from Pikes Peak and the rough and ready life of the mines. But that would be a mistake. In all but the most precarious and temporary camps, the supply of fine drink was an item of paramount concern to what was by certain standards an unhealthily large proportion of the population, and items like champagne, Jamaica rum, maraschino liqueur, and lemons were often available when things like vegetables, eggs, and soap weren't.

Rocky Mountain Punch retained its popularity as a banquet-drink through the end of the century, both in its native precincts and among the artificial canyons of the urban East.

(FOR A MIXED PARTY OF TWENTY.)

(FROM A RECIPE IN THE POSSESSION OF MAJOR JAMES FOSTER.)

THIS DELICIOUS PUNCH IS COMPOUNDED AS FOLLOWS:

5 BOTTLES OF CHAMPAGNE

1 QUART OF JAMAICA RUM

1 PINT OF MARASCHINO

6 LEMONS, SLICED

SUGAR TO TASTE

Mix the above ingredients in a large punch-bowl, then place in the centre of the bowl a large square block of ice, ornamented on top with rock candy, loaf-sugar, sliced lemons or oranges, and fruits in season. This is a splendid punch for New Year's Day.

NOTES ON INGREDIENTS: Use superfine sugar, or substitute gum syrup. How much is needed will depend on the dryness of the champagne and the sweetness of the maraschino liqueur, which might be sufficient all by itself. If it's not, begin with 2 ounces and adjust upward by taste.

NOTES ON EXECUTION: Steep the lemon slices in the combined rum and maraschino for at least 4 hours before assembly. For improvising a block of ice, see Philadelphia Fish-House Punch (page 89).

CHATHAM ARTILLERY PUNCH

Finally, a Punch not from Jerry Thomas. The Chatham Artillery of Savannah was a Social-Register militia of considerable antiquity (it was formed in 1786) that spent far more time parading and partying than it did loading cannons and shooting them, at least until those hotheads up the coast in Charleston fired on Fort Sumter. After seeing considerable action in its neck of the woods, part of the battery was captured in 1864 and the rest surrendered in 1865. Eventually, it was reconstituted, going on to serve in the Spanish-American War, World War I, World War II, and on, until the present, As I write this, it—or rather its successor, the 118th Battalion of the Georgia National Guard—is deployed in Iraq.

Back in the day, it was not a unit that deprived itself of the good things in life, as long as such were to be had. As Charles Jones recalled in 1867, at the beginning of the Civil War "the *cuisine* of the company was perfect" and "the well fed Artillery-man, enjoying his champagne punch within the comfortable casemates, little thought of the coming day when even a glass of Confederate whisky could not be obtained."

I don't know precisely when the below recipe made its debut or its connection to Jones's "champagne punch," but by the end of the century the Chatham Artillery's house Punch was a byword for its seductiveness and potency. One Georgia newspaper assured its readers in 1883 that "there is such a beverage made and known as artillery punch. We are living witnesses to the fact that it is no misnomer. When it attacketh a man it layeth him low and he knoweth not whence he cometh or whither he goeth." That was Admiral Dewey's experience of it, anyway, when he visited Savannah in 1900, just as it was Chester Arthur's a few years before and William Howard Taft's a few years after. The *Baltimore American* summed up its reputation in a poem, or at least a limerick:

When you visit the town of Savannah
Enlist 'neath the temperance banneh,
For if you should lunch,
On artillery punch,
It will treat you in sorrowful manneh.

The city's boosters conceded its strength, but claimed that the skill with which the locals concocted it mitigated the damage; that "in Savannah, it puts a man to bed like a gentleman; outside of Savannah it makes him a howling imbecile, a laughingstock for the populace, and a victim for the police barracks."

Although the Punch's composition was supposedly no secret, I have been unable to find a formula for it earlier than 1897, when a member of the Georgia Pharmaceutical Society contributed sketchy and manifestly incomplete instructions for it to a trade journal. The version below, printed a decade later, is somewhat better, although it nonetheless bears clear signs of corruption. (Its source admits as much when it says that "its vigor in those days [i.e., when the Chatham Artillery was founded] was much greater than at present, experience having taught the rising generation to modify the receipt of their forefathers to conform to the weaker constitutions of their progeny.")

1 GALLON CATAWBA WINE, LIGHT COLOR

1 QUART ST. CROIX RUM

4 CANS SLICED PINEAPPLES

2½ DOZEN LEMONS

3 ORANGES

1 BOTTLE OF MARASCHINO CHERRIES

2 CUPS OF STRONG GREEN TEA

4 BOTTLES OF CHAMPAGNE (AMERICAN WILL DO AS WELL AS IM-PORTED)

Mix the juices of the lemons, pineapples and liquor of the cherries with the Catawba wine, St. Croix rum and tea, then sweeten to taste.

This is known as the stock, and improves with age.

Before serving, this should be cooled in a refrigerator, or by placing a piece of ice in it.

When ready to serve, put a piece of ice in the punch bowl, then pour in the stock, leaving room for a prorate part of the Champagne. As each charge is put into the bowl, oranges and pineapples sliced into small particles, and cherries, should be added in proportion to the amount used.

The stock should be kept at least two days before serving.

SOURCE: PERCY HAMMOND AND GEORGE C. WHARTON, *POKER, SMOKE AND OTHER THINGS*, 1907

NOTES ON INGREDIENTS: First off, the Catawba presents a challenge. If you can find some (it's still made on a small scale), use it. Otherwise, any sweet and fruity domestic wine of a tolerable quality will do, especially if it's pink (paging white zin . . .). Then the pineapple: It should be fresh, not canned. For this amount, 2 whole pineapples should do, sliced into chunks. As for the maraschino cherries, these are not present in the 1897 version. Instead, a quart of whiskey (use rye) is added. Here's that greater vigor. That same recipe also calls for sufficient strawberries to flavor and color the Punch (a quart should do, cored and cut in half). This must be right, since it gives the Punch a rich red color, and red is the traditional color of the artillery. If used, you'll need more sugar.

NOTES ON EXECUTION: Pretty much as directed, except adding the pineapple chunks and strawberries (if used) at the beginning instead of the canned and bottled juices, and omitting the pineapple particles and cherries at the end. This would benefit, as all Punches do, by preparing an oleo-saccharum at the beginning (see Philadelphia Fish-House Punch (page 89); start with ½ cup sugar). If you're incorporating strawberries, muddle them in with the lemon peel and the sugar, add the citrus and strain before proceeding with the rest of the assembly.

CHAPTER 4

THE CHILDREN
OF PUNCH: COLLINSES,
FIZZES, DAISIES, SOURS,
COOLERS, AND COBBLERS

The glass of Punch went forth in the new land and multiplied, begetting a whole host of other drinks. Even the Cobbler, an unpunchy drink if ever there was one, can be seen as one of its off-shoots, combining as it does wine, sugar, ice, and a couple of slices of citrus shaken in.

I. THE LESSER PUNCHES: FIXES AND SOURS
(AND THE KNICKERBOCKER)

One of the many questions that could have easily been answered by knowledgeable and careful inquiry at the time and now is probably past recovery is, Wherefore the rise of the "short drink" in mid-Victorian America? Was it due to the increasing popularity of the Cocktail? Or was it merely a symptom, an acknowledgment of the accelerating pace of urban life? Whatever the reason, the decade or two before the Civil War saw American barkeepers making, and American tipplers tippling, pocket versions of those two mainstays of bar-drinking, the Mint Julep and the glass of Punch, versions made and served not in the large bar-glass, but the small one.

Nineteenth-century Americans dearly loved to make up names for things (viz, the map of North America), and these drinks rapidly took on identities, and as it were, lives of their own. You'll find the baby Julep listed herein as the Smash, which is the only name it was ever known by. The lesser Punches, however, were more numerous in their generation and their classification is not easy.

The two earliest classes of lesser Punch—the Fix and the Sour—entered the historical record at the same time, in a Toronto saloon's drink list that is dated, by hand, to 1856 (see under Evolved Cocktails for more on this extraordinary document), which means there is no surefire way of determining which one came first. But when comparing ancient manuscripts, one of the principles scholars rely on is the idea that the *lectio dificilior*, the "more difficult reading," is the one most likely to be older, since the monks who copied out the manuscripts tended to simplify what they didn't understand. According to this principle, the Fix should have seniority over the Sour, since it is the more involved drink to make. The fact that its distinguishing feature is the same ornamental garnish that graced Willard-era Punches works to support this conclusion.

BRANDY, GIN, SANTA CRUZ, OR WHISKEY FIX

Dificilior or not, the Fix, or "Fix-Up" (which gives us a clue as to its etymology) isn't exactly complicated—it's merely a short Punch with fancy fruit garnish. As such, it's a surprisingly mysterious beverage: It appears in just about all the bartender's bibles published before Prohibition and is among the few drinks listed as essential for the bartender to know in Paul Lowe's influential *Drinks: How to Mix and Serve* from 1909—and yet devil a drinker do you find actually ordering one. (I suspect that most people, not well up on their technical mixology, would have simply described it as a "fancy Sour," which may explain why we don't hear of it.)

(USE SMALL BAR-GLASS.)

    1 TABLE-SPOONFUL [1 TSP] OF SUGAR

    [JUICE OF] ¼ OF A LEMON

    ½ A WINE-GLASS [1 TBSP] OF WATER

    1 WINE-GLASS [2 OZ] OF [SPIRITS]

Fill a tumbler two-thirds full of shaved ice. Stir with a spoon and dress the top with fruit in season.

SOURCE: JERRY THOMAS, 1862 (COMPOSITE)

NOTES ON INGREDIENTS: The 1887 edition of Thomas's book adds "3 dashes [say, 1 tsp] of Curaçoa," which ain't a bad idea. By the 1880s, recipes were calling for the sugar to be replaced by ½ ounce of pineapple syrup. This, too, works well. For garnish, pieces of pineapple and orange, lemon peel (which is rubbed around the rim of the glass before being dropped in), and berries in season are idiomatic.

As for spirits: The canonical ones are brandy (cognac, preferably), Holland gin, Santa Cruz rum and, eventually, plain old domestic whiskey. Without input from its drinkers, it's impossible to say which was ultimately most popular.

BRANDY, GIN, SANTA CRUZ, OR WHISKEY SOUR

"When American meets American then comes the whisky sour." Thus declared the *Atlanta Daily Constitution* in 1879, and it wasn't wrong. From roughly the 1860s to the 1960s, the Sour, and particularly its whiskey incarnation, was one of the cardinal points of American drinking, and, along with the Highball, one of the few drinks that could come near to slugging it out with the vast and aggressive tribe of Cocktails in terms of day-in, day-out popularity. It began pulling away from its siblings among the lesser Punches early: In 1858, we find it popular enough that the *New York Times* could attach the epithet "Brandy-

No. D 375. Porcelain Lemon Squeezer.
Price..20c
Iron japanned frame, with porcelain bowl. An old reliable article.

By 1902, when this handy cast-iron and porcelain juicer was included in a hotelware catalogue, it was obsolescent; a generation or two earlier, though, it must have been a revelation. (Author's collection)

sour" to the name of a certain Mr. Brisley and expect people to know what that meant. In 1863, matters had already reached the point that the local paper from across the river in the great and liberal city of Brooklyn considered "compounder of cocktails, skins and sours" an acceptable circumlocution for "barkeeper."

Two things appear to have driven the Sour's quick elevation to indispensability: It was simple, and it was flexible. "The . . . sour," wrote Jerry Thomas, "is made with the same ingredients as the . . . fix, omitting all fruits except a small piece of lemon, the juice of which must be pressed in the glass." So: spirits, sugar, water, lemon, ice. The only real question here is the ratio of sugar to lemon. But that one's a doozy (it still is—if you want to get a mixologist riled, tell him he's put too much sugar in his Sour). There were essentially two schools: those who took the name seriously, and those who considered it akin to a child's protestation that she's not tired at all, really. The former, among whom we may count the author of the *Steward & Barkeeper's Manual* and whoever reworked the Professor's book, call for the juice of half of a lemon and a teaspoon or so of sugar—a tart and tasty drink. But Jerry Thomas himself, and most who followed him—Harry Johnson, George Kappeler, Bill Boothby—show what is perhaps a more realistic view of human nature and make their Sours sweet, restricting the lemon juice to a few dashes or a quarter of a lemon's worth at most, and making sure that there's plenty of sweet to balance it out.

One notable innovation was to cap a Whiskey Sour with a float of red wine, to give it what one Chicago bartender called "the claret 'snap' " (in the language of the saloon, red wine was always called "claret," no matter how distant its origins from the sunlit banks of the Gironde). This worthy, who was interviewed in 1883, claimed ownership over this bit of fanciness, adding that "men who drink our sours expect a claret at every bar, and when it is not put in they ask for it. It's getting circulated now, and other places are adopting our flourish." (One is entitled to be skeptical, as he claimed to have invented the Manhattan as well, but there does exist another description of a Chicago bartender assembling a Whiskey Sour that same year, and lo and behold, he tops it off with claret, too.) Whoever invented it, this "Continental Sour," "Southern Whiskey Sour," or—the name it finally settled on in the early 1900s—"New York Sour" was broadly popular. As our Chicago barkeep noted, "the claret makes the drink look well and it gives it a better taste."

In the 1890s, some of the fecundity with which bartenders were generating new Cocktails and Fizzes touched the humble Sour as well, and where before there had been only the basic versions, named after the spirits that animated them, suddenly the bars are festooned with signs for Blackthorn Sours (with sloe gin, pineapple syrup, and a splash of apricot liqueur), Sours a la Creole (brandy and Jamaica rum with lime juice and "a little ice cream on top"), Dizzy Sours (rye with a dash of Benedictine and a Jamaica rum float), Jack Frost Whiskey Sours (apple "whiskey"—i.e., applejack—with an egg and cream), and the like.

But by this point the Sour was already being attracted away from its orbit around Punch and into a new one around the Cocktail. This realignment was greatly facilitated by a trend that began early: The *Steward & Barkeeper's Manual* instructed that "in the manufacture of fixes and sours a small bar-glass or ordinary tumbler is employed, and a strainer placed in the glass to drink through." This use of the strainer was popular for a time, but by the 1880s bartenders had taken control of the device back from the drinker and were serving their Sours up, in a special Sour glass—basically, a footed glass, rather deeper than a Cocktail glass (to make room for the drink's somewhat more generous proportions, for the garnish that it had swiped from the Fix, and for the seltzer with which it was sometimes lightened). After 1905 or so, most new short drinks with citrus became Cocktails (see Cocktail Punches) and the Sour's flirtation with fanciness ceased.

I've provided the formula from the *Steward & Barkeeper's Manual* since it's a little more precise than Thomas's.

ONE WINE GLASS [2 OZ] **OF** [SPIRITS]

HALF WINE GLASS [1 OZ] **OF WATER**

ONE TABLESPOONFUL OF SUGAR

HALF OF A LEMON

Squeeze a portion of the lemon into the tumbler, which should be a quarter full of ice, and rub the lemon on the rim of the glass. Stir with a spoon. . . . In the manufacture of fixes and sours a small bar-glass or ordinary tumbler is employed.

SOURCE: *STEWARD & BARKEEPER'S MANUAL*, 1869 (COMPOSITE)

NOTES ON INGREDIENTS: By the 1880s, 1 tablespoonful of sugar was considered excessive, and the amount was reduced by half to two-thirds, and indeed 1 teaspoon or 1½ teaspoons is sufficient; I will not dictate as this is a personal matter. The water, included at the beginning to help the sugar dissolve, was soon replaced by a squirt of seltzer which, once bartenders switched to syrup for sweetening (use 1 to 2 teaspoons of gum), migrated to the top of the drink. The canonical Sour spirits were brandy (the early favorite), Holland gin, applejack (this made for a "Jersey Sour"), bourbon (generally, but not always favored over rye—a New York Sour, for instance, calls for rye), and Santa Cruz rum (these last two being the latter-day favorites). The 1887 edition of Thomas's book adds a dash of curaçao.

For an **Egg Sour**, use 1 ounce each of brandy and curaçao for the spirits and add a whole egg. In 1922, the great Anglo-Belgian (shades of Hercule Poirot!) bartender Robert Vermiere suggested that "a few drops of white of egg improve all Sours." This, the European school of Sour-making, was the one that recolonized America after Prohibition, and the Sour with a head on it was a standard specialty of FDR-era Cocktail lounges. (It should be pointed out, however, that as early as 1904 the *Chicago Tribune* was talking about an artificial, presweetened "acid and white of egg mixture" that was sold to bars by the gallon; but it was never considered good form to use such a thing.)

NOTES ON EXECUTION: For a midcentury Sour, begin by squeezing the lemon into a small bar-glass, add the sugar and water, stir, then finish with spirits and ice. Done. The claret, always a nice touch, is best applied with a dasher top. Failing that, careful pouring from a jigger (use about ½ ounce) over the back of a spoon will do. The idea is to have a "pleasant-looking, red-headed drink," as the *Chicago Tribune* observed in 1883.

For one of the advanced sours of the 1880s, use syrup and shake everything but the float, if using one (and don't forget the curaçao!). Strain into a 4-or 5-ounce footed glass, add a healthy splash of seltzer if you like, float the float if you want that, and finish with a piece of pineapple, a couple of orange wedges, and a few berries.

KNICKERBOCKER

In 1852 or 1853, the list of mixed drinks obtainable at one of Boston's fancier saloon/restaurants found its way into the newspapers. It was widely reprinted, generally as an example of the moral decline that the nation was sliding into as it hit the three-quarters of a century mark. Among the many drinks listed (some versions have as few as fifty-six, others are in the high sixties) are quite a few whose formulae have eluded history, fascinating compounds like the "Jewett's Fancy" (Jewett was the Boston-based publisher of *Uncle Tom's Cabin*), the "Vox Populi," the "Tippe Na Pecco," and even the famous "Fiscal Agent." But a few, at least, would later find their way into Jerry Thomas's book, among them the Knickerbocker (its recipe-double in the book, the White Lion, shows up in an augmented version of the list published in 1855, as coming from a California saloon). If this Boston Knickerbocker is the same as the Professor's, that makes it in fact the first of the lesser Punches on record. Its origins are likely to lie in New York, then thickly populated with Knickerbocker thises and Knickerbocker thats. Even the ice company was named Knickerbocker, and the drink calls for a fair amount of the stuff—but then again, the 1850s also saw the knee-breeches become knickerbockers, and it's entirely possible that the drink took its name from them, it being an abbreviated, "knickerbocker" sort of Punch (indeed, Charles B. Campbell, in his 1867 *American Bartender*, attaches a "Punch" to its name). In any case, for a while there in the 1850s and 1860s it was a popular drink, even turning up, in somewhat bastardized form, in England. But then, for whatever reason, it faded away, and the last one hears of it is in 1882, when a writer for the *New York World* admonished, "in the resume of what is good to drink in the summer-time the Knickerbocker should not be forgotten." An old-timer, no doubt. But the thing is, he's not wrong: With its rum and its lime juice, its syrups and liqueurs, the Knicker-bocker is the spiritual progenitor of the Tiki drink. Think of it as an 1850s Mai Tai—similar drink, different island.

(USE SMALL BAR-GLASS.)

½ A LIME OR LEMON, SQUEEZE OUT THE JUICE, AND PUT RIND AND JUICE IN THE GLASS

2 TEA-SPOONFULS OF RASPBERRY SYRUP

1 WINE-GLASS [2 OZ] SANTA CRUZ RUM

½ [1 OZ] TEASPOONFUL OF CURAÇOA

Cool with shaved ice; shake up well, and ornament with berries in season. If this is not sweet enough, put in a little more raspberry syrup.

SOURCE: JERRY THOMAS, 1862

NOTES ON INGREDIENTS: Choose the lime over the lemon. Some find this recipe too tart. Rather than adding more raspberry syrup (which can be purchased in larger organic markets or easily made by macerating raspberries in rich simple syrup), I prefer to increase the curaçao to 2 teaspoons. Raspberries, blackberries, orange pieces, even pineapple can be part of the garnish. The only difference between Thomas's Knickerbocker and his **White Lion** is that the latter replaces three-quarters of the raspberry syrup with pulverized sugar. I'll take the knee-pants.

Campbell makes his with half brandy and half port, with pieces of orange and pineapple in the glass; delicious, but no Knickerbocker.

NOTES ON EXECUTION: This drink should be built and shaken in the glass for authenticity. But if you don't have a shaker small enough to cover a 6- to 8-ounce tumbler and would prefer not to pour it back and forth between glasses, the floor, your shirt, and the boss's wife, g'ahead and cheat and make it in the big shaker. It really doesn't make a damn bit of difference to the final drink. Just don't shake the lime rind in with everything else; it can make the drink bitter if bruised.

II. DAISIES AND FIZZES

If the Sour has one fault, it's that it lacks zip (this of course is also its virtue; zip is a fine thing, but all zip all the time can get to be a bit much). Whereas Punches are capacious enough in size and conception to allow clever combinations of liquors to be deployed, not to mention several kinds of juice and extra dashes and fillips of this and that, the Sour is a drink designed for mass production: straightforward, efficient, and a little bland. But charge your basic Sour with fizz-water, and it sparkles and dances in the glass, bland simplicity transforming itself into clean directness. This is particularly true if you strain the Sour before you charge it.

This secret was long known to the makers of Gin Punch, and, indeed, as embodied in the John Collins had been revealed to the American tippling public since the late 1850s. But it didn't come into its own until after the Civil War, and when it did there was—as so often in American saloon culture—a certain amount of confusion about what to call it. Was it a John Collins? A Daisy? A Fizz? Why not all three? Eventually, each of these names would be applied to its own class of drinks, all broadly similar but nonetheless possessing the small, idiomatic differences that are the mixographer's delight.

We've already examined the Collins option (which has its own nomenclatural confusions). Now for the other two. We'll begin with the Daisy, since it's the first to make it into the historical record.

THE DAISY

Charlie was detailing his romantic troubles to a couple of friends. Naturally wanting to help, Harry ordered "three cocktails, strong, cold, and plenty of it!"

"Stop," interrupted Charlie, as the waiter was about to leave the room, "Stop, no cocktails for me. I'll take a glass of lemonade!"

"A glass of what?" thundered Harry.

> "Ha! ha! ha! Lemonade. Well that's a good thing for a man in the dumps! Wouldn't you rather have a concentrated zephyr, in a daisy, or an iced dew drop. Nonsense, man. . . . Lemonade, indeed."

Thus Henry Llewellyn Williams in his 1866 novel, *Gay Life in New York, or Fast Men and Grass Widows*. I must applaud Harry's judgment. While many a nineteenth-century formula for concentrating zephyrs has survived, as this book readily attests, the Iced Dew Drop appears lost forever. Not so the Daisy, which flourished for a time, practically died out, and then came roaring back in spectacular, albeit disguised, form, and is almost always just the thing for a man or woman in the dumps or out of them (as old-time bartender Jere Sullivan recalled in 1930, Daisies were "cooling, refreshing and peculiarly tasty").

After Williams's novel, the next we hear of the Daisy is in the 1876 supplement to Jerry Thomas's book, where its formula reveals it to be a Sour—with brandy, whiskey, gin, or rum—that is sweetened in part with orange cordial, strained, and fizzed. The only way that this differs from the book's Fizzes is in those "2 or 3 dashes of orange cordial." But Thomas's book doesn't tell the whole story. Where the Fizz went on to become a staple of bar-drinking, in some hands the Daisy—one hears most often of the Brandy Daisy, but the Whiskey and Gin versions also turn up from time to time—evolved into something of a dude's drink, a little bit of fanciness that came empinkened with grenadine and decanted into some sort of recherché, ice-filled goblet or mug and tricked out with fruit and whatever else was in the garnish-tray. By the time Prohibition rolled around, both kinds—the old, orange liqueur-up kind and the newer, grenadine-rocks kind, were in circulation.

It's worth going into this much detail about the Daisy because of something that happened in Mexico while the Great Experiment was running its course in *el Norte*. First off, in 1929 or thereabouts, the new American-financed gambling and golf resort at Agua Caliente, outside Tijuana, introduced its house cocktail, the "Sunrise Tequila." Tequila. Lime juice. Grenadine. A little creme de cassis. Ice. Soda. In other words, a tequila Daisy, modern type. Second, a little after repeal, journalists and other travelers who visited Mexico started talking about a "Tequila Daisy," and in 1936 this even pops up north of the border, in Syracuse, New York, of all places. Unfortunately, nobody bothers to record which kind of Daisy they're drinking, the old-school one, which was often served in Cocktail glasses with only a minimal amount of fizz, or the new-school one, like Agua Caliente's Sunrise. This is important because of the Spanish word for "daisy." If they were drinking them old-school, you see, they were drinking tequila, orange liqueur, lime juice (much more common than lemon in Mexico), and maybe a little splash of soda—and ordering them as "margaritas."

BRANDY, GIN, WHISKEY, OR RUM DAISY (OLD SCHOOL)

The original Daisy of the 1870s.

(USE SMALL BAR-GLASS.)

3 OR 4 DASHES [1 TSP] **GUM SYRUP**

2 OR 3 DASHES [1½ TSP] **ORANGE CORDIAL**

THE JUICE OF HALF A LEMON

1 SMALL WINEGLASS [2 OZ] **OF** [SPIRITS]

Fill glass half full of shaved ice.

Shake well and strain into a glass, and fill up with Seltzer water from a syphon.

SOURCE: JERRY THOMAS, 1876 (COMPOSITE)

NOTES ON INGREDIENTS: Jerry Thomas made all his Daisies according to the same pattern; for the orange cordial, I like to use Grand Marnier. Whoever it was that revised his book, however, recommended varying the cordial according to the spirit used, calling for maraschino with rum (specifically Santa Cruz) and gin (Hollands), with orgeat syrup replacing the gum in the latter. With whiskey, there's no cordial at all, but again orgeat steps in for the gum. Other mixologists liked other cordials; Harry Johnson, for example, was particularly fond of yellow Chartreuse in a Daisy, although he used an awful lot of it: ½ ounce, on top of ½ tablespoon of sugar, and all to balance out 2 or 3 dashes of lemon juice.

In Jerry Thomas's Daisies, anyway, the cordial is intended as an accent, not as the main sweetener. As always, the precise amounts will be a matter of taste.

Thomas's reviser suggests finishing the Brandy Daisy with "2 dashes of Jamaica rum." Rum with brandy? You bet.

By the way, the term *small wineglass* appears to be a reaction to the obsolescence of that measure; within a few years recipe writers would be claiming that a wineglass was 4 ounces (by then they were measuring spirits in 2-ounce jiggers, just to be safe).

NOTES ON EXECUTION: The big question here is what kind of glass to put the thing into. In 1876, it would have been the standard small bar-glass. In 1887, the guy who revised Thomas's book has his strained into a "large cocktail glass." Others went for a Fizz glass, a Punch glass, or a "fancy bar-glass." I prefer the Cocktail glass, since it limits the amount of fizz that goes into the drink, ensuring that it sparkles yet still has a Cocktail-like throw-weight to it. It should be noted that in the context of 1887, a large cocktail glass held approximately 3½ ounces.

BRANDY, GIN, RUM, OR WHISKEY DAISY (NEW SCHOOL)

The fancy Daisy of the 1910s.

BRANDY DAISY	RUM DAISY
GIN DAISY	WHISKEY DAISY

ALL THE ABOVE DAISIES ARE MADE AS FOLLOWS:

JUICE ½ LIME AND ¼ LEMON

1 TEASPOONFUL POWDERED SUGAR

2 DASHES [1 TSP] GRENADINE

1 DRINK [2 OZ] OF LIQUOR DESIRED

2 DASHES [½ OZ] CARBONATED WATER

Use silver mug, put in above ingredients, fill up with fine ice, stir until mug is frosted, decorate with fruit and sprays of fresh mint and serve with straws.

SOURCE: HUGO ENSSLIN, *RECIPES FOR MIXED DRINKS*, 1916

NOTES ON INGREDIENTS: Where Ensslin says "powdered," we would today say "superfine." Others used a good deal more carbonated water in their new-school Daisies. Still others—Jacques Straub, for one—used none at all. It's your choice. I like a goodly splash in mine. For the fruit decoration, berries in season, pieces of orange and pineapple, and maraschino cherries are all appropriate (as, for that matter, are kiwi, starfruit, and Buddha's hand, if not idiomatic).

GIN, WHISKEY, BRANDY, OR SANTA CRUZ RUM FIZZ

San Francisco has a knack for generating great bartenders. If Jerry Thomas was the first, or one of them, he was by no means the last. One of the good ones at the turn of the last century was Ernest P. Rawling. Judging by his 1914 *Rawling's Book of Mixed Drinks*, he was a sensible, patient sort who gave a good deal of thought to the right and wrong ways of doing things. But he also had a poetic side: "While the Cocktail is unquestionably the most popular drink on the Pacific coast today," he wrote,

> the next in favor is surely the Fizz—the long drink par excellence. At any time or in any place where the tongue and throat are dry; when the spirits are jaded and the body is weary; after a long automobile trip on hot and dusty roads; it is then that the Gin Fizz comes like a cooling breeze from the sea, bringing new life and the zest and joy of living.
>
> And in the "morning after the night before," when the whole world seems gray and lonesome, and every nerve and fibre of the body is throbbing a complaint against the indiscretion, just press the button and order a Gin Fizz—"Not too sweet, please!" It comes. Oh, shades of the green oasis in the sandy desert of life!

Truer words were never written. Not about the Fizz, anyway. Of course, that green-oasis effect only works if you're having just one. Maybe two. But not forty. Definitely not forty.

That's how many Gin Fizzes "Professor" Denton, of Brooklyn, New York, used to put away in a day, back in the early 1890s. Of course, he was "the champion gin fizz drinker in America," as he used to bill himself while he went around the Williamsburg bars cadging drinks, so he was perhaps exceptional (and not an example to be emulated, seeing as he died from internal hemorrhaging after betting that he could drink a Fizz and eat the glass, too). But Gin Fizzes are definitely moreish. Have one and you want another and that way danger lies. That's the essence of the Fizz—as the Japanese ambassador reportedly said upon trying one in the early 1890s, "it buzzes like a fly and stings like a wasp."

If the Gin Fizz, or "Fiz," as Jerry Thomas called it, was *primus inter pares*, before long there was no shortage of other Fizzes in circulation, based on all the canonical liquors including applejack, with variations. Silver, Golden, Morning Glory, Police Gazette, Elks', Electric Current, Green, Sitting Bull, Ramos— the list goes on. But then again, they needed a lot of 'em. A Fizz, you see, was what a sporting man would moisten the clay with directly upon arising—an eye-opener, corpse-reviver, fog-cutter, gloom-lifter. A hangover cure. Into the saloon you'd go, the kindly internist behind the bar would manipulate a bottle or two, and zam! There stood the glass, packed with vitamins, proteins (assuming you went for one with egg in it, such as a Silver Fizz, below), and complex sugars, foaming brightly and aglow with the promise of sweet release. Civilization proceeds, but not always forward.

(USE SMALL BAR - GLASS .)

4 OR 5 DASHES [1½ TSP] **OF GUM SYRUP**

JUICE OF HALF A LEMON

1 SMALL WINEGLASS [2 OZ] **OF** [SPIRITS]

Fill the glass half full of shaved ice, shake up well and strain into a glass. Fill up the glass with Seltzer water from a siphon and drink without hesitation.

SOURCE: JERRY THOMAS, 1876 (COMPOSITE; THIS WAS THE DRINK'S FIRST KNOWN APPEARANCE IN PRINT)

NOTES ON INGREDIENTS: Thomas doesn't say what kind of gin to use here, but judging by his contemporaries it would have been Old Tom; one does not see Hollands recommended for this drink—not that it makes a bad Fizz, but the lighter English styles give it more snap.

A **Crushed Strawberry Fizz** is a standard Gin Fizz with two or three strawberries muddled into it (use at least 2 teaspoons of gum). It was a specialty of New York's venerable St. Nicholas Hotel in the 1880s.

NOTES ON EXECUTION: Use a narrow-mouthed, 6- to 8-ounce glass. This can and should be chilled in advance, but when receiving the drink it should not have ice in it, nor should any be added once the glass is full. A Fizz is meant to be drunk off quickly, like a Cocktail, not lingered over, like a Collins.

If making a Crushed Strawberry Fizz, begin by quickly muddling the strawberries in with the lemon juice and syrup. Add gin and ice, shake well, and double-strain it (with the Hawthorne strainer in the shaker and the Julep strainer held over the glass).

It was an old Fizz-maker's trick to not sweeten the drink until the very end, when a large spoonful of superfine sugar would be stirred in. If there's enough soda in the drink and not too much extraneous matter (eggs, cream, and such), this should make the drink fizz up most impressively.

SILVER FIZZ

In 1883, Fred Hildreth, head bartender at one of Chicago's top salons, mentioned the Silver Fizz to a man from the *Tribune* as one of the "popular fancy drinks" of the day. It would remain so for another forty years, during which it did yeoman service as a lifeline for the overhung.

(USE LARGE BAR-GLASS.)

ONE-HALF TABLE-SPOON OF SUGAR

2 OR 3 DASHES [½ OZ] OF LEMON JUICE

1 WINE-GLASS [2 OZ] OF OLD TOM GIN

1 EGG (THE WHITE ONLY)

Three-quarters glass filled with fine shaved ice; shake up well with a shaker, strain it into a good sized fizz glass, fill up the glass with Syphon Selters [sic] or Vichy Water, mix well, and serve.

SOURCE: HARRY JOHNSON, *NEW AND IMPROVED BARTENDER'S MANUAL*, 1882

NOTES ON INGREDIENTS: For an industrial-grade *katzenjammer*, try taking Johnson's **Golden Fizz:** Simply replace the egg white with the yolk and, optionally, the gin with whiskey. The result is a very soothing drink, and much tastier than it sounds.

NOTES ON EXECUTION: As with all egg drinks, this one will take some serious shaking.

MORNING GLORY FIZZ

An early and quite successful attempt at mixologizing with Scotch. Other than the likelihood that this is a Harry Johnson original (for whom see the Bijou Cocktail, page 256), little about the drink is known. As with any drink that goes by the name "Morning Glory," this is a hangover-helper.

(U S E   L A R G E   B A R - G L A S S .)

In all first-class barrooms it is proper to have the whites of eggs separated into an empty bottle, providing you have a demand for such a drink as above, and keep them continually on ice, as by doing so, considerable time will be saved; mix as follows:

THREE-QUARTERS TABLE-SPOONFUL OF SUGAR

3 OR 4 DASHES [½ OZ] OF LEMON JUICE

2 OR 3 DASHES [¼ OZ] OF LIME JUICE

3 OR 4 DASHES OF ABSINTHE [½ TSP], DISSOLVED WELL WITH [A] LITTLE WATER

THREE-QUARTER GLASS FILLED WITH FINE SHAVED ICE

1 EGG (THE WHITE ONLY)

1 WINEGLASS [2 OZ] OF SCOTCH WHISKEY

PLATE No. 7.

Shake up well with a shaker; strain it into a good-sized bar-glass; fill up the balance with Syphon Selters [sic] or Vichy water, and serve.

The above drink must be drank as soon as prepared, so as not to lose the effect of it. The author respectfully recommends the above drink as an excellent one for a morning beverage, which will give a good appetite and quiet the nerves.

SOURCE: HARRY JOHNSON, *NEW AND IMPROVED BARTENDER'S MANUAL*, 1882

NOTES ON INGREDIENTS: One must assume that the Scotch here is

MORNING GLORY FIZZ.

The Morning Glory Fizz, As Mixed (right) and Served (left). From Harry Johnson's *New and Improved Illustrated Bartender's Manual*, 1888. (Courtesy Ted Haigh)

the blended kind, which was then beginning its assault on American shores. Don't worry about dissolving the absinthe in water.

For the equally effective **Saratoga Brace Up**, found in the 1887 edition of Thomas's book, use a whole egg, replace the Scotch with brandy, lose the lime juice, cut the absinthe down to 2 dashes, and add a couple of dashes of Angostura. Okay, that's a lot to change, but the results are worth it.

NOTES ON EXECUTION: Begin with the juices and 1 teaspoon or so of water, stirring the sugar into it. Shake vigorously.

NEW ORLEANS FIZZ, ALIAS RAMOS GIN FIZZ

In 1887, a New Orleans bartender by the name of Henry Charles Ramos—everyone called him Carl—and his brother took over a saloon at the corner of Gravier and Carondelet streets in the heart of the "Faubourg Americain," the city's Anglo-dominated business district. Business at the Imperial Cabinet Saloon (which was named after a brand of whiskey, among other things) went on pretty well for a while, and then it went really, really well. For whatever reason, New Orleans really took off as a tourist destination in the late 1890s, and suddenly everyone was interested in its quaint, historic saloons (even if they were only a dozen years old). Maybe this was because the Midwest was going Dry at an alarming rate. In any case, one of the biggest beneficiaries was Carl Ramos: suddenly his bar, a courtly, decorous joint that closed at eight every evening, was packed to the gills with punters all clamoring for one of his house special Fizzes. In 1900, The *Kansas City Star* dubbed the Imperial Cabinet "the most famous gin fizz saloon in the world" and went on to add, "Ramos serves a gin fizz which is not equaled anywhere."

All that business meant work: Ramos's "One and Only One," as he dubbed his version of the Fizz, took a lot of shaking.

You see, it supplemented the gin and citrus juice—split between lemon and lime, a common epicurean touch at the time—with the two ingredients that are hardest to mix: egg white and cream. Individually, not such a problem, and certainly nothing new (as early as 1891, William Schmidt had published a Cream Fizz recipe; see the Silver Fizz [page 114] for the egg white). But use both, and you're going to need some muscle to get them to emulsify. Which is precisely what Ramos had: For each of his bartenders—in 1900, during Mardi Gras, he was employing six on a shift—there was a "shaker boy," a young black man whose sole job was to receive the fully charged shaker from the bartender and shake the bejeezus out of it. Contemporary accounts say that this went on for fifteen minutes, but I'm willing to bet it only seemed that long, especially to the guy who had to do all the work.

In 1907, Ramos moved a couple of blocks to larger quarters, taking over the operation of the Stag Saloon, across from the St. Charles Hotel (the Stag was owned by the notorious Tom Anderson, "Mayor" of Storyville). Business was even better than before: During Mardi Gras, 1915, he had thirty-five shakermen on. Evidently, the procedure had changed: Now, one man shook until his arms were tired and passed it to another, in a long chain. It was something to see.

When Prohibition came, unlike Duncan Nichol, who took the Formula of his Pisco Punch to his grave, Ramos told everyone exactly how to make 'em. For this, he deserves the title *benefactor generis humani*, a benefactor of the human race. Here's his formula as he dictated it to a reporter for the New Orleans *Item-Tribune* a few years before his death in 1928.

(1) ONE TABLESPOONFUL POWDERED SUGAR

THREE OR FOUR DROPS OF ORANGE FLOWER WATER

ONE-HALF LIME (JUICE)

ONE-HALF LEMON (JUICE)

(1) ONE JIGGER [1½ OZ] OF OLD TOM GIN. (OLD GORDON MAY BE USED BUT A SWEET GIN IS PREFERABLE)

THE WHITE OF ONE EGG

ONE-HALF GLASS OF CRUSHED ICE

ABOUT (2) TABLESPOONSFUL OF RICH MILK OR CREAM

A LITTLE SELTZER WATER (ABOUT AN OUNCE) TO MAKE IT PUNGENT

TOGETHER WELL SHAKEN AND STRAINED (DRINK FREELY)

To those who may have forgotten, a "jigger" is a stemmed sherry glass holding a little more than one ounce.

SOURCE: *NEW ORLEANS ITEM-TRIBUNE*, 1925

NOTES ON INGREDIENTS: For "powdered," read "superfine." Otherwise, as the man says. Plymouth gin works well in this as a substitute for the Old Tom. And take that business about the drops of orange flower water seriously—too much of it and that's all you'll taste.

NOTES ON EXECUTION: "Shake and shake and shake until there is not a bubble left but the drink is smooth and snowy white and of the consistency of good rich milk," as Mr. Ramos told the reporter. This takes at least a minute. When making this for guests, I like to pass the shaker around and let everyone have at it until their arms get tired. Both Ramos's recipe and all the accounts of practice at his bar imply that the seltzer was shaken in with the drink, but modern practice is to strain the drink into a tall glass and then add the seltzer, giving it a quick stir. In either case, this drink isn't meant to actually fizz.

III. Two Popular Coolers

Among the drinks Hinton Helper encountered in Gold Rush–era San Francisco was something called a "Cooler." Unfortunately, he gives no description of it. But it's a pretty safe assumption that it had ice, and liquor of some kind, and maybe some soda water. That's what all the others had, anyway. It took a while for this loose derivation of the old soda water and citrus Gin Punch to propagate, but by the turn of the century the bartender's bibles were full of Coolers; of simple, tall things that are of little mixological interest but are mighty refreshing on a hot day, especially with air-conditioning still a generation or two over the horizon.

Every town had one. Chicago had its "Mamie Taylor," with Scotch and lime and ginger ale (Taylor was a comic actress of the 1890s). Atlantic City had its Horse's Neck, which was simply ginger ale with a long, long lemon twist—although many liked theirs with a "stick" of rye or gin in it. New York had its **Remsen Cooler**, named after a member of the Union League. (Old Tom, long, long twist, plain soda—Harry Johnson thought this was a Scotch drink, but he was confusing it with the "Ramsay Cooler," made with Ramsay whisky, from the Port Ellen distillery on Islay; unfortunately, his confusion has infected the annals of mixology.) There was a **Boston Cooler**, with rum and lemon and soda, a **Narragansett Cooler** (bourbon, orange juice, ginger ale), and so on. You could fill a book with them, if you were of a mind to. There are two, however, that are worth special notice, one because of its overwhelming popularity and the other because of its story.

THE JOE RICKEY (AND THE GIN RICKEY)

"Colonel" Joe Rickey was a wheeling-dealing Democratic lobbyist from the town of Fulton, in Callaway County, Missouri. He was a veteran of the Confederate army, liked the races, knew how to play poker, and could fill a back room with smoke with the best of them. Somewhere along the line, he invented a simple cooler that he would have bartenders make for him. Various places have been given as the scene of inspiration: The bar across the street from the Southern Hotel in St. Louis, the St. James Hotel in New York (this little hostelry, right up Broadway from the Hoffman House, was a favorite resort of the Sporting Fraternity), Joe Chamberlin's in Washington. I have no doubt at one point or another the Colonel instructed the bartenders in all those places how to make his drink. He instructed bartenders *everywhere* how to make it. But the first place he

seems to have done it, at least so as anyone noticed, was at Shoe-
maker's, a quiet, skew-angled old place on Pennsylvania Avenue
in Washington, D.C., famed for the quality of its whiskey and
the political wattage of its clientele (some called it the "third
Room of the Congress"). There, some time between 1883, when
Rickey hit town, and 1889, when the drink made it into the
Washington Post, Rickey had George Williamson, the saloon's
beloved head barkeeper, start making 'em for him.

They couldn't be simpler: a slug of whiskey, and only
whiskey (some say rye, some say bourbon, but there is agree-
ment that Rickey preferred the fine Belle of Nelson brand), the
juice of half a lime or a whole one if the limes were small, some
ice, and some soda water. Done. You'll note the absence of sugar.
That's because it was intended as a Cooler, and as Rickey went
around saying, "Any drink with sugar in it . . . heats the blood,
while the Rickey, with its blood-cooling lime juice, is highly ben-
eficial" (thus the *Brooklyn Eagle*'s Washington correspondent in
1892). In any case, the drink spread from "Shoo's" (as Shoe-
maker's was known) to all Washington, from Washington to
New York, and then to points all over the globe. Except Kansas.
At least, that's what the *Kansas City Star* said in 1890: "When a
Kansas man orders a 'Joe Rickey' he instructs the barkeeper to
leave out the ice, the lime juice and the soda."

Kansans notwithstanding, the drink was a sensation. Rickey
moved to New York and went into the soda-water business and got
his face on a whiskey label. In 1903, though, he took carbolic acid
in his room at the Hoffman House and died. His health had been
failing and his finances troubled. Or maybe it was just that everybody was going around putting gin in his drink, and had been doing so for at least eleven years. The drink, anyway, lived on, and
deservedly—that business of sugar heating the blood is probably
bunk, but its absence certainly makes for a drink of unparalleled
coolness, while the soda works to dilute any excess acidity.

The mixture is simple. It consists of one half a lime, whisky, ice and
soda. When properly and carefully mixed it is said to come nearer

supplying what a drinker wants in hot weather than anything else yet discovered.

SOURCE: *WASHINGTON POST*, 1889

NOTES ON INGREDIENTS: Bourbon or rye, rye or bourbon. Half a normal-sized lime is plenty. For a **Gin Rickey**, use gin.

NOTES ON EXECUTION: The *Brooklyn Eagle*'s man explained it perfectly: "The juice of [half] a lime is squeezed into a goblet, which is then filled with crushed ice. Then a portion of whiskey or gin, in quantity to suit the taste, is poured in. The glass is then filled up with club soda or carbonic water."

FLORODORA

In 1900, *Florodora*, a thoroughly silly bit of musical fluff imported from the London stage, opened at New York's Casino Theater. Monster hit. It wasn't the plot, which involved perfume manufacture, phrenology, and a skein of tangled attractions, set half on the fictitious Philippine island of Florodora and half in Wales. *(Wales?)* It wasn't Leslie Stuart's music, although that was popular enough to make him rich. (He blew it all in the approved manner, on champagne, horses, and chorus girls.) It wasn't the leads, the dancing, or the scenery—not the fixed scenery, anyway. You see, Cyrus W. Gilfain, who owns the island of Florodora, has a daughter, Angela. And Angela has six friends who go everywhere together—six well-developed young friends with shapely ankles, who all happen to be brunettes five feet four inches tall, with a penchant for dressing in identical costumes. In an era when sex was sex and public entertainment was most certainly not sex save in the most abstract terms, the "Florodora Sextette" was hot, hot stuff.

The six girlies involved—Daisy Green, Marjorie Relyea, Vaughn Texsmith, Margaret Walker, Agnes Wayburn, and Marie

Wilson—were catnip to New York's rich young (and not-so-young) sports, and they knew it. Wilson parlayed a stock tip from James R. Keene into a $750,000 score, and then turned around and married his horseracing pal Frederick Gebhard. Green caught a Denver financier, Wayburn a South African diamond magnate, and Texsmith a silk-manufacturer, all seven-figure men. Marjorie Relyea won out with a Carnegie, who promptly died and left her a pile. We don't know exactly what happened to Miss Walker, but Broadway legend has it that all six pretty maidens married millionaires; the odds are certainly in her favor.

If ever there was a show that demanded to be commemorated with a drink, and preferably a fragrant, slightly silly one that hits like a roll of quarters in a clutch purse, it was this one. Lo and behold:

> A party of professional people were in a Columbus avenue restaurant in New York the other night after the show. One of the "Florodora" pretty maidens was in the crowd, and her persistent refusal to partake of anything but lemonade irked the rest.
>
> "If you'll get me something brand new," she said, "I'll drink it." Jimmy O'Brien, the head inventor of drinks, was called. He thought until the noise of his thinking drowned the whir of the electric fans.

Then he turned out this drink. That was in 1901, as reported by the *New York Evening World*. Alas, the article was silent as to which of the pretty maidens it was, but she sure had the chorus girl thing down, didn't she?

Put three or four dashes [2 tsp] of raspberry syrup in the bottom of an ordinary glass, squeeze in the juice of a whole lime, add just enough Plymouth gin to catch the taste [1½ oz] and half fill the glass with finely cracked ice.

Then pour in the best ginger ale until the glass is brimming. Vibrate the mixture with a long bar spoon until it is ice cold and turn it into a cold stein. Float a slice of orange and a pitted cherry on top, put the

stein to your lips, shut your eyes and take an express transport to Elysium.

SOURCE: *NEW YORK EVENING WORLD*, 1901

NOTES ON INGREDIENTS: If you want to turn this into a **Florodora, Imperial Style**, replace the gin with cognac. You should probably replace the ginger ale with champagne, while you're at it: The recipe, from Jacques Straub's 1914 *Drinks*, doesn't mention it, but "Imperial" or "Royal" drinks almost always have champagne.

NOTES ON EXECUTION: You can also build the whole thing in the glass you serve it in.

IV. THE COBBLER

"America is fertile in mixtures: what do we not owe her? Sherry Cobbler, Gin Sling, Cocktail, Mint Julep, Brandy Smash, Sudden Death, Eye Openers." So said Charles Reade, the Victorian novelist, in 1863. If he were writing today, of course, the list would be rather different: Apple Martini, Screaming Orgasm, Dirty Girl Scout, Irish Car Bomb—like that: insert your own pointed observation on the decline of public morality in America. At least, if past performance is any guarantee of future results, we can be fairly certain that our mixological indiscretions won't live on to embarrass us. Reade's list represented the state of the art of mixed drinking in his day. What survives? The Julep (once a year, anyway), and the Cocktail, in the form of the Old-Fashioned (although outside of Wisconsin not one bar in twenty can make a proper one anymore). But for the "Sudden Death," alas, not even a recipe remains, and the others exist only in the fragile, age-browned pages of old bar books.

If someone had waved Reade's little list under the nose of the average drinking man of 1863 and made him choose one drink to survive the test of time, odds are heavy he would've gone for the Sherry Cobbler. It was, Harry Johnson observed in the 1888 edition of his *Bartender's Manual*, "without doubt the most popular beverage in the country, with ladies as well as with gentlemen." And not just this country, either—"the sublimity of the sherry cobbler" as one old Virginian called it, was a worldwide hit. In 1855, a traveler through Panama pokes his head into "a drinking saloon," only to find "the sallow bar-keeper . . . concocting a Sherry-Cobbler for a fever-stricken Yankee." In 1862, it's a gang of Aussies piping 'em into a visiting English cricket team. And in 1867, if the French judges at the Exposition Universelle de Paris deemed our Hudson River School paintings worth but a single medal, and that of the second class, the French crowd lined up at the Exposition's American Bar held different views regarding our Sherry Cobblers: They were going through 500 bottles of sherry a day.

All well and good, but what exactly is the Sherry Cobbler? Nothing but sherry, sugar, a lot of ice, a bit of fruit (a slice or two of orange muddled in with the ice and a few berries on top), and a straw. The straw is key: As the *Grand Island Times* (that's in Nebraska) pointed out in 1873, the "straw is a very useful article—when one end is bathed in a Sherry Cobbler." But not only was it useful, it was also something much more important. It was *new*. Now, I've never seen a definitive history of the drinking straw, but from what I've been able to gather, the Sherry Cobbler was the killer app that brought it into common use. When Mr. Tapley builds one for Dickens's Martin Chuzzlewit, "plunging a reed into the mixture . . . and signifying by an expressive gesture that it was to be pumped up through that agency by the enraptured drinker," poor Martin's astonished. They didn't *do* that sort of thing in Europe. Leave it to those mad, ingenious Yanks.

The ice was pretty new, too. Nobody seems precisely sure where the Cobbler got its name, but the most plausible theory posits that it's from the little "cobbles" of ice over which it's built. It's significant that the drink seems to have been first introduced in the late 1830s, the decade that saw the "frozen water trade" take off in America: At least, the first reference to it I've found comes from 1838, and in 1840 one Brantz Mayer, of Baltimore, in an article in the New York weekly *New World* entitled "What Is a Sherry Cobbler?" calls it "the greatest 'liquorary' invention of the day" and wonders "How happens it that 't was not discovered before?" Without ice, a glass of sweetened sherry with a little orange bruised into it doesn't hold much excitement. Add ice, and it's fascinating.

In the fullness of time, the Cobbler treatment got applied to an array of other wines; Jerry Thomas lists a Catawba Cobbler, a Claret Cobbler, a Hock Cobbler (i.e., with a German white wine) and a Sauternes Cobbler. Most of these pop up in travelers' accounts from the 1850s, so somebody was drinking them, anyway. He even lists a Whiskey Cobbler, which is rather going against the nature of the drink (to this we may add a Brandy Cobbler, which seems to have been current in New York in the 1850s, and even a Gin Cobbler—although that one's English, and they had a way with American drinks, and not a good way). But the Sherry version remained far and away the most popular, and indeed, along with the Mint Julep, was one of the two drinks that introduced America and the world to the pleasures of taking ice in your alcoholic beverages as a matter of course.

But we've gone and left poor Mr. Chuzzlewit hanging: "Martin took the glass with an astonished look; applied his lips to the reed; and cast up his eyes once in ecstasy." While I wouldn't go that far, I'd certainly rather have a Sherry Cobbler than not and sometimes—when it's beastly hot, or when I'm in the mood for a caress rather than a left hook—a lot rather.

SHERRY COBBLER

The basic trunk from which all other Cobblers branched.

(U S E   L A R G E   B A R - G L A S S .)

2 WINE-GLASSES [4 OZ] OF SHERRY

1 TABLE-SPOONFUL OF SUGAR

2 OR 3 SLICES OF ORANGE

Fill a tumbler with shaved ice, shake well, and ornament with berries in season. Place a straw as represented in the wood-cut.

SOURCE: JERRY THOMAS, 1862

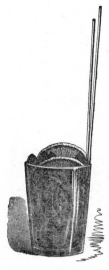

The Sherry Cobbler.
From *The Bon Vivant's Companion,* 1862.
(Author's collection)

NOTES ON INGREDIENTS: The amount of sugar (superfine) used should vary according to the kind of sherry. There were two kinds of sherry in general use: pale and brown. While it's notoriously difficult to pin down historical styles of wine, it's safe to say Thomas's recipe is calibrated to the dry, pale kind—a fino or an amontillado. With these I like a little less sugar, but not much less—say, 2 teaspoons. If using a sweeter, darker sherry, such as an oloroso or, especially, a Pedro Ximenes, use still less sugar—1 teaspoon or less. The same rules apply to Cobblers made with other still wines.

For a **Catawba Cobbler** (*"Can* there be sin in such a nectar?"* asked the *Knickerbocker* in 1855), you're basically out of luck, quality Catawba wine having gone the way of the passenger pigeon (although I hear stirring noises . . .). For a **Hock Cobbler**, though, use a nice Moselle, and a Bordeaux or other big red wine for the **Claret Cobbler**. For a **Whiskey Cobbler**, be aware that Thomas's recipe calls for a full 4 ounces of the stuff, and is a heavy cargo to carry. It calls for no ornamentation.

Mr. Mayer, of Baltimore, instructs that "every particle of [the ice] is broken up into lumps not larger than a pea" and makes no mention of orange in his ur-Cobbler, merely pouring the sherry over "the fine cut peeling of half a lemon" and letting it sit for a couple of minutes.

NOTES ON EXECUTION: As Thomas writes, "The 'cobbler' does not require much skill in compounding, but to make it acceptable to the eye, as well as to the palate, it is necessary to display some taste in ornamenting the glass after the beverage is made." See the illustration, which shows "how a cobbler should look when made to suit an epicure." The best way to execute this is by dissolving the sugar in an equal amount of water in a cocktail shaker, adding the wine and orange slices, filling it with cracked ice, and shaking vigorously (the shaking will muddle the fruit). Then pour it unstrained into a tall glass, lance it with a straw, and berry it up. The *Steward & Barkeeper's Manual* suggests that the berries be shaken in with the rest. That makes for a fruitier drink, but a less attractive one.

CHAMPAGNE COBBLER

This one requires a somewhat different technique.

(ONE BOTTLE OF WINE TO FOUR LARGE BAR-GLASSES.)

　1 TABLE-SPOONFUL [1 TSP] OF SUGAR

　1 PIECE EACH OF ORANGE AND LEMON PEEL

Fill the tumbler one-third full with shaved ice, and fill balance with wine, ornament in a tasty manner with berries in season. This beverage should be sipped through a straw.

SOURCE: JERRY THOMAS, 1862

NOTES ON INGREDIENTS: This is a nice one to make with a rosé champagne.

NOTES ON EXECUTION: It should be reinforced that the above is *per glass*, not per bottle. Dissolve the sugar first in a splash of water (or, of course, use a like amount of gum syrup).

CHAPTER 5

A HANDFUL OF EGG DRINKS

I have given what were generally known as "egg drinks" a little section of their own, as they are neither Punches nor part of the lineage of the Cocktail. In segregating them, I am mirroring their place in the psyche of the Jerry Thomas–age drinker. Formerly a major part of day-to-day drinking, by the middle of the nineteenth century drinks made with eggs had seen their role greatly diminished. There were exceptions. Some Fizzes used eggs, or at least parts of them. There was a **Flip** of sorts, that took the mighty quaff of Colonial days—when Flips were made from quarts of ale and gills of strong rum, thickened with eggs and sugar and poured back and forth from pitcher to pitcher—and shrank it to something that would fit in a Cocktail glass (to make one, shake up an egg with a wineglass of liquor or fortified wine of your choice, a splash of syrup, and plenty of ice; strain and grate nutmeg over the top). And there was the Tom & Jerry, the cold-weather favorite that carried the egg drink's banner into the twentieth century, if not always at full height. But the only time that egg drinks really recaptured their former importance was on Christmas and New Year's Day, when they were mandatory.

EGG NOGG

"Dec 25—Cloudy & thawy—very muddy—Christmas day—good many drunken ones around town & some few arrests for drunk & disorderly—got up 12—read paper—went down to Charley Ockel's [saloon] & got some egg-nog." Thus did Alf Doten, then living in Virginia City, Nevada, begin his Christmas in 1866. But that's how *everyone* began their Christmas, if they could afford it and knew where to get their hands on some eggs (in the days before 7-Eleven, not a given) and weren't infected with temperance principles. The very idea of Christmas or New Year's Day without the stuff . . . It just wouldn't be a holiday.

When Jerry Thomas wrote in 1862 that Egg Nogg "is a beverage of American origin, but it has a popularity that is cosmopolitan," he was not wrong; if early European travelers to the United States viewed it as one of the novelties Americans were inflicting on the art of drinking, by the 1860s it was a drink of universal, if strictly seasonal, popularity (when Thomas added that in the North "it is a favorite of all seasons," he was certainly overstating the case). It was popular enough to have spawned numerous variants, most of them sharing the characteristic that Doten recorded on Christmas Day 1871: "Egg nog is deceiptful." In fact, that's what people always liked about it, as can be seen in the earliest account of the drink I know of, in an article printed in the *Pittsburg Gazette* in 1801 describing the "Late, Mad Circuit of Judge Brackenridge through Washington County," in the course of which this distinctly unsober judge finds himself at a country inn. "He ordered egg nogg to be made; upon tasting it he swore and damned so horribly that the whole family were terrified at his profaneness and all this merely because the egg nogg had not whiskey enough in it." (Using whiskey in the Egg Nogg was strictly a backwoods practice; swells and epicures preferred brandy and rum, or fortified wines in theirs. But any port in a storm, as the saying goes—in validation of which, there's even a mezcal Egg Nogg on record, made by Texan prisoners in Mexico, back in the Lone Star days. One shudders.)

Of Thomas's six Egg Noggs, I have included the three best, one for a largish group and two for individual drinks.

BALTIMORE EGG NOGG

I'm not sure if I completely agree with Thomas that "Egg Nogg made in this manner is digestible, and will not cause headache," or that "it makes an excellent drink for debilitated persons, and a nourishing diet for consumptives," but I will say that it is thoroughly delicious.

(FOR A PARTY OF FIFTEEN.)

Take the yellow of sixteen eggs and twelve table-spoonfuls of pulverized loaf-sugar [3–4 oz superfine sugar], and beat them to the consistency of cream; to this add two-thirds of a nutmeg grated, and beat well together; then mix in half a pint of good brandy or Jamaica rum, and two wine-glasses [4 oz] of Madeira wine. Have ready the whites of the eggs, beaten to a stiff froth, and beat them into the above-described mixture. When this is all done, stir in six pints of good rich milk. There is no heat used.

SOURCE: JERRY THOMAS, 1862

NOTES ON INGREDIENTS: The 1887 edition of Thomas's book suggests, correctly, that 10 eggs are enough; in any case, they should be "large," not "jumbo." As for the spirits: I prefer to split the difference, going with 5 ounces of cognac and 3 ounces of rum. In 1862, there was a far greater variety of Madeiras available than there is today. I like a Bual in this.

EGG NOGG

The individual version.

(USE LARGE BAR-GLASS.)

1 TABLE-SPOONFUL OF FINE WHITE SUGAR, DISSOLVED WITH

1 TABLE-SPOONFUL COLD WATER

1 EGG

1 WINE-GLASS [2 OZ] OF COGNAC BRANDY

½ WINE-GLASS [1 OZ] OF SANTA CRUZ RUM

⅓ TUMBLERFUL OF MILK

Fill the tumbler ¼ full with shaved ice, shake the ingredients until they are *thoroughly mixed together*, and grate a little nutmeg on top. Every well ordered bar has a tin egg-nogg "shaker," which is a great aid in mixing this beverage.

SOURCE: JERRY THOMAS, 1862

NOTES ON INGREDIENTS: For Thomas's **Sherry Egg Nogg**, replace the cognac and rum with two wineglasses of oloroso sherry and use only the yolk of the egg. Then "quaff the nectar cup."

NOTES ON EXECUTION: This is the only drink in Thomas's book that explicitly calls for the use of the Cocktail shaker.

GENERAL HARRISON'S EGG NOGG

Benjamin "Old Tippecanoe" Harrison ran for president in 1840 on the "log cabin and hard cider" ticket, the idea being that he was a common man of the people who just wanted to drink cider and sit on the porch of his cabin. The people bought it.

(USE LARGE BAR-GLASS.)

    1 EGG

    1½ TEA-SPOONFUL OF SUGAR

    2 OR 3 SMALL LUMPS [½ GLASS] OF ICE

Fill the tumbler with cider, and shake well. This is a splendid drink, and is very popular on the Mississippi river. It was General Harrison's favorite beverage.

SOURCE: JERRY THOMAS, 1862

NOTES ON INGREDIENTS: The cider should of course be hard. Try to get something artisanal, made from whole cider apples, not concentrate.

TOM & JERRY

The reporter came right out and asked him; what was he gonna do, say no? The Professor went into his spiel:

One day in . . . 1847 a gentleman asked me to give him an egg beaten up in sugar. I prepared the article, and then . . . I thought to myself, 'How beautiful the egg and sugar would be with brandy to it!' I ran to the gentleman and, says I, 'If you'll only bear with me for five minutes I'll fix you up a drink that'll do your heart-strings good.' He wasn't at all averse to having the condition of his heartstrings improved, so back I went, mixed the egg and sugar, which I had beaten up into a kind of batter, with some brandy, then I poured in some hot water and stirred vigorously. The drink realised my expectations. It was the one thing I'd been dreaming of for months. . . . I named the drink after myself, kinder familiarly: I had two small white mice in those days, one of them I had called Tom and the other Jerry, so I combined the abbreviations in the drink, as Jeremiah P. Thomas would have sounded rather heavy, and that wouldn't have done for a beverage.

By the early 1880s, when Alan Dale—the reporter in question—encountered him, Thomas must've been telling that story for thirty years. When his obituaries were written, he was unquestioningly credited with the invention of this popular drink. (Indeed, this anecdote appears almost verbatim in his obituary in the *New York Times.*) In his book, he says that people even called it "Jerry Thomas." In a way, he *was* the drink. I'm sure he got to the point that he was almost believing that he invented it himself.

But he didn't, as this little item from the Salem, Massachusetts, *Gazette* demonstrates:

At the Police Court in Boston, last week, a lad about thirteen years of age was tried for stealing a watch, and acquitted. In the course of the trial, it appeared that the prosecutor [i.e., the plaintiff] sold to the lad, under the name of "Tom and Jerry," a composition of saleratus [i.e., baking soda], eggs, sugar, nutmeg, ginger, allspice and rum. A female witness testified that the boy . . . appeared to be perfectly deranged, probably in consequence of the 'hell-broth' that he had been drinking.

Thomas, you'll recall, was born in 1830. This was published on March 20, 1827. Nor is this an isolated quote: numerous references to the drink from the 1830s and 1840s have turned up, all from

New England. It's quite possible, therefore, that Thomas mixed *his* first Tom & Jerry in 1847, while he was learning the bar business in new Haven, in the heart of the Tom & Jerry Belt. But *the* first? No way. No matter; if he didn't invent the drink, he certainly did more than any other man to promote it.

From after the Civil War until the late 1880s, come the cold weather in October or November, every saloon worth wrecking with a hatchet would get down the china Tom & Jerry bowl and the little "shaving mugs" that went with it (these sets were commercially available since at least the early 1870s) and the newspapers would start making spavined jokes about Thomas and Jeremiah, "two well-known sports" who had just showed up in town and "whose acquaintance should not be cultivated too deeply." From then until spring, the bowl would be full of the foamy batter (or "dope," as it was sometimes known), ready to be spooned into the little mugs, stiffened with booze, and heated with a little water or milk from the little boiler on the bar. Everyone loved it.

But eventually tastes changed, and right around the time Jerry Thomas passed away, his semi-namesake began to share the fate of other drinks of its age and level of fanciness, to the point that in 1902 the *New York Sun* could write that it "seems to have vanished as absolutely as the dodo." Fortunately, that was over-pessimistic; you could still find it at the more traditional places until Prohibition, and even now, in the heart of the Upper Midwest, there are bars that make Tom & Jerry every holiday season.

(U S E   P U N C H - B O W L   F O R   T H E   M I X T U R E .)

5 LBS [2 LBS] SUGAR

12 EGGS

½ SMALL GLASS [1 OZ] OF JAMAICA RUM

1½ TEA-SPOONFUL OF GROUND CINNAMON

½ TEA-SPOONFUL OF GROUND CLOVES

½ TEA-SPOONFUL OF GROUND ALLSPICE

Beat the whites of the eggs to a stiff froth, and the yolks until they are thin as water, then mix together and add the spice and rum; thicken with sugar until the mixture attains the consistence of a light batter. N. B.—A tea-spoonful of cream of tartar, or about as much carbonate of soda as you can get on a dime, will prevent the sugar from settling to the bottom of the mixture. This drink is sometimes called Copenhagen, and sometimes *Jerry Thomas*.

To deal out Tom and Jerry to customers:
Take a small bar-glass, and to one table-spoonful of the above mixture, add one wine-glass [2 oz] of brandy, and fill the glass with boiling water; grate a little nutmeg on top. Adepts at the bar, in serving Tom and Jerry, sometimes adopt a mixture of ½ brandy, ¼ Jamaica rum, and ¼ Santa Cruz rum, instead of brandy plain. This compound is usually mixed and kept in a bottle, and a wine-glassful [2 oz] is used to each tumbler of Tom and Jerry.

SOURCE: JERRY THOMAS, 1862

NOTES ON INGREDIENTS: By today's standards 5 pounds is a crazy amount of sugar. Two pounds should be plenty. The water can be replaced with hot milk, and often was by the turn of the twentieth century. It's better that way, although there's a certain austere ruggedness to the water version (if using water, add an extra pound of sugar, to give the drink a little more body).

NOTES ON EXECUTION: Whether you use water or milk, the mugs (an eBay item if ever there was one) should be rinsed with boiling water before being filled, to warm them.

CHAPTER 6

TODDIES, SLINGS,
JULEPS, AND SUCH

B efore the Cocktail, there was the Toddy—or the Sling—or the
Julep—or the Sangaree. Or anything else you wanted to call a
glass of beverage alcohol with a little sugar in it, a little water if
needed, and maybe a scrape of nutmeg over the top or a sprig or
two of mint stuck in the glass.

The very simplicity of these drinks led to a good deal of confusion between them, particularly when regional and national differences in nomenclature are factored in (a Yankee's Sling, an
Englishman's Toddy, and an Irishman's Skin might be made in the
exact same way). Indeed, the three editions of Jerry Thomas's book
give a sheaf of overlapping recipes for Toddies and Slings in particular that differ only in the temperature of the H_2O, the choice of
base spirit, and the presence and absence of nutmeg.*

The works of his contemporaries only add to the confusion. While

---

* For the record, the precise variations acknowledged in Thomas's book are: hot Apple
Toddy, cold and hot Brandy Toddy, cold Whiskey Toddy, cold Gin Toddy, cold (and presumably hot) Brandy Sling, hot Whiskey Sling, and cold Gin Sling.

the general rule of this book is to present definitive, original recipes in unmodified form, if ever there's a place to break it, this is it. Since it's fair to say that, in general (although, ironically, not in Jerry Thomas's book), Toddy was perceived as a hot drink that you could also make cold, and Sling as a cold one that you could also make hot, I've used that as a sort of stick with which to thresh this large and incestuous family of drinks out into two master recipes, a Hot Toddy and a Cold Sling, each based on Jerry Thomas's 1862 edition but incorporating some of the handy hints from elsewhere. If you want a Cold Toddy or a Hot Sling, just make a Cold Sling or a Hot Toddy and change the name, manipulating the nutmeg *ad libitum*.

There are a few major variations, including the popular Sangaree, that achieved a life of their own; I've allowed them to roam free, below.

I. Rum, Brandy, Whiskey, or Gin Toddy, Hot

Some time at the beginning of the 1750s, the great Early American portrait painter Charles Willson Peale—then a lad of twelve or so—put a vital question to a local Annapolis doctor. "What is the best drink for health?" The doctor, a gentleman of Scottish extraction, did not hem or haw. "Toddy, mun. The spirit must have something to act on, and therefore acts on the sugar and does nae injury to the stomach." It's a charming theory, anyway; how nice if it were true (another round of Piña Coladas over here, Ramon!). But whatever its benignity, Toddy hot in the winter and cold in the summer was one of the invariables of American drinking

CRESCENT SHAPE BAR KETTLE.
Made of heavy copper and nickel plated. Shaped so that it can be placed on top of stove to be heated; crescent groove made to fit around stovepipe.
Dimensions........................7 inches high
" 14   "   diameter.
Faucet of latest and best make.
Price, each.................................$3.69

Hot drinks, too, required special equipment. This handy heater was designed to go on top of the ubiquitous potbellied stove. (Author's collection)

from the middle of the eighteenth century until the end of the nineteenth—and, in some places, beyond. When I was a child, which was not so long ago as all that (we had *Batman* on the TV and Johnnie Eagle plastic M-14s to shoot our little friends with), my New England–born mother would, in circumstances of extreme chill, administer Toddy to my brother and me under the guise of Hot Buttered Rum. It was strictly medicinal, of course, and very much on the weak side, but nonetheless.

Toddy—aka Sling, Sangaree, Skin, or Bombo, all more or less the same thing—is a simple drink in the same way a tripod is a simple device: Remove one leg and it cannot stand, set it up properly and it will hold the whole weight of the world. This mixture of spirits, hot or cold water, sugar, and perhaps a scraping of nutmeg is the irreducible minimum of true mixology. Take away any ingredient and you're left with something less than a mixed drink. Except the nutmeg, that is—just as had occurred with the Bowl of Punch, the element of spice was soon recognized as inessential. But without the sugar, it's just spirits and water. Sure, you can fit this out with a fancy name—call it a Grog or a Highball—but it's still just watered booze. Without the water, it's essentially a liqueur (provided you can get the sugar to dissolve in the first place), and not fit for serious drinking. And without the spirits—well, no. But get everything right (and Lord knows it's easy enough) and it's a drink all right. Indeed, like all truly great drinks, it's sometimes a good deal more than that.

Under the proper circumstances, a Hot Toddy—particularly one constructed upon a foundation of good Highland malt whisky—is one of the clearest signs I know that there is a providential plan to the universe. Of course, those circumstances include things like faulty central heating, dripping eaves, gray mists, chill drafts, and moth-eaten cardigan sweaters, all of which are in short supply in modern American life. But it's almost worth artificially creating them just to feel the blissful warmth seeping farther into every muscle and nerve with each sip until, as far as your body is concerned, you're laying out on the Grand Anse beach in Grenada, not hunched against a cold and cutting nor' easter. The old days were hard, but the people who lived them found ways of making them tolerable.

Apparently of Scottish origin (although its print debut is found in a July 1750 issue of the *Boston Weekly Post Boy*), the "fashionable" Toddy—as the Newport, Rhode Island, *Mercury* dubbed it in 1764—was a fixture of American tippling for a century or more. It didn't hurt that, unlike Punch, the Toddy required no perishable ingredients or complicated formulae. Rum (or whiskey if you were out on the frontier, brandy if you were posh, applejack if you were from New Jersey, gin if you were of African or Dutch extraction, etc.). As much sugar as you liked, or had—no worries here about balancing out the acidity of lemons or limes. Water, hot or cold. If you had some nutmeg, fine; if not, fine, too. If there was no sugar, honey or even blackstrap molasses would do. You could make it strong or you could make it weak and sip it all day, as John Ferdinand Smyth found the Virginia planters doing in the 1780s. You could make it one glass or mug at a time, or—well, consider the way Pennsylvanian Joseph Price spent May 11, 1802: "had 3 Pints Whis[key], they Complaind of Cold very much, at Mothers Got a bowl hot Toddy then they Came home with me and I Made them 2 Bowls, made their harts Glad & away they went." (Who's "they"? He never does tell us; perhaps he should've waited until May 12 to update his diary.) In fact, the first published recipe for Toddy that I've been able to find, the one in Samuel Stearns's 1801 *American Herbal*, makes a hefty quart of the stuff. One hopes that that wasn't intended for one person.

By Jerry Thomas's day, the Toddy had settled into a comfortable middle age. The size was reduced to what could comfortably fit in one hand, the sugar moved up the social scale to pure white, and, while there were a few holdouts in New England who plumped for Medford rum and some ethnics who went for gin (with the pot-stilled, whiskeylike Hollands, this is decidedly more pleasant than it sounds), most people preferred to stoke their Toddies with good domestic rye or, preferably, bourbon (some felt rye "doesn't suit" as well in hot drinks), or even better, imported French brandy. In fact, Brandy Toddy was often prescribed by doctors for its medicinal value (some ideas die hard).

Then, in the late 1870s, for whatever reason—the verminous phylloxera's devastation of the vineyards of France, increasing Anglophilia, a sudden and uncharacteristic onrush of good sense—America at large discovered what a few had always known: that by far the best spirit in a Hot Toddy is pure Scotch whisky. Under the guise of Hot Scotch, the Hibernian version of the Toddy quickly rose to near-universal popularity as the sovereign remedy for a frosty night; indeed, until the golf-and-Scotch Highball craze of the 1890s it was just about the only way Scotch whisky was drunk in America. Judging by the contents of his bar's cellar, which included barrels of a nice fifteen-year-old Caol Isla malt, Jerry Thomas was an early adopter (Andrew Johnson was another, although I don't know if he took it up pre- or post-impeachment). Mark Twain came later to it, but made up for the delay by his regular devotion (according to his friend William Dean Howells, for years he took it before bedtime, deeming it "the only soporific worth considering"; in an age without benzodiazepines, he wasn't wrong). The only dissenters were the Irish-Americans, who maintained, like the "old rounder" quoted in an Ohio paper in 1888, that "Irish whisky can stand hot water better than any other under the sun."

That rounder was onto something. In the 1880s, you see, the old, unblended Scottish malt whisky, made in a traditional copper pot still with its kettle and gooseneck and spiral condensing worm, was being edged out by blended Scotch, wherein the malt was cut by the much lighter and purer stuff that the new "patent" stills were turning out, while the Americans had switched to mostly patent-still production, as had some rum distillers. The Irish, however, were still selling their whiskey unblended. This might seem a bit technical, but it's anything but: after years of experience with the Hot Toddy, I've found that the one sure secret to success is to use pot-stilled spirits in it. The heavier body they possess gives the drink a silky texture that is hard to resist.

(USE SMALL BAR-GLASS.)

1 TEASPOONFUL OF SUGAR

½ WINEGLASS [3–4 OZ] OF WATER

1 WINE-GLASS [2 OZ] OF [SPIRITS]

Stir with a spoon.

SOURCE: JERRY THOMAS, 1862 (COMPOSITE)

NOTES ON INGREDIENTS: Again, pot-stilled spirits are essential here. Cognac or single-malt Scotch: always (this is an excellent use for a very peaty Scotch, particularly if it's at cask strength). Dark rum, Irish whiskey, and Hollands: on a case-by-case basis (Redbreast Irish whiskey is pure pot-still, and fabulous here). Bourbon and rye: well, they're kind of a special case, because they almost always come out of a patent still, but at a lower proof than usual (and hence with a heavier body); in fact, some of them have just the right thickness you need (Woodford Reserve is a particular favorite here, but then again, it's supposed to be part pot-still.). Vodka, London Dry gin, etc.: No. Tequila: It certainly might work, but you go first.

As for the sugar, you've got options here, too. For one thing, you can do without, as Mark Twain liked to (it was a Western thing). I don't recommend that; not so much because I like a sweeter drink, but because the sugar adds thickness, and a thin Toddy is a sad Toddy. Some modern mixologists suggest sweetening Whisky Toddies with honey; personally, I think it clashes with the malt. Certainly the Professor and his colleagues never call for anything but sugar. Generally, this would have been the standard quick-dissolving powdered white sugar, but the presence of boiling water means that other kinds will work as well. I favor Demerara or raw sugar in my Toddies—they're a little less sweet and a little more rich and complex (you can also get Demerara in cubes or, even better, irregular little lumps that just scream out "authentic").

Water. The ideal proportion seems to be about one part spirit to one and a half to two parts water. Keep it as hot as possible. If you prefer nutmeg on your Toddy, well, according to the Professor that's a Sling. His 1887 reviser, however, disagrees; myself, I find nutmeg works well with rum, brandy, or Hollands, but not so well with whisky. When you do use it, grate it fresh. Never use the stuff in a jar; you might as well be following the jocular (I hope) advice the British traveler J. E. Alexander gave in 1833: "If there is no nutmeg convenient, a scrape or two of the mudler (wooden sugar-breaker) will answer the purpose."

NOTES ON EXECUTION: As he so often did, the 1887 reviser added clear and useful instructions: "First rinse the glass with hot water, put in the sugar, fill the glass half-full of boiling water, add the [spirits] and stir. Serve with a spoon." If you're using a glass, make sure it's a heavy, tempered one. In general, I prefer a mug, which will keep the drink warm longer (try not to use a "World's Best Dad" mug or other such cultural detritus; it cheapens the effect). If you've got a toddy-stick, now's the time to use it. Beyond that, there's little to say. If you like lemon peel in yours, that's a **Skin** (page 144).

APPLE TODDY

From the beginning of the Republic, if not before, until the turn of the last century, if not after, one of the particular treats Americans looked to with which to solace their winters was Apple Toddy—a drink that has since disappeared with scarcely a trace. Indeed, before the Mint Julep and the Cocktail assumed the role it was so popular that it was something of a signifier of Americanness. That, certainly, is how it appears in the 1792 comedy *The Yorker's Strategy*, its earliest citation.

As befits a truly democratic drink, the Apple Toddy was enjoyed up and down the social scale. If we find the British traveler Captain J. E. Alexander ("Late of the 16th Lancers") noting that, on the Mississippi in 1831, "mint julep and apple toddy were the favourite liquors of the refined; cocktail and gin-sling were relished by the *Dii minorum gentium*" [i.e., the "lesser gods"], we equally find the Gettysburg *Republican Compiler* singling it out just a few years later as the kind of swill drunk by the Democratic (with a capital "D") mob. Whichever end of the scale you put senators on, to see Senator Beck of Kentucky drink one was "supposed to be a liberal education," as one newspaper put it in the 1880s. When other drinks of similar vintage fell by the wayside, the Apple Toddy continued on into the era of electric light and moving pictures, just as popular as ever.

But then Prohibition came, and in all the excitement people had little time for such things as an Apple Toddy. After repeal, whether roasting apples and mixing them up with sugar, water, and booze was too old-fashioned, too much work, or everybody just forgot, I do not know. But Apple Toddy was seen no more.

(U S E   S M A L L   B A R - G L A S S .)

1 TABLE-SPOONFUL OF FINE WHITE SUGAR

1 WINE-GLASS [2 OZ] OF CIDER BRANDY

½ OF A BAKED APPLE

Fill the glass two-thirds full of boiling water, and grate a little nutmeg on top.

SOURCE: JERRY THOMAS, 1862

N O T E S   O N   I N G R E D I E N T S : Though Jerry Thomas and the *Steward & Barkeeper's Manual* both favor "cider brandy" or applejack, the great Willard, whose iced version is one of four of his recipes to survive, preferred plain grape brandy. If you can only get the blended applejack Laird's sells, use Calvados instead, or listen to Willard (preferably with a nice VSOP cognac); if you can get one of Laird's fine straight apple brandies, proceed with that. Whatever you use, it's worth bearing in mind what the *Steward & Barkeeper's Manual* stated in 1869: "This drink ought never to be made with a suspicion of weakness. It is only drank [sic] in cold weather, and needs to be a little strong to be satisfactory to the epicurean" (its recipe called for a full 4 ounces of hooch).

Half an apple per drink should do. Just peel and core the apples, wrap them in wet brown paper as Willard suggests (otherwise they'll fall apart) and bake them in a 350-degree oven for 30 to 45 minutes, until completely soft (or, as Willard suggests, roast them in the embers of a fire). For sugar, see the notes on ingredients for Hot

Toddy (page 141); whichever kind you use, use 1 tablespoonful as Thomas indicates; this is no place to skimp on the sweetness. In his 1869 *Cooling Cups and Dainty Drinks*, the Englishman William Terrington suggests using boiling cider instead of water; that might just be a bit too much apple.

NOTES ON EXECUTION: Put the sugar in a heated mug or heavy tumbler, add a splash of boiling water and stir (use a toddy-stick, if you've got one, or a muddler); add the spirits and the apple and stir some more until its pulp is dissolved. Fill with another 1 or 2 ounces boiling water, stir and grate nutmeg over the top.

WHISKY SKIN

Late one night in early 1855, one Richard Stark was tending bar at a sporting-life joint on Broadway at Howard Street in New York, when three men walked in. One of them, a yegg by the name of Richard McLaughlin—alias "Pargene"—stepped up to the bar and, as Stark later testified, "called for a whisky skin." When the seventeen-year-old bartender slid it over to him, Pargene dashed it in his face, saying, "You son of a bitch—if your master was here I would scald his eyes out, too!" A few days earlier, you see, Pargene had bumped into the bar's owner outside the Astor House and called him "a pretty son of a bitch." In return, the man had laughed at him, and, as the *New York Daily Times* later recounted, "tapping him by the side of the nose, said, 'I'm too sweet for you,'" and turned his back on him. The comment rankled. A couple months later, Pargene and a few other toughs managed to catch up with Stark's master at another Broadway bar, the Stanwix Hall, which was right across the street from the Metropolitan Hotel, where Jerry Thomas would soon be working. They didn't scald him with a Whisky Skin, either—after some tussling, they ended up shooting him three times. Thus ended the life of William "Bill the Butcher"

Poole, of *Gangs of New York* fame; his last words, "I die a true American." Jerry Thomas must have approved.

The Whisky Skin is nothing more than a Hot Toddy with a strip of lemon peel in it. As a name, it came on the scene in the mid-1850s, with the drink dashed in poor young Stark's face being only the second known attribution (the first is from the *Brooklyn Daily Eagle* in 1854). The drink itself is surely Irish, a small version of the almost-lemonless punch popular there. According to Thomas, who only gave the Scotch version, it was also known—in Boston, anyway—as a "Columbia Skin."

For a time Whisky Skin was a popular drink, celebrated on stage (it made a cameo in *Our American Cousin*, the play Lincoln was watching when he got shot) and in verse. It's still a damned good one.

(USE SMALL BAR - GLASS .)

1 WINE-GLASS [2 OZ] OF SCOTCH WHISKEY

1 PIECE OF LEMON PEEL

Fill the tumbler one-half full with boiling water.

SOURCE: JERRY THOMAS, 1862

NOTES ON INGREDIENTS: The 1887 edition specifies "Glenlivet or Islay"—i.e., a mellow, rich malt on the one hand, or a briny, peaty one on the other. Both will work just fine. It also adds an **Irish Whiskey Skin**, which is made the same way, but with the necessary substitution. If you can get the pure pot-still Redbreast, do so. Neither Thomas nor the 1869 *Steward & Barkeeper's Manual* call for sugar in their Skins; others disagreed. Personally, I like 1 teaspoon of Demerara sugar in mine; call me what thou wilt. As for the lemon peel—a long strip pared away from the fruit without any of the white pith is what's wanted here. It's worth the effort.

NOTES ON EXECUTION: Proceed as for the standard Hot Toddy. The lemon peel should go in with the sugar, to ensure maximum extraction of flavor.

BLUE BLAZER

Perhaps the most colorful part of Herbert Asbury's account of
Jerry Thomas's life is the bit where a "bewhiskered giant laden
with gold lust with three layers of pistols strapped around his
middle" stomps into the El Dorado and roars "Bar-keep! . . .
Fix me up some hell-fire that'll shake me right down to my gizzard!" The Professor measures his man and tells him to come
back in an hour, whereupon, in front of a crowd filled with antic-
ipation and booze, he proceeds to prepare a mixture of Scotch
whisky and boiling water, light it on fire, and hurl the blazing
mixture back and forth between two silver mugs "with a rapid-
ity and dexterity that were well nigh unbelievable." The mixture
is a success. "Right down to my gizzard! Yes, sir, right down to
my gizzard!" the miner finally manages to whisper.

That's not how the Professor remembered it. As he told Alan
Dale, he invented the drink while "in a fit of musing." He was fiddling around one day with a cupful of Scotch, you see, and an

BLUE BLAZER.

The Professor mixes a Blue Blazer. From *The Bon
Vivant's Companion*, 1862. (Author's collection)

empty glass, and "dream-
ily" he just happened to
light the whisky on fire.
As he watched "the pale
blue flame flickering and
dancing," he then poured
it back and forth between
vessels "until the whiskey
was thoroughly burned."

Whatever the circum-
stances of its creation,
considered from the un-
sentimental perspective of
mixology, the Blue Blazer
is not much of an inven-

tion, being merely a Scotch Whisky Skin to which has been applied the bartender's standard procedure for mixing cold drinks. And, of course, fire. No matter: That fire was enough to make this a spectacular barroom stunt, especially in those gaslit days. As Thomas wrote, "A beholder gazing for the first time upon an experienced artist, compounding this beverage, would naturally come to the conclusion that it was a nectar for Pluto rather than Bacchus"—and it was well worth taking credit for. Thomas even kept a photograph of him making one right over the bar (I assume the engraving found in his book was based on it).

One thing, though: In his 1867 *American Bartender*, Charles B. Campbell, of San Francisco, includes a slightly more complex version of the drink with the comment, "This drink is solely my own." Hmm.

Whoever invented it, the Blue Blazer starts turning up in print in the late 1850s and enjoyed a certain amount of popularity through the 1870s, with bartenders doing to it what bartenders do—that is, making it with everything but Scotch (rum and brandy were particularly popular). Eventually, with the new, cool, spoon-twirling school of bartender taking over in the 1880s, bartenders lost the desire and skill to perform this dangerous and racy stunt. As one Kansas City bartender reminisced in 1883, "There used to be a dozen men in Kansas City who thought nothing of doing that, but you never see them now. Why a bartender on Main St. tried it the other day for fun and nearly burned his hand off." He couldn't say nobody warned him: It says right there in Jerry Thomas's book, "The novice in mixing this beverage should be careful not to scald himself. To become proficient in throwing the liquid from one mug to the other, it will be necessary to practise [sic] for some time with cold water."

(USE TWO LARGE SILVER-PLATED MUGS, WITH HANDLES.)

1 WINE-GLASS [2 OZ] OF SCOTCH WHISKEY

1 WINE-GLASS [1½ OZ] BOILING WATER

Put the whiskey and the boiling water in one mug, ignite the liquid with fire, and while blazing mix both ingredients by pouring them four or five times from one mug to the other, as represented in the cut. If well done this will have the appearance of a continued stream of liquid fire.

Sweeten with one teaspoonful of pulverized white sugar, and serve in a small bar tumbler, with a piece of lemon peel.

SOURCE: JERRY THOMAS, 1862

NOTES ON INGREDIENTS: If possible, I try to use a cask-strength single-malt whisky with this; the extra alcohol makes it much easier to set alight (the cask-strength Laphroaig works splendidly). Campbell calls for Scotch and Irish whiskeys mixed in equal parts. This is fine, but unnecessary. As with the Hot Scotch, I prefer a raw or Demerara sugar in this one.

NOTES ON EXECUTION: The Blue Blazer is all about the execution. First off, the mugs: I use one-pint pewter tankards, tulip-shaped as in the engraving. The flared rim makes them pour more neatly; here, you really, really want that. Campbell suggests two "silver-plated mugs, with handles and glass bottoms" (eBay is full of pewter mugs, glass-bottomed or not; the silver plating is not strictly essential). The greatest trick here—besides not burning the house down, that is (I always make these over a baking tray full of water)—is to avoid putting the fire out. For that, I try to make them two at a time, with a little more whisky than water, putting the water and sugar in before the booze. This ensures a goodly amount of hot alcohol fumes to ignite. When pouring, be gentle and only pour about half the drink at a time, "being particular," as Campbell says, "to keep the other [mug] blazing during the pouring process." Then approach the tea cups or small, heavy glasses you have laid out in advance and prepared with a strip of lemon peel in each and—Campbell again—"pour mixture into glass blazing, and cover with [mixing] cup," to extinguish it. Whatever you do, do it quickly—the handles have a habit of getting pretty damned hot, pretty damned fast.

Oh, and remember to dim the lights. It makes it easier to see the flames, both for your audience (and there's no point in making this drink without one) and, of course, for yourself. You want to see the flames.

II. Gin, Brandy, Whiskey, and Rum Sling, Cold

About that quart of Toddy in Stearns's *American Herbal* being for one person. The thing is, it might have been. Americans drank far too much in the early years of the Republic and days like Joseph Price's May 11, 1802, with the three pints of whiskey, were far from uncommon. This gave his fellow Pennsylvanian Benjamin Rush pause. Signer of the Declaration of Independence, surgeon-general to the Continental army (well, part of it, anyway), Professor of Medical Theory and Clinical Practice at the University of Pennsylvania, etc., etc., Dr. Rush was one of those amazing do-it-all gents without whom America could not have been built. He was also no dope. While the rest of his countrymen were engaged on a national binge that would put a U of T fraternity to shame, he had reservations. Nor did he keep them to himself. In 1785—astonishingly early; the American temperance movement wouldn't get into gear for another forty years—he published *An Inquiry Into the Effects of Spirituous Liquors Upon the Human Body*. While by no means coming out in favor of total abstinence, he did have qualms about Dr. Hamilton's most healthful of drinks: "To every class of my readers," he wrote, "I beg leave to suggest a caution against the use of Toddy." Sure, he knew a few men who, "by limiting its strength constantly, by measuring the spirit and water, and . . . by drinking it only with their meals," got off lightly. Others, though . . . Take the Philadelphia gentleman of Rush's acquaintance, "once of a fair and sober character," who took Toddy as his "Constant drink." Toddy led to Grog (a simple mix of rum and water). Grog led to Slings, Slings led to "raw rum," and next thing you know he was drinking "Jamaica spirits" with a tablespoonful of ground pepper in each glass ("to take off their coldness," he averred). Then he died.

The funny thing about this *descensus Avernae*, if there is a funny thing, is Rush's description of the Slings his unfortunate acquaintance had been drinking: They were "equal parts rum and water, with a little sugar"—in other words, merely a strong Toddy (in those days a Toddy was, it appears, made with two or three parts water to one part spirits). If there was any other important difference between them, nobody in on the secret seems to have seen fit to confide it to posterity. Even Jerry Thomas, with his vast knowledge and experience, could only come up with a rather arbitrary rule that Sling had nutmeg and Toddy did not (something the man who revised his book in 1887 promptly contradicted). No matter—the Sling, particularly the gin variety (first attested to in 1800), soon became one of the iconic American drinks, consumed morning, noon, and night everywhere American was spoken (Rush was a voice shouting in the wilderness, and the American wilderness was vast).

Sling, which most likely takes its name from the act of "slinging" one back, seems to have been a purely American drink (or at least a purely American name for it); not only was Dr. Rush apparently the first to notice it in print, but "gin sling" appears as one of the "peculiarities" an 1808 article in the Philadelphia *Port-Folio* noted as characteristic of the American way with the language. Peculiar or not, it was something Americans couldn't stay away from. From the end of the eighteenth century until well past the middle of the nineteenth, whenever somebody made even passing mention of the alcoholic concoctions characteristic of the American people, "Sling" was sure to be one of first words out of the inkwell. It didn't hurt its notoriety that it was often partaken of in the morning, right upon arising.

Like the Toddy, if the Sling had a particular corner of America to call its own, it remains well-hidden to the mixographer. Sure, Washington Irving in his *Knickerbocker's History of New York* might try to pass it off on the Marylanders, and the abstemious Newport, Rhode Island, *Mercury* on the Virginians (while claiming that New Englanders stuck to tea, thank you very much). But at pretty much the same time—the first decade or so of the 1800s—a paper in Saratoga County, New York, only 150-odd miles away from both New York and Newport, could talk about seeing a man take two Slings "before breakfast" as if it were as common as brushing your teeth. Okay, bad comparison, seeing as the first American patent for a toothbrush wasn't registered until the 1850s; but you get the idea. In New York City, the Sling even passed as a health drink—as the *Evening Post*'s editorial department noted in 1825, "It is stated with unshaken confidence, as the result of actual and repeated experience, that half a tumbler of gin sling, well powdered with grated nutmeg, proves a speedy and an efficacious styptic in that dangerous and alarming complaint, a bleeding of the lungs." Dr. Hamilton would have been pleased.

That "actual experience" was only to be more repeated once ice made the transition from luxury to staple. By the 1830s, it had formed an indissoluble union with the Cold Sling; having tried Gin Sling with water and Gin Sling with ice, I can see why. By the end of the century, the rise of the Sling's offspring—the Cocktail— rendered it a subject of nostalgia. But for a good while there, it sufficed—and, if made with a certain amount of care and consumed with a certain amount of blended sympathy and archeological curiosity, it still does. Don't forget the nutmeg.

(USE SMALL BAR-GLASS.)

1 TEASPOONFUL OF POWDERED WHITE SUGAR

½ WINE-GLASS [1 OZ] **OF WATER**

1 WINE-GLASS [2 OZ] **OF** [SPIRITS]

1 SMALL LUMP OF ICE

Stir with a spoon.

SOURCE: JERRY THOMAS, 1862 (COMPOSITE)

NOTES ON INGREDIENTS: Gin, of course. Historically, it would've been Hollands, but in an iced drink, where body is less of an issue, you can get away with something like Plymouth (or, better still, a 60-40 mix of Plymouth and Irish whiskey, which yields a fair enough field approximation of Hollands). Jerry Thomas also lists whiskey, which is plenty good, although here it's the American ones that shine—the same sharp woodiness that makes them a bit scary in a hot drink rescues a cold one from insipidness. My personal preference is for rye, but bourbon slings up nicely as well. Beyond that, the historical record offers "Madeira Sling" (attested in 1804), which is more properly a Sangaree; "Mint Sling" (also from 1804), identical with the Julep; and even the occasional Rum Sling or Brandy Sling (the only other one the Professor lists). The mention of Brandy Sling brings up a deeper issue. Good cognac is expensive these days, and if I'm going to mix it up in a drink, I'm afraid I want something a bit spicier than a plain old Brandy Sling. In fact, while Hot Toddy is an essential drink, I've always found its close cousin Cold Sling—dare I say it—rather uninspiring. It happens in the best of families, I guess.

Water and ice can be adjusted. Spirits tended to be stronger in the Professor's day and could take more dilution, so with the weak stuff we get today a quarter of a wineglass—½ ounce—of water should do. Before the ice machine, every bartender had to carve his own ice cubes, which means the Professor's "small lump" might very well be our "baseball." In any case, two or three regular-sized cubes are enough. And the nutmeg has to be fresh-grated, as above, or don't bother.

I should note here that in English hands, the formula for the Sling was expanded to include citrus juices and, later, liqueurs, thus making it nothing more than Punch in a glass. Thus it appears in the 1862 *Cook's Guide, and Housekeeper's and Butler's Assistant* by Charles Elme Francatelli (Queen Victoria's chef) and numerous other early transatlantic works of mixography. It's from this tradition that the famous Singapore Sling is descended.

NOTES ON EXECUTION: If you're using lump sugar, muddle it with the water before adding the spirits (see the **Cocktail**). Some preferred to shake their Slings, while old-timers would deploy the toddy-stick.

III. JULEPS AND SMASHES

Somebody somewhere was kidding. A "julep," you see, was medicine, pure and simple, and it always had been. It was medicine when

Rhazes put it in his *Kitab al-Mansuri* in 900 (his Juleps had no offense in them, being merely violets macerated with water and sugar); it was medicine in the fifteenth-century Latin translation of his book; it was medicine in 1583, when Philip Barrough noted in his *Methode of Physicke* that "a iulep doeth not much differ from a syrupe, but that it is lesse boyled . . . and because also it is made without the permixtion of

MINT JULEP.

The Mint Julep. From *The Bon Vivant's Companion*, 1862. (Author's collection)

anie other decoction with it"; it was medicine in 1619, when a character in John Fletcher's *Humorous Lieutenant* predicted a battle-wearied enemy would "no doubt fall to his jewlips"; it was medicine in 1698, when Samuel Lee pontificated on the inability of "life-exhausting blood-lets" and "cold, mortal Juleps" to stave off death and judgment ("O vain man!"); it was medicine in 1765 when William Alexander treated some poor bastard for his ills with "camphorated julep" and "musk julep"; it was medicine in 1770 when Peter Thomson, a surgeon, was prescribing juleps compounded with things like egg yolks, "Chymical Oil of Cinnamon," and "Salt of Wormwood."

It was not medicine, however, in 1796, when the anonymous American author of *The Wedding, An Epic Poem* rhymed "nymphs in gardens picking tulips" with "maids preparing cordial juleps." Nobody wants

THE PRESCRIPTION.

The Prescription Julep. From *Harper's Magazine*, 1857. (Author's collection)

to drink salt of wormwood or suchlike at a wedding, no matter how dull it is. After centuries of usage as a term connoting medicine, somehow, in America, "julep" morphed into a word for something you drank for fun. In 1784, John Ferdinand Smyth, a Briton, published his impressions after a tour of America. In Virginia, he observed, upon arising the man of the lower or middling class "drinks a julap, made of rum, water, and sugar, but very strong." Now to call this, which is mixologically identical with a Sling, a "julep" was like calling a morning bong-hit "glaucoma medicine." Sure, medicinal Juleps often contained alcohol, and had since the 1600s. But they also contained various objectionable things and were taken under a doctor's orders, for specific complaints. The American Julep began in the same kind of sophistry that allowed drinking a morning Cocktail to be called "taking one's bitters." Not every drinker was so dishonest: In 1804, only two years after we first hear of mint going into a Julep (in a letter by a William and Mary student, no less, who thought his classmates too devoted to them), we find the *Adams Centinel*, a Pennsylvania paper, making reference to "Mint Sling." For a time, people fought the good fight and called a Sling a Sling, but by the 1820s it had become a Julep for good.

Richard Barksdale Hartwell has written a scholarly and entertaining monograph on the Mint Julep that ably chronicles this drink's glory years before the Civil War, so I will not repeat the story; suffice it to say that the Julep spread from the South to all parts of the Republic, and then the world. It was the most popular drink in America from the early nineteenth century until the Civil War, and—along with the Sherry Cobbler—spread the gospel of the iced drink everywhere it went (the estimable Willard, of the City Hotel, was serving iced Juleps as early as 1831). But what is not generally realized is, despite its agrarian, Southern image, how much a part of city drinking the Julep was. Willard, Cato Alexander, and Shed Sterling of the Astor House were all famous for their Mint Juleps. Even after the Civil War, New Yorkers, Chicagoans, and other urbanites were still good for a staggering number of the things every summer. It really wasn't until the early twentieth century that the Julep's star began to fade. Sure, people had complained of its decline before then—the 1887 edition of Thomas's book reprints one such article—but people always complain of such things (in 1902, the *New York Sun* went so far as to assert that not even Jerry Thomas had known the secret of concocting a proper Julep).

In the earlier part of the nineteenth century, when the Julep was primarily a brandy drink and rarely a whiskey one, one heard of various sorts of fancy Juleps; of variations with dashes of this and that, fancy fruit garnishes and the whole panoply of mixological swank. Always the sign of a living drink, this faded away after the war and the drink became something of a fossil. I've included a couple of the variations.

PRESCRIPTION JULEP

This little piece of medical humor comes from "A Winter in the South," a serial *Harper's Monthly* ran in 1857. It also happens to be the tastiest Mint Julep recipe I know. Cognac and rye whiskey are a marriage made in heaven, the cognac mellowing the rye and the rye adding spice to the cognac.

THE DOCTOR ACCORDINGLY WROTE OUT A PRESCRIPTION FOR THE CASE, AS FOLLOWS:

SACCHA ALB. ℥ IJ	WHITE SUGAR, 2 OZ [½ OZ]
CUM AQUA FONTANA, QUANT. SUFF	WITH SPRING WATER, AS MUCH AS NECESSARY [1 OZ]
COGNIAC FORT. ℥ ISS	STRONG COGNAC, 1½ OZ
SPIR. SECALICUS, ℥ SS	SPIRITS OF RYE, ½ OZ
FOL. MENTHAE VIRIDIS, AD LIB	MINT LEAVES, AS DESIRED

FIAT INFUSUM ET ADD.

GLACIES PULV. QUANT. SUFF.

OMNIA MISCE

INFUSE [the sugar, water, and spirits with the mint], THEN ADD AS MUCH POWDERED ICE AS NECESSARY AND MIX IT ALL UP.

Repeat dose three or four times a day until cold weather.

"Quackenboss, M.D."

SOURCE: *HARPER'S MONTHLY*, 1857

NOTES ON EXECUTION: Dissolve the sugar in the water, lightly press the mint leaves in the resulting syrup, add the spirits and the ice, and stir. If desired, you can add another hedge of mint to the top. And have at it with a straw.

MINT JULEP

This is Jerry Thomas's version, which remained more or less the bartender's standard for the rest of the century; note the absence of fancy silver cups, icicles of frost and all the other labor-intensive bells and whistles with which the drink became endowed once it passed from the bartender's repertoire into the householder's. The variations Thomas records include the Gin Julep, which would have been made with Hollands, and as such is surprisingly tasty (it is attested to as early as 1828); the Brandy Julep, which is a Mint Julep without all the fancy trimmings, among which some even include mint (in which case, as the *Steward & Barkeeper's Manual* sagely observed, "It is like the play of Hamlet, with the prince left out"); the Whiskey Julep, which before the Civil War was considered rather vulgar and after was considered delicious; and the Georgia Julep, which was made with brandy and the now-extinct peach brandy (the aged eau-de-vie, not the sticky liqueur).

(USE LARGE BAR-GLASS.)

1 TABLE-SPOONFUL OF WHITE PULVERIZED SUGAR

2½ TABLE-SPOONFULS OF WATER, MIX WELL WITH A SPOON

Take three or four sprigs of fresh mint, and press them well in the sugar and water, until the flavor of the mint is extracted; add one and a half wine-glass of brandy [3 oz], and fill the glass with fine shaved ice, then draw out the sprigs of mint and insert them in the ice with the stems downward, so that the leaves will be above, in the shape of a bouquet; arrange berries, and small pieces of sliced orange on top in a tasty manner, dash with Jamaica rum, and sprinkle white sugar on top. Place a straw as represented in the cut, and you have a julep that is fit for an emperor.

NOTES ON INGREDIENTS: For the **Brandy Julep**, the **Gin Julep**, and the **Whiskey Julep**, omit the fruits and dashes of rum. For a Julep "scientific style," with "the latest New Orleans touch," as tantalizingly described in a memorable passage in Mayne Reid's 1856 novel *The Quadroon*, add a slice of orange and one of lemon and see below.

NOTES ON EXECUTION: Pressing the mint renders it rather bedraggled; I prefer to discard it and use a couple of fresh sprigs at the end, rather than reinserting the pressed ones. The "scientific julep" is shaken back and forth between two glasses, mint, "ice, brandy, lemons, and all," and then the rim of the glass it rests in is wiped with "a thin slice of pineapple . . . cut freshly from the fruit." This has the double effect of clearing any undissolved sugar or bits of mint from the rim of the glass and leaving the fruit's "fragrant juice to mingle its aroma with the beverage." You can of course use a Boston shaker here, serving the drink out of the mixing glass.

PINEAPPLE JULEP

Properly, this is not a Julep at all—but as we've seen, neither is a Julep, strictly speaking. Whatever it is (I'd call it a Cup), it's delightful.

(**F O R   A   P A R T Y   O F   F I V E .**)

Peel, slice and cut up a ripe pineapple into a glass bowl, add the juice of two oranges, a gill [4 oz] of raspberry syrup, a gill [4 oz] of maraschino, a gill [4 oz] of old gin, a bottle of sparkling Moselle, and about a pound of pure ice in shaves; mix, ornament with berries in season, and serve in flat glasses.

SOURCE: JERRY THOMAS, 1862

N O T E S   O N   I N G R E D I E N T S : For the maraschino, use the liqueur, not the polymer in which "cherries" are suspended. The old gin would be a Hollands. For sparkling Moselle, substitute something sweetish and sparkling; I like a rosé champagne in this.

BRANDY, GIN, OR WHISKEY SMASH

In 1862, Jerry Thomas prefaced his section on the Smash with the simple declaration that "this beverage is simply a julep on a small plan." This is true, as far as it goes: The Smash, also known as the Smasher and the Smash-Up (it gets its name from the way the mint was smashed up in the shaking), bears the same relation to the Julep that the Fix does to the individual Punch. It's a quick bracer, rather than a slow-sipper; you don't hear of Smashes coming with straws.

But Thomas's cursory assessment of the drink leaves one with an insufficient appreciation of its importance. From its first appearance in the mid-1840s until after the Civil War, the Smash was just about the most popular thing going. In the 1850s, at the height of the Smash's popularity, all the "pert young men," the Broadway dandies, San Francisco swells, and junior New Orleans *grandissimes*, seemed to spend the warm months of the year with a Smash glued to one hand and a "segar" to the other. In fact, the Smash became rather an icon of dissipation, as in the bit in *Harper's Monthly* from 1859

FANCY BRANDY SMASH.

The Fancy Brandy Smash (the serving glass is on the left and the mixing glass on the right). From Harry Johnson's *New and Improved Illustrated Bartender's Manual*, 1888. (Courtesy Ted Haigh)

about one young son of privilege's experience in college, "where he acquired the proper proficiency in Greek, Latin, Mathematics, slang, billiards and brandy smashes." Eventually, it was pulled back into the orbit of its parent, the Julep, and one ceased to hear much about it.

(USE SMALL BAR-GLASS.)

½ TABLE-SPOONFUL [1 TSP] OF WHITE SUGAR

1 TABLE-SPOONFUL [2 TSP] OF WATER

1 WINE-GLASS [2 OZ] OF BRANDY

Fill two-thirds full of shaved ice, use two sprigs of mint, the same as in the recipe for mint julep. Lay two small pieces of orange on top, and ornament with berries in season.

SOURCE: JERRY THOMAS, 1862

NOTES ON INGREDIENTS: The sugar should be superfine. As for spirits: The Brandy Smash was by far the most popular, followed in later years by the Whiskey Smash (bourbon or rye). The Gin Smash also appears from time to time. As with the Gin Julep, Hollands is indicated. The orange-and-berry ornamentation (which goes on at the end) is not strictly necessary, and in fact Thomas's Whiskey Smash omits it.

NOTES ON EXECUTION: Dissolve the sugar in the water first (or, of course, use 1 teaspoonful or so of gum), then shake. This, however, yields a drink that is less than pleasing visually, so some mixologists of the drink's heyday preferred to stir it. I still like to shake mine, but I'll strain it over fresh ice (cracked) and insert a new sprig of mint at the end.

IV. SANGAREE

Sangaree—the name comes from the Spanish *sangria*, which pretty much gives us the origins of the drink—is a concoction of strong wine (usually port, but also sherry and Madeira), sugar, water, and nutmeg that was drunk in Britain by gentlemen and sea-captains and in America by infants, invalids, and Indians. Now, it's possible that I'm exaggerating a bit. When it came to infants and children, I have to concede that there were those who considered giving them Sangaree an "unreasonable and dangerous practice." But the very fact that this condemnation, published in the *Journal of Health* in 1830, was deemed necessary speaks volumes. For invalids, at least, it was just fine—even for ones being treated for alcoholism, if *Harper's Monthly* is to be believed (see the February 1864 issue). And for Indians, well, supplying them with the drink was positively doing them a kindness, if we can judge by the visit a delegation of important "red men of the woods" made to a cannon-foundry near Washington in 1824. After the tour, refreshments were served, "cautiously prepared in the form of sangaree, lemonade, etc." The Indians might perhaps have preferred whiskey, the *National Journal* opined, but "this weaker sort of drink is better for [them]."

Examined chronologically, this "mild and gentlemanly foreigner," as one Jackson-era newspaper dubbed it, might as well have been a native. While it first appeared in the English-speaking world in London in 1736, when the *Gentleman's Magazine* noted "a new Punch made of strong Madeira wine and called Sangre," just seven years later we find our old friend Dr. Hamilton dispatching a bowl of it—the Spanish "sangre" already corrupted to "sangaree"—in suburban Baltimore. That's an unusually quick transatlantic crossing for a drink—unless, as is entirely possible, it was already over on this side of the pond; unless Mr. Gordon got his "Sangre" from the Caribbean, where Spaniard and Englishmen mixed with great frequency. Early evidence is lacking, but by the early 1800s Sangaree (usually based on Madeira) is a constant feature in travelers' tales of the Caribbean. Wherever it was born, Sangaree was an American before there *were* Americans. But it never quite settled in here; never took out citizenship papers, cleared itself a patch of woods and set about putting in rows of corn. It's indicative that there's no "Whiskey Sangaree" in Jerry Thomas's book. Brandy and gin, yes. But whiskey, no.

By the Civil War, Sangaree was getting a little long in the tooth. Not that it disappeared entirely, mind you; it just sort of went into a pleasant retirement. As longtime East Coast bartender Jere Sullivan recalled in 1930, "In the Author's experience it was found principally the order of the elderly business man, after the counters were closed in the late afternoon." But not every drink has to play the classic American go-getter, all youth and drive and swagger. The Sangaree maintains a certain Old-World courtliness that has its appeal.

PORT WINE SANGAREE

In Jerry Thomas's day, this was by far the most common version.

(USE SMALL BAR-GLASS.)

1½ WINE-GLASS [4 OZ] OF PORT WINE

1 TEASPOONFUL OF SUGAR

Fill tumbler two-thirds with ice.

Shake well and grate nutmeg on top.

SOURCE: JERRY THOMAS, 1862

NOTE ON INGREDIENTS: This is not the time to break out that crusted vintage port. Plain old ruby port of a decent quality is what you want here. Thomas also suggests a **Sherry Sangaree**, made exactly the same way. Should you give the variation a spin, adjust the amount of sugar you use according to your sherry: more for a fino or an amontillado, less for a cream or a Pedro Ximenez. Likewise, if you want to get all eighteenth century with a **Madeira Sangaree**, the dry Sercials and Verdelhos will require a bit more sugar than the sweeter Buals and Malmseys. Whatever wine you use, the *Steward & Barkeeper's Manual* suggests 4 ounces of it rather than Thomas's 3; a sound suggestion that should not be ignored.

One variation that had enough currency for Jerry Thomas to deem it worth mention involves replacing the imported Iberian wines with rather the more quotidian tipples, porter, or ale. The venerable **Porter Sangaree**, alias "Porteree," was a "good and very wholesome Beverage" (as the *Boston Intelligencer* dubbed it in 1819) of English origin—wholesome enough for the *Journal of Health* to approve its administration to children. After the Civil War, one sees little of the Porteree outside of plagiaristic bartender's guides. As late as 1906, though, its sibling the **Ale Sangaree** had enough charm for one nostalgic toper to remember it as "the finest summer preparation that ever went down a man's throat." He recommended that the "divine, amber-colored fluid" be made with Scotch ale, noted for its mild creaminess (in other words, avoid the heavily hopped American microbrews). The thing of it is, he wasn't entirely wrong. While I might deny the Ale Sangaree the superlative *finest*, it's at least worthy of the comparative *finer*—it's a surprisingly delightful testament to the transformative power of sugar and nutmeg and there's many a younger, sportier summer drink that could learn a thing or two from it.

As for **Brandy Sangaree** and **Gin Sangaree**, which Thomas also mentioned but pretty much nobody else did (again, discounting his plagiarists). Just make the requisite Sling, omit the nutmeg, and "dash about a teaspoonful of port wine, so that it will float on top" (there are some—and I'm one of them—who consider it a kindness to float a little port on an Ale Sangaree as well). The brandy one is particularly tasty—score one for the Professor—although it is improved by using more port and squeezing in a dollop of orange juice.

NOTES ON EXECUTION: Dissolve the sugar in a splash of water before proceeding (if using Demerara, as I like to, you'll have to muddle). For a Porteree or Ale Sangaree, use a pint glass and omit the ice. Nutmeg all around.

V. THREE YANKEE FAVORITES

To round out this gathering of old-timers, here's a trey of the native drinks of Jerry Thomas's people; musty, slightly eccentric concoctions that savor of white clapboard houses, short summers, closed mouths, and dark woods. I've listed them in rough order of palatability.

HOT SPICED (OR BUTTERED) RUM

The addition of butter to hot drinks goes back at least to the days of Henry VIII, when we find one Andrew Boorde recommending buttered beer or ale as a remedy for hoarseness. By Samuel Pepys's day, buttered ale, with sugar and cinnamon, had made the transition from medicinal drink to recreational one. History is silent as to where and when the spirits came into the picture, but eighteenth-century New England would have to rank high on any list of suspects. By the time Jerry Thomas got around to committing his knowledge to paper, Hot (Spiced) Rum had largely been displaced by Hot Scotch as America's winter warmer of first resort, but there were still a few who swore by it. Unlike those who continued to stick by the Black Strap (page 166), these loyalists weren't entirely wrong.

(U S E   S M A L L   B A R - G L A S S .)

1 TEASPOONFUL OF SUGAR

1 WINE-GLASS [2 OZ] OF JAMAICA RUM

1 TEASPOONFUL OF SPICES (ALLSPICE AND CLOVES)

1 PIECE OF BUTTER AS LARGE AS HALF OF A CHESTNUT

Fill tumbler with [3–4 oz] hot water

SOURCE: JERRY THOMAS, 1862

NOTES ON INGREDIENTS: In its heyday, this drink's devotees preferred old Jamaica to the somewhat lighter Santa Cruz and anything to the rougher stuff from New England. In any case, you'll want a pot-still rum such as Inner Circle, from Australia, if you can find it (get the 115-proof); otherwise, any dark, Demerara-style rum will do (El Dorado is cheap and effective). There are those who prefer cider to water; it's not necessary.

For a simple Hot Rum, omit the butter and the mixed spices, although Thomas suggests you still grate nutmeg on top. A perfectly acceptable drink, but frankly this is a case where more is definitely more.

NOTES ON EXECUTION: Proceed as for a standard Hot Toddy, adding the spirits, butter, and spices in with the liquor before topping off with boiling water. If you want to make these the fun way—the way, as it were, I learned at my mother's knee—simply put everything into a mug, including water (not heated), and plunge a red-hot poker into it. This is not recommended after the second round.

STONE FENCE

Roused from bed by the yelling and the shooting, the officer stood his ground, pants in hand. "I demand you surrender this fort," shouted the sabre-waving giant before him. "In whose name, sir, do you demand this?" "In the name of the Great Jehovah and the Continental Congress!"

And so (as Allen told it in his autobiography) fell Fort Ticonderoga, thus securing the Colonies' back against a British thrust from Canada, which would have most likely proved fatal to their hopes of independence. And we owe it all to the Stone Fence. It was over large noggins of this rustic and potent beverage that, according to legend and a good deal of historical fact, Ethan Allen—the giant with the cutlery—and his Green Mountain Boys planned their early morning assault. Had they been sober, the idea of a relative handful of lightly armed backwoodsmen taking on a professional garrison armed with cannons might not have seemed like such a winning proposition. But they drank, and dared, and won. (Okay, so it turned out the garrison was completely unsuspecting and they waltzed right in—but they didn't know that when they started out, did they?)

By the time the Civil War rolled around, the Stone Fence was a ghost of its former self. When Ethan Allen and his crew asked for it, they were asking for a savage mixture of hard cider and New England rum. Four generations later, if the testimony of Jerry Thomas in the matter is to be believed, the Stone Fence was bourbon whiskey diluted with sweet—that is, nonalcoholic—cider. Suave and smooth, but comparatively feeble; if Colonel Allen and his crew had been drinking it this way, their meeting at the Catamount Tavern might have given rise merely to a polite but firm letter to the fort's commander, rather than a personal visit.

1 WINE-GLASS [2 OZ] OF WHISKEY (BOURBON)

2 OR 3 SMALL LUMPS OF ICE

Fill up the glass with sweet cider.

SOURCE: JERRY THOMAS, 1862

NOTES ON INGREDIENTS: In 1775, of course, there was no bourbon. To make a Revolutionarily correct Stone Fence, you'll need rum of the usual old-school kind and hard cider, the funkier the better—as in, ferment your own. Alas, the only rum I know savage enough to do this justice is the acrid and funky 115-proof Bundaberg, from Australia, which you can't get in the United States (see how the laws conspire to make us good?). As late as 1869, the *Steward & Barkeeper's Manual* observed that a tart and full-flavored (and alcoholic) crab apple cider was "frequently used in preference to ordinary cider," but for the Professor's version, your standard health-food store sweet cider will do. And this isn't the place to trot out your fanciest bourbon.

BLACK STRAP (AKA THE BLACK STRIPE)

New Englanders have somehow acquired a reputation for being a bit on the effete side compared to other Americans. All it takes is one taste of this to understand how deeply wrong that is. Mind you, it's not that the drink is violently harsh, or even particularly strong. It's just . . . crude. Like a three-legged stool, or succotash. Anyone who could call " 'Lasses and rum, with a leetle [sic] dash of water"—the formula in question—"the sweetest drink that ever streaked down a common-sized gullet" is by definition no milquetoast. Now granted, that quote's from an 1833 humor piece—a lying contest between a down-east "Nutmeg"

and a Georgia "Cracker"—but in this case fiction is merely truth with a slightly more colorful turn of speech. The Nutmegs so loved their Black Strap that, according to the memoirs of Henry Soulé, a New England parson, bowls of it were even circulated at weddings. One shudders. At any rate, it's inconceivable that any family tree that was irrigated with the stuff could ever devolve to the point of effeteness, even after ten generations.

(USE SMALL BAR - GLASS .)

    1 WINE GLASS [2 OZ] OF SANTA CRUZ RUM

    1 TABLE-SPOONFUL OF MOLASSES

This drink can either be made in summer or winter; if in the former season, mix in one table spoonful of water, and cool with shaved ice; if in the latter, fill up the tumbler with boiling water. Grate a little nutmeg on top.

SOURCE: JERRY THOMAS, 1862

NOTES ON INGREDIENTS: Again, for full authenticity you'll need a rum that you could stand a fork up in; real pirate-juice. The molasses should be Caribbean—like a nice Barbados blackstrap—and the water should be from an outdoor pump (okay, that's not strictly necessary). For a hot Black Strap, use about 2 ounces of water, for cold—a drink I shudder to recall—1 ounce and plenty of cracked ice.

NOTES ON EXECUTION: Whether hot or cold, stir the molasses and the water together before adding the spirits.

CHAPTER 7

COCKTAILS AND CRUSTAS

A nyone who has spent any time pondering the origins of the Cocktail—be it for the months or years it takes to write a book or the minutes or seconds it takes to internalize a Dry Martini—will agree that it's a quintessentially American contraption. How could it be anything but? It's quick, direct, and vigorous. It's flashy and a little bit vulgar. It induces an unreflective overconfidence. It's democratic, forcing the finest liquors to rub elbows with ingredients of far more humble stamp. It's profligate with natural resources (think of all the electricity generated to make ice that gets used for ten seconds and discarded). In short, it rocks.

But if the Cocktail is American, it's American in the same way as the hot dog (that is, the Frankfurter), the hamburger (the Hamburger steak), and the ice-cream cone (with its rolled *gaufrette*). As a nation, we have a knack for taking underperforming elements of other peoples' cultures, streamlining them, supercharging them, and letting 'em rip—from nobody to superstar, with a trail of sparks and a hell of a noise along the way. That's how the Cocktail did it, anyway.

Dr. Stoughton's Elixir Magnum

You could say, I suppose, that the Cocktail has been around since antiquity; that it was already old when Scribonius Largus, one of the emperor Claudius's physicians, suggested that a stomachache would be soothed by dissolving black myrtle berries and pills made up of dates, dill, saffron, nigella seeds, hazelwort, and juniper in sweet wine and chugging it down. Before you turn the page, muttering, "I know Cocktails, and that's no Cocktail," hear me out. Nowadays, "Cocktail" means anything from "whatever is served in a conical, stemmed glass" to "a mixed drink containing alcohol" (as in, "Cocktails are five dollars for our Economy customers," where the term indicates a plastic cup full of ice and soda and a tiny bottle of booze on the side). But that lexical flexibility wasn't always the case. In the nineteenth century, when the word first became joined to a drink, it denoted something far more specific: spirits or wine, sweetened with sugar, diluted (if necessary) with water, and spiced up with a few dashes of "bitters"—that is, a medicinal infusion of bitter roots, herbs, barks, and spices. Under that definition, Scribonius's potion, with its bitter hazelwort, has a lot more right to the title than most of the things you'll find on the average modern Cocktail menu (e.g., the "Chocolate Martini").

But this book is about the American Cocktail, not the *Galli-cauda Romana*, so we'll leave the nostrums of antiquity to find their own historian and fast-forward some 1,600 years to Restoration-era London, where the more immediate roots of our national beverage lie. At first glance, those roots appear to be well buried. There's no end of drinking going on, to be sure. Ale (unhopped and traditional) and beer (hopped and controversial) were consumed morning, noon, and night by all classes, supplemented whenever economic circumstance allowed by copious draughts of wine, the stronger the better. But distilled spirits, if consumed at all, were taken neat in drams, or—in fast company—mixed up in bowls of Punch. There was nary a Cocktail to be seen.

That said, consider the drink known as "Purl." Now, Purl has come down to us as a Dickensian mixture of hot ale, gin, sugar, and eggs, with nutmeg on top. But in the seventeenth century, it was something rather different: a sharply bitter ale infused with wormwood and other botanicals and drunk in the morning to settle the stomach, if settling was needed. It was popular enough for Samuel Pepys to mention it in his diary (then again, there's pretty much nothing alcoholic he doesn't mention).

The humble Purl had a city cousin, "Purl-Royal." This was pretty much the same drink, except instead of ale or beer it was based on "Sack"—a relatively sweet Sherry that was fortified with brandy. If you were to taste Purl-Royal today, you'd have no trouble at all classifying it: vermouth. (In fact, "vermouth" is derived from *vermut*, the German word for "wormwood," which the modern beverage originally contained in some quantity.) As "Wormwood-wine," Purl-Royal was another thing Pepys drank. He also drank gin; had he but thought to mix them, the Age of Reason might have been rather different (imagine Voltaire on Martinis!). Interestingly enough, Pepys drank vermouth and gin in the same year, 1663, with the same person, Sir William Batten; one might wish to speak with Sir William.

But Royal or not, Purl would be nothing but a byway in the history of drink if not for Richard Stoughton, who kept an apothecary's shop at the Sign of the Unicorn in the London borough of Southwark. One of the novel features of the age was a lively trade in proprietary medicines; pre-mixed, one-size-fits-all concoctions that you could buy in stores, rather than having to go to a doctor and stand around while he customized something for you (these were essentially the first branded goods). In 1690, Stoughton decided to get in on the action. His entry, the "Elixir Magnum Stomachicum," aka "Stoughton's Great Cordial Elixir," was an alcoholic infusion of twenty-two botanicals, the chief among them apparently being gentian. It turned out he was onto something: At a shilling apiece, the characteristic long-necked, globular little bottles of dark yellow liquid (or was it red?—accounts differ) sold briskly enough that, eight years later, he was able to put himself through medical school at Cambridge. In 1712, Stoughton applied for and received a Royal Patent for his creation—only the second to be granted to a medicine.

Like most patent medicines, Dr. Stoughton's was originally marketed with a certain latitude regarding its applications—after all, why limit your business? Pretty much whatever you had, it was for it—particularly if your distemper had anything whatsoever to do with the stomach, which the elixir would "rectify" from all its "Indispositions," or the blood, which it would cleanse from its "Impurities, [such] as Scurvies." Over the years, however, users seem to have discovered that it was good for one set of symptoms in particular. In 1710, Stoughton's advertising, which had previously hinted at this somewhat less-exalted indication, came right out and said it: the Elixir is "Drank by most Gentlemen . . . to recover and restore a weaken'd Stomach or lost Appetite . . . occasioned by hard Drinking or Sickness, &c." and "[carry] off the effects of bad Wine, which too many die of." In other words, a hangover cure—and, considering that this was the Age of Punch, no doubt a necessary one.

But whatever its therapeutic qualities, or lack thereof (one is entitled to a certain skepticism), Stoughton's Elixir had something else going for it: It tasted good. Not straight, of course—the stuff was quite concentrated. But you could mix it in with your water or tea, yielding what Stoughton called "the Bitter draught." Where's the fun in that, though? Much better to pour a little into your hair-of-the-dog, thus yielding "the best Purl in Ale, and Purl Royal in Sack, [being] very pleasant and wholesome, [and] giving each of them a fragrant smell and taste, far exceeding Purl made of Wormwood." What's more, with the Elixir, you could make your Purl "in a Minute"—no more assembling bunches of herbs or weeks of steeping. Just tip a little into your drink, give it a stir, and you're done.

I don't want to make too much of this; a glass of Purl-Royal with 1 teaspoon or less (the recommended dose) of Stoughton's "bitters," as they soon came to be known, is not the same thing as a Cocktail. For one thing, it's got no charisma. Royal or not, drinking Purl was more a health-maintaining duty, like taking your vitamins, than a wicked sport, like playing out a string of Sidecars and Widow's Kisses. Plus, it's got no booze in it. Of course, neither does the Champagne Cocktail, and nineteenth-century mixographers—including Jerry Thomas—had no problem including that in their Cocktail sections. But when Dr. Stoughton suggests his bitters be taken in "a dram of Brandy," then we've got to pull up our reins. Of the four ingredients of the American Cocktail, here are the two most important, already consorting together in a glass, almost a full century before the drink surfaces in America. Just to make things more interesting, before too long we have evidence that people were already adding a third.

When Scotland rose in rebellion in 1745, the Scots clan leader Simon Fraser, Lord Lovat, lent himself warily to the Jacobite cause. In April of the next year, when Scotland's hopes and a large number of Frasers were shot to bits on the bleak moor of Culloden, he made sure to be nowhere near the battlefield ("None but a mad a fool would have fought that day," he is reported to have said). But he was nonetheless captured by the British, imprisoned, and condemned to have his head chopped off in the Tower of London. This was his right as a Peer of the Realm; had he been less exalted in rank, he would've been hung. Anyway, on the eve of his execution in March 1747, the eighty-year-old Lord Lovat was, understandably, somewhat troubled in mind.

"But pray," he asked one of his attendants (according to a pamphlet published at the time), "have you got any Wine for me in the Morning; and some Bitters, if I should want to carry any to the Scaffold?" There were no bitters left in the bottle, so he sent somebody out with a shilling for a bottle of "Stoughton's Elixir"—still the leading kind of bitters, although not without competition (Stoughton himself had died in 1720, but his squabbling heirs carried the business on without him). In the meanwhile, though, the warder came up with a bottle of "burnt brandy and bitters" that had been lying around since the Lord's trial.

Now, to make Burnt Brandy, you set brandy on fire (often with a live cinder or coal, leading to its alternate name, "Coal Brandy") and melt sugar over the resulting flame; when the flame gets low, you stir the sugar in and drink it. Originally, this was a medicine: from the mid-1600s to the mid-1800s, it was what any respectable physician would prescribe for congestion or stomach disorders. But even with much of the alcohol burned off it was still taken recreationally (Pepys drank it that way; why are we not surprised?). So, brandy and sugar, mixed up with bitters and kept in a bottle. This is awfully like the bottled Brandy Cocktail of Jerry Thomas's day, only that used water to reduce the proof and this used fire.

In any case, the next morning, as Lord Lovat discussed the disposal of his clothing, tested the sharpness of the axe, and reviewed the arrangements for handling his head (he "desir'd that . . . when taken off, [it] might be receiv'd in a Cloth"), he had recourse to that bottle. If ever there was a time . . .

THE COCKTAIL IS BORN

After Lord Lovat's decapitation, bittered booze dropped out of the historical record for a few key decades. Was the actual Cocktail—spirits, bitters, sugar, and water combined—born in Britain? It's more than possible, and there's even a passing reference to a drink called "cauld [that's Scots for 'cold'] cock" in William Creech's 1791 essay collection, *Edinburgh Fugitive Pieces*, for us to puzzle on. But if it was of British birth, it was born ahead of its time and nobody paid much attention; it would have to be transported to the New World to receive its due.

The American Colonies had long been supplied with all the necessary components of the Cocktail, including thirst. Spirits were everywhere, sugar was cheap, and water was plentiful and clean (not always the case in the mother country). You could even get genuine Stoughton's Elixir. Well, more or less—patent or no patent, its near-universal popularity ensured that it was imported, but also that the concoction was widely counterfeited and imitated.

In fact, a whole lot of bitters were being consumed in America, and outside the major cities, it's doubtful if any of it generated so much as a farthing in royalties. In the Colonies, do-it-yourself was the mode of the day. The forests abounded in medicinal roots, barks, and herbs; the alcohol to infuse with them was cheap and plentiful as long as you weren't too particular about what it was made from; and if you needed a recipe, there was one right there in John Wesley's *Primitive Physic* (since this John Wesley and the one who founded Methodism were one and the same, the book had wide distribution). Judging by the extant published recipes (admittedly from a generation or two later) Americans liked more booze and less bitter in their mix. By the Revolution, in America at least, the Southwark apothecary's bitter drops had undergone a transformation from product to genre, from Xerox to xerox, Kleenex to kleenex. And once the Colonies rose up in revolt, the homemade stuff had the field to itself, since imports stopped entirely—at least to the rebels; there are records of Stoughton's Elixir being shipped to the king's troops by the caseload.

Wars make history, but they also obscure it. Among all the bold and desperate events, it's easy for little things to get lost. One of those little things involved bitters. At some point between Lexington and Concord and Yorktown, it became acceptable for Americans to swallow a full dram of these high-proof domestic bitters as a morning eye-opener. When Americans take to something, they don't hold back. If a dash of bitters in a glass of wine is good in the morning, then a full two ounces of the stuff will be better. After all, it's medicine, right? And medicine is good for you—particularly if it makes you feel good. (Some facets of American life never change.)

The early years of the Republic were drinking times, and intemperate or not, eye-openers and humor-qualifiers were the order of the day, with Bitters and Slings leading the pack by a few comfortable lengths. At some point during those years, somebody somewhere thought to pour some of the former into the latter. Whether this seminal moment was inspired by the example of Purl Royal or Burnt Brandy and Bitters, or it was entirely a manifestation of native genius is immaterial; what is important is that Americans recognized the delightfulness and versatility of this formula; that we nurtured it and cherished it and allowed it to thrive.

It didn't hurt that—well, it didn't hurt—that by diluting what was already diluted and sweetening it up, one turned a medicinal drink that didn't taste good into one that tasted great and still kept a therapeutic cover without actually being good for you (that is, assuming that a glass of bitters was in some way good for you). As one Victorian mixographer sagely observed, "It is a cosmopolitan practice to pamper the appetite under pretence of preserving the health." The morning bitters-and-sling man could pretend, not least to himself, that he wasn't a morning dram drinker (which would be bad); that he was only following the path of wisdom by taking a little preventative medicine. In fact, people were calling the morning Cocktail "a glass of bitters" well into the next century, even though they had merely a shade of bitters in them.

THE WHERE AND THE WHEN

When did this transformational act occur, and how did the resulting mixture get the name *Cocktail* welded on to it? This is some of the most wrangled-over territory in American cultural history. But rather than rehearse what has already been hashed to death, I'll try to simply lay forth the known facts—the earliest testimonies to a drink called "Cocktail"—and let them dictate the conclusions (for a more detailed discussion, see Appendix I). As a kind of control, let's begin with the *Pennsylvania Gazette*, which in 1788 published a fairly comprehensive list of the spirit-based recreational drinks of America. In it we find mention of, among others, Toddy, Grog, Sling, Bitters, and "stinkibus," whatever that might be, but no Cocktail as of yet.

Fifteen years later, on April 28, 1803, the *Farmer's Cabinet*, a newspaper out of Amherst, New Hampshire, printed a little humor item purporting to be a page from the diary of a "lounger"—basically, an affluent young ne'er-do-well. In it, the author (probably Joseph Cushing, the paper's editor) has this character waking up lateish after an "Assembly" the night before and feeling "queer." At nine, he has a cup of coffee, which doesn't help. Let's give the highlights of the rest of the morning as the diarist himself wrote it:

10. Lounged to the Doctor's—found Peter—talked of the girls—smoked half a cigar—felt rather squally: Van Hogan

came in—quiz'd me for looking dull—great bore.—11. Drank a glass of cocktail—excellent for the head . . . Went to the Squire's—girls just done breakfast. *Mem.* Girls not so bright after dancing. . . . Went to the Col's . . . drank a glass of wine— talk'd about Indians—call'd Miss———a Squaw—all laugh'd—damn'd good one— . . . jogg'd off. Call'd at the Doct's . . . —drank another glass of cocktail.

That "glass of cocktail" at 11 a.m. is the very first on record— provided, of course, that it is indeed a real Cocktail. The *Farmer's Cabinet* doesn't tell us what went into it, and for a while there in the very early part of the century that name appears here and there attached to drinks that in later years any self-respecting saloon denizen would have looked at with slantendicular gaze had it been proffered to him as a Cocktail—e.g., "rum and honey," which may be a fine drink but ain't no Cocktail. But I find it strongly suggestive that the two things we can deduce about the *Cabinet's* "glass of cocktail"—that it's therapeutic in the morning and that it's favored by a loungy, sporty, dissolute set—were precisely those that defined the Cocktail for most of the ensuing century.

If the Cocktail was well-enough known by 1803 for the *Cabinet* to include it without explanation, not everybody was in on the secret, as Harry Crosswell discovered in 1806. On May 6, Crosswell, the controversial editor and writer of the Hudson, New York, *Balance and Columbian Repository*, a political paper of the Federalist/ anti-Democratic persuasion, printed a snarky little item at the expense of the (Democratic) loser of a local election, in the form of an expense/profit ledger. Under "Gain," it simply reads "Nothing"; under loss, besides the election, there's a categorized list of drinks (candidates used to buy drinks for prospective voters—a custom I for one wouldn't mind seeing return to fashion), including "411 glasses bitters" and, more important, "25 [glasses] cock-tail." Now, I have no idea whether the list of drinks was a real one, but it was at least a realistic one. Nothing else on it (it also included rum and brandy Grogs and Gin Slings) was in any way obscure or controversial.

Those glasses of Cocktail, though, were unfamiliar enough to snare one reader, who wrote in about it in a letter Crosswell printed the next week, on May 13:

> I have heard of a *jorum*, of *phlegm-cutter* and *fog driver* [these last are nothing more than nicknames for an eye-opener or morning jolt—DW], of *wetting the whistle*, or *moistening the clay*, of a *fillip*, a *spur in the head, quenching the spark in the head*, of *flip*, etc., but never in my life, though I have lived a good many years, did I hear of *cock-tail* before. Is it peculiar to this part of the country? Or is it a late invention? Is the name expressive of the effect which the drink has on a particular part of the body? Or does it signify that the democrats who take the potion are turned topsyturvy, and have their heads where their tails should be?

All good questions, except the last—which was of course the one that Crosswell's answer chiefly focused on:

> *Cock tail*, then, is a stimulating liquor, composed of *spirits* of any kind, *sugar, water*, and *bitters*—it is vulgarly called *bittered sling*, and is supposed to be an excellent electioneering potion, inasmuch as it renders the heart stout and bold, at the same time that it fuddles the head. It is said also, to be of great use to a democratic candidate: because, a person having swallowed a glass of it, is ready to swallow anything else.

Would that Crosswell had answered the correspondent's other questions in like detail; this chapter would be much shorter. Nevertheless, it's still one of the most famous and oft-repeated quotations in the history of American tippling. There are, however, a few things left to tease out of it. Setting aside the blogospheric political hyperbole and even the definition itself, which would with one or two minor adjustments describe what people thought of when they thought of a Cocktail for the next four generations, let's focus on that "bittered sling." As we've seen, Bitters were one thing and

Sling was another; so "bittered sling" was rather like "Jägered Kamikaze" or "Vodka and Red Bull": two drinks, mixed together and consumed not by frat boys but by the 1806 equivalent, Democrats, who were proverbial for the woo-hooness of their brand of populism. The next reference came eleven days later, when the *Sun*, a Democratic paper from Pittsfield, Massachusetts (some thirty miles west of Hudson), printed a letter taking Croswell to task for various political crimes and, along the way, getting in a swipe at him for "publishing grog stories," and strictures on "cock tail." Clearly, a known—even slightly notorious—drink, or else the insult would be meaningless. After that, seven years of silence, unless you count the early morning glass of "whiskey and bitters" John Melish was offered in central Pennsylvania in 1811 (this appears to have been a local specialty: eight years later Adlard Welby found the same people, more or less, drinking the same thing). The oft-cited 1809 date for the word's appearance in Washington Irving's *Knickerbocker's History of New York* is wrong.* Finally, in 1813, Cocktail popped up again, this time in the metropolis: the "News for [read 'from'] New York" page of the *Tickler*, a Philadelphia humor rag, contained a comic account of a dispute between a couple of mooks "about the superior virtues of gin-sling and cock-tail."

Something about the drink must've struck New Yorkers as amusing, because its next appearance was in a bit of philosophico-medical doubletalk printed in the *New-York Courier* in 1816, in which the author claims to prove the "duality of souls" by his not being able to remember what he does at night, after a daily routine that began with "a cocktail or two every morning before breakfast" and ended with, "just before going to bed, two or three brandy tods." There were plenty of other potables in between, not neglecting "a cocktail or two . . . before dinner." But the drink was popular in Massachusetts, too, judging by its appearance (as "bitter sling") in an 1818 ad for a Natick merchant (the ad, in verse, was considered amusing enough to be widely reprinted) and in an 1820 issue of the Worcester *National*

---

* Irving's book was indeed first published in 1809, but he frequently and extensively revised it and Cocktail was one of the things he shoehorned in later.

Aegis. Whatever the precise circumstances of its birth, it's clear that the Cocktail enjoyed its first fame in the rough triangle between Boston, Albany, and New York, and in the absence of any evidence to the contrary we must consider that its homeland. As for that name— the simplest explanation is that it is taken from the common slang term for a mixed-breed horse, it being a mixed-breed sort of drink; but you'll find my argument for this in Appendix I.

THE COCKTAIL IN NEW YORK AND POINTS SOUTH AND WEST

The Cocktail made the jump from journalism to literature in 1821, when James Fenimore Cooper wrote it into his Revolutionary War novel, *The Spy*, as "that beverage which is so well known, at the present hour, to all the patriots who make a winter's march between the commercial and political capitals of this great state [i.e., New York and Albany] and which is distinguished by the name of 'cocktail.' " At the very end of the same year, Dr. Samuel Mitchill (another polymath physician who, like Benjamin Rush, deserves a chapter of his own) included it in a widely reported satirical lecture he gave in New York against "Anti-fogmatics," or morning drinks. Ironically, as diarist Philip Hone noted upon Mitchill's death in 1831, "for several years past he was a confirmed drunkard."

Once the Cocktail found its way to the metropolis, it made itself right at home. Thus in 1824 we find a porter eulogizing a dead friend as "the kindest soul that ever poted a gin cock-tail." In 1827, it's one Captain Morgan, or someone the *New-York Chronicle* thought looked a lot like him, following up an evening at the theater by eating a "mince treat" and "toss[ing] off four brandy cocktails"— quite a performance for somebody whose body half the country was looking for (the supposed murder of William Morgan by Masons was the O. J. Simpson case of the late 1820s). The next year, the *Chronicle* was making knowing references to the "cocktail snooze." The year after that, the *Manhattan Courier* fixed the Cocktail in its social milieu when it lamented how the city's old ale houses, where the "venerable burgher" could while away his thoughts with "the smooth pipe and the bright pewter mug," had fallen to the hotel bar, where it was all

Segars of bright Havana, lit from a taper at the bar, and smoked by a youngster, who having dispatched his cock-tail, mint julap, or gin sling . . . thrusts both hands into his breeches pockets, takes his strides up and down the bar room, and rolls the volume of grey smoke from the corner of his mellow mouth.

The Cocktail might have gotten a foot out of the morning-drink ghetto, but it was still unfit for polite company. As Robert Montgomery Bird had one of his characters say in his 1837 novel, *Shepperd Lee*, "None but vulgarians drink strong liquors; slings, cock-tails, and even julaps are fit only for bullies. Gentlemen never drink any thing but wine."

But by then, it seems, America was a nation of bullies and vulgarians. Outside of a few square blocks in New York, Boston, and a couple of other cities where society attempted to maintain a European *bon ton*, and the occasional knot of Temperance men here and there, Juleps and Slings were in universal use—and so, it appears, was the Cocktail. If travelers are to be trusted, in the 1820s, while history was looking elsewhere, the Cocktail stole out of New York and followed the rivers, canals, wagon-tracks, and foot-trails that were binding the new nation together and pitched its tent wherever it found its people, ending up in places as far-flung as Niagara Falls and Balize, Louisiana, a godforsaken patch of mud and reeds and wooden shacks at the spot where the Mississippi meets the Gulf. That's where Captain J. E. Alexander of the Royal Army, traveling from Havana to New York via the Mississippi, was greeted with these friendly words: "Halloo, man! are you here? Which are you for, cocktail or gin-sling? Here is the Bar, you must liquorise"—said bar being a shack equally as unprepossessing as the rest. That was in 1831, by which point the Cocktail was everywhere, even Canada (it first turns up there in the mid-1820s).

THE COCKTAIL GROWS UP
In the thirty years between Captain Alexander's book and Jerry Thomas's, some things about the Cocktail remained constant.

By way of introduction to the Cocktail section of his book, Thomas notes,

> The "Cocktail" is a modern invention, and is generally used on fishing and other sporting parties, although some *patients* insist that it is good in the morning as a tonic.

However threadbare, that old cloak of medicinal respectability still hung from its shoulders, and when it wasn't ministering to suffering humanity it still traveled with the same sporty crowd. (Those "other sporting parties" no doubt included the notorious ones—with which Thomas must have been intimately acquainted—formed by the "fancy" to travel to illegal boxing matches. The Cocktails would have been bottled; the merriment, not.)

During those decades, though, the actual drink itself changed in several small ways and one very big one—that one being, of course, the permanent and indissoluble incorporation of ice into its fabric. It's difficult to pinpoint precisely when this happened. The conventional wisdom is that it was in the 1830s, when everything else got iced. However, a close examination of recipes and descriptions of Cocktails from the Antebellum era suggests that it was actually a generation later—in fact, out of the dozens of references to Cocktails and their consumption I've been able to find from the 1830s and 1840s, only two suggest that the drink was ever served iced: one from New York in 1843 (which has it served with "a few nobs [sic] of ice as pure as crystal") and one from the frontier a couple of years later.

In fact, not only were Cocktails generally served un-iced, they were occasionally even served—perish the thought—*hot*. With boiling water. Since a Cocktail is nothing more than a spiced Sling, and I consider a hot Sling or Toddy to be a sanctified thing, I don't know why this makes me shudder. It must be years of Pavlovian conditioning; of associating the word *cocktail* with the thrilling rattle of ice. But when I read Charles Fenno Hoffman's description in his 1835 *A Winter in the West* of the "smoking 'cocktail'" he was handed in a country tavern near Kalamazoo, I quail inside. In any case, this perversion was not a common one and had disappeared by 1857. At least that's when a New York bartender was recorded replying to an order for a Hot Brandy Cocktail with, "Hot what, sir?" and, "No, sir, they are never made hot."

Even as late as 1855, when the Julep and the Cobbler had made American iced drinks famous throughout the world, the stuff's presence in the Cocktail is still not a given. Consider, for instance, the handful of dog-Latin prescriptions for mixed drinks the *Spirit of the Times*, the popular sporting paper, published as a joke in 1855 (you got your doctor to sign them, you see, and took them to the nearest drugstore and handed it . . . well, it seemed amusing at the time). There's the Mint Julep, which calls for ice (you'll find the recipe on page 156). But the Brandy Cocktail and Gin Cocktail merely call for "*aqua frigida*"—cold water. Add John Bartlett's *Dictionary of Americanisms*, from 1860, which defines the drink as "A stimulating beverage, made with brandy or gin, mixed with sugar and a very little water," a few similar references from the time, and you have legitimate grounds for doubt.

But the 1850s were a go-ahead decade, and that drive to the future extended to perpendicular drinking. In 1852, the *Southern Literary Messenger* already saw the writing on the wall when it noted, not without regret, that

> Virginia, at one time, may have possessed a better head than most, for strong potations; but that day is long since gone by. Once, the mint julep was proverbial, but western invention has long since won far superior trophies in the cocktail, the sherry cobbler, and snake and tiger.

This is perhaps true more in the metaphorical sense than the literal one—it's hard to make a case for the Cobbler as a Western drink, and the "snake and tiger" is otherwise unknown—but it's true nonetheless. The Gold Rush may not have changed every aspect of American life, but it sure galvanized the Sporting Fraternity. As

Bayard Taylor observed when he toured the diggings in 1849, in the easy-come-easy-go atmosphere of California, "[w]eather-beaten tars, wiry, delving Irishmen, and stalwart foresters from the wilds of Missouri became a race of sybarites and epicureans." This was manifested most characteristically in their sudden and surprising "fondness for champagne and all kinds of cordials and choice liquors." One of the places this expressed itself was in the Cocktail, a luxury that at a bit or two a pop even a busted-flush gambler or empty-pan prospector could afford.

That taste for the finest extended to ice: John Borthwick, a Scot who spent much of the early 1850s in California, later recalled of the mining town of Sonora that "Snow was packed in on mules thirty or forty miles from the Sierra Nevada, and no one took even a cocktail without its being iced." In any case, by the end of the decade an iced Cocktail was no longer an item of wonder, not just in California but in the rest of the country as well (though there were exceptions). The advent of ice brought in a few other changes: Since granulated sugar doesn't dissolve well in cold liquor, "mixologists," as they could now be called (the word, you'll recall, was coined in 1856), learned to replace it with syrup—and why stop with plain sugar syrup? Why not throw in a little raspberry or almond syrup, if you've got it, or even a few dashes of some fancy imported cordial? And once you've predissolved the sugar, you won't need that toddy-stick to break up the lumps anymore; you can stir the drink with a simple teaspoon or, more theatrically, pour it back and forth between two glasses, or a glass and one of those new tin "shakers." And since the cocktail is a short drink, meant to go down the hatch before it has time to warm up, you won't need to leave the ice in it and can spare its *devotés* the shock of it bumping up against their teeth by straining it into another glass.

This is where Jerry Thomas steps in. *How to Mix Drinks* is the first book to contain a section of recipes devoted to the Cocktail. There are a grand total of thirteen of 'em, all but one iced, and that one's bottled for traveling. Nowadays, of course, you can get more Cocktails out of an airport bartender, and there are books floating around with titles like *1,001 New Vodka Cocktails*. But thirteen is actually a lot: If Thomas had set pen to paper ten or fifteen years earlier, he would've been hard-pressed to offer four or five—a Brandy Cocktail, a Gin Cocktail, perhaps a Champagne Cocktail, and maybe even a Whiskey Cocktail, although that one was still not quite ready for polite society. But writing when he did, he could offer that bottled Cocktail, three plain old Cocktails, a couple of "fancy" Cocktails, a "Japanese" Cocktail (made without sake or anything else from the land of the rising sun), some Cocktails that extend the basic formula to include bases other than straight booze, and a few Crustas, which Thomas defines for us as "an improvement on the 'Cocktail' "—the improvement lying chiefly in the addition of "a little lemon juice" and some fiddling around with lemon peel and sugar. In the 1876 edition, Thomas adds three so-called Improved Cocktails (this improvement, too, is a subtle one). Finally, the 1887 revision reflects the Cocktail's displacement of Punch as the Monarch of Mixed Drinks by moving Punches to the back of the book and putting Cocktails in their rightful place at the front. What's more, the later edition featured twenty-three Cocktail recipes, including five with the new wonder ingredient: vermouth, which would bring the Cocktail into the twentieth century, transforming it utterly in the process. In 1914, on the eve of Prohibition, Jacques Straub's up-to-date *Drinks* would offer more than twelve times that many.

Rather than attempt to untangle all these chronologically, I've divided Thomas's recipes into four loose families, from the plain old Cocktail and its variations, to the Evolved Cocktail, to the Crusta and other citric cocktails to the Manhattan, the Martini, and the whole frisky tribe of vermouth Cocktails. As elsewhere, I've fleshed out each category with a few other important recipes that the Professor didn't include, either because he wouldn't or he couldn't. Had he lived out his threescore-and-ten (and maybe a little extra), I know he would've gotten around to them, so this is really just covering the rest of his shift.

PREQUEL: THE ORIGINAL COCKTAIL

When the peripatetic Captain Alexander got to New York, he proved that he wasn't too refined to pote the humble Cocktail. Of course, it didn't hurt that he had Willard himself to mix them for him. Fortunately for us, Alexander repaid the favor by recording four of the Great One's recipes for posterity, the Cocktail among them, and printing them in the book he got out of his trip. Vague as it is, his is the first true recipe for the Cocktail to see print. More important, it agrees with the drink's 1806 definition, showing that that was no fluke or historical outlier but a glimpse at the trunk of the drink's family tree.

You will note, of course, the absence of ice. To the Jackson-era tippler, the Cocktail occupied an entirely different compartment in the brain from its close cousin the Mint Julep: the Julep is a "cooling drink"; the Cocktail is a "tonic." Cooling drinks, meant to be sipped and savored, take ice. Tonics, on the other hand, are set into action with a flick of the wrist; they belong to medicine, not gastronomy. That said, I still like 'em better with ice. But if there's none to be found and I've got everything else, I have before me the example of antiquity to indicate that I need not panic.

For the receipt-book let the following be copied: . . . *Cocktail* is composed of water, with the addition of rum, gin, or brandy, as one chooses—a third of the spirit [2 oz] to two-thirds of the water [3 oz]; add [4-5 dashes] bitters, and *enrich* with sugar [½ oz] and nutmeg . . . . N.B. If there is no nutmeg convenient, a scrape or two of the mudler (wooden sugar-breaker) will answer the purpose.

SOURCE: J. E. ALEXANDER, *TRANSATLANTIC SKETCHES* (LONDON, 1833)

NOTES ON INGREDIENTS: As with the Sling, Holland gin and brandy were by far the most popular spirits used for Cocktails. Thanks to the lower proof of today's brandies and genevers, you should cut the water back as indicated if you're using them. The whiskey version of the Cocktail ran a distant (and later-appearing: the earliest reference comes only from 1838) third; if you're not afraid of being considered vulgar, though, you can make your Cocktail with Anchor's Old Potrero whiskey, which is over-proof even for the time, and authentic—and delicious.

For the bitters, you'll need Stoughton's, which you will of course have to make yourself (see Chapter 9). If this seems like a long way to go for a Cocktail, Angostura or Peychaud's will work just fine, seeing as their formulae date to 1824 and sometime in the 1830s, respectively. While Captain Alexander is singularly unhelpful as to how much of them to use, Charles Frederick Briggs's 1839 novel, *The Adventures of Harry Franco*, is a little more forthcoming: When the naïve and proper young Harry finally deigns to "liquorate" with a Cocktail, he watches the bartender point up the gin, sugar, and water with "a few drops of a red liquid, which he poured out of a little cruet like an ink bottle with a quill stuck in the cork." (Before too many years had passed, this improvised dasher-top would be replaced by a manufactured one.)

Oh, and that business about the "mudler"? Pay it no never mind. He's kidding. I think.

NOTES ON EXECUTION: Exactly as for the Sling, but with bitters.

I. PLAIN, FANCY, IMPROVED, AND OLD-FASHIONED

If you set out to order a Martini in, say, 1988, there would've been a little back-and-forth across the bar about which spirit you wanted, the presence or absence of ice in the glass, and the desired level of dryness, and it would've been done. Sure, there were options available if you'd been willing to go there—remember the Hennessy Martini? But odds are good the bartender wouldn't have been following you. Those options were restricted; there were as yet none of that sickly and dismal tribe of Chocolate Martinis, Mango Martinis, Saketinis, and Appletinis that have in recent years transformed the Martini from a recipe into a category. In 1862, that's what ordering a Cocktail was like, only the drinks that were lurking to usurp its name were far less grim.

Of Thomas's original thirteen recipes, six are for combinations of spirits, sugar, bitters, and (frozen) water; Cocktails more or less as Harry Crosswell would've understood them, give or take some lumps of ice. Unfortunately, when it comes to the mixological details, there's no consistency to be found among them—some are stirred, some are shaken; some are on the rocks, some are straight up; some are labeled "Fancy" and yet are no fancier in their ingredients or execution than others not so privileged. In short, a mess. If you factor in the three "Improved" Cocktails from the 1876 edition, I won't say it gets any more confusing, because it's already as confusing as can be, but it's certainly not less so. Rather than perpetuate this, I've knocked all their heads together, lined them up, and got them to behave, but it's probably true that Thomas's original chaos is a better representation of the actual state of Cocktailistics at the time (or any time); it's just not so useful when you're actually mixing drinks. To that end, I've reduced everything to three templates: the (Plain) Cocktail, the Fancy Cocktail, and the Improved Cocktail.

PLAIN BRANDY, GIN, OR WHISKEY COCKTAIL

The default Cocktail formula from the Civil War until Prohibition, although one increasingly tainted by fanciness—in fact, Thomas himself fancied things up a bit by calling for "1 or 2 dashes of Curaçoa" in his recipes for plain Brandy Cocktail and Gin Cocktail, but not, interestingly enough, in his Whiskey

Cocktail. There were parts of the country where dashing orange curaçao into somebody's drink without clearing it with him first would see you staring down the barrel of a Colt Navy Revolver quicker than you could say "cooked asparagus." Bearing that in mind, I've reserved curaçao for the Fancy Cocktail (page 190).

Not the least of the many things for which Thomas's book is noteworthy is providing the first reference to the twist, without which a basic Cocktail seems insipid and even dare I say it, slightly tiresome. The precise process whereby this little strip of lemon peel, long so crucial to the epicurean concoction of Punch, came to replace the grating of nutmeg as the capstone of the Cocktail is obscure to history, but if nothing else it can be read as evidence of antebellum America's growing wealth and commercial development. A single nutmeg costs far more than a single lemon, true, but it will garnish dozens of Cocktails to that lemon's eight or twelve, and it doesn't need to be delivered fresh every few days. But no matter. Early bar guides are just as silent on technical minutiae such as the proper way to cut the things. With some digging, we learn that it should be "small" and "thin"—in fact, it's just the "yellow part of the rind" we want. Come to think of it, what more do we need?

(USE SMALL BAR-GLASS.)

3 OR 4 DASHES [1 TSP] **OF GUM SYRUP**

2 DASHES OF BITTERS (BOGART'S)

1 WINE-GLASS [2 OZ] **OF** [SPIRITS]

1 OR 2 DASHES [½ TSP] **OF CURAÇOA**

Squeeze lemon peel; fill one-third full of ice, and stir with a spoon.

SOURCE: JERRY THOMAS, 1862 (COMPOSITE)

NOTES ON INGREDIENTS: Given the paucity of detailed early recipes, it's difficult to say exactly when syrup replaced lump or powdered sugar in the Cocktail; Thomas, a working bartender who understood the need for speed, preferred syrup. "Bogart's" is

Thomas's (or his publisher's) mistake for "Boker's," the leading aromatic bitters of the day, which had largely supplanted Stoughton's for Cocktail use. Since they're no longer available, Fee Bros' Aromatic Bitters make a pretty good approximation, though Angostura or Peychaud's will work just fine, too. My slight preference is for Peychaud's when using brandy, Fee's when using gin, and Angostura when using whiskey.

A decent, not-too-expensive cognac is what Jerry Thomas would've used (although his bar's cellar was well-stocked with fine old cognacs), and so should you. Don't try to go too cheap, or you won't like the results.

For myself, I'm exceedingly partial to Hollands in this drink and in fact consider it so made to be one of the most seductive potations known to natural science. The way the bitters mask the juniper and let the gin's maltiness come forth is particularly enticing. On the other hand, a proper Whiskey Cocktail has its own charms, particularly if you're making it, as Thomas would have, with a fine old rye (among the barrels of rye in his cellar were several of the highly esteemed Maryland Club and some nine-year-old Tom Moore from Kentucky, not to mention the eight-year-old stuff he and George bottled under their own name). But bourbon works just as well, and in fact many tipplers of the day preferred it. I should note that most other spirits, including some far beyond Thomas's ken, respond well to the basic Cocktail treatment. You can even make a surprisingly pleasant plain Cocktail with vodka, and a palatable one with Chinese rose petal *chiu*.

The curaçao here is a sign of creeping gentrification and can and should be omitted (but see the Fancy Cocktail, page 190).

NOTES ON EXECUTION: Going by his book, Thomas couldn't make up his mind whether the Cocktail is shaken or stirred. His brandy Cocktail calls for the spoon, his gin and whiskey ones the shaker. Nor are his professional colleagues much help: While, for example, the author of the 1869 *Steward & Barkeeper's Manual* makes it a flat rule that, "A cocktail should never be shaken," A. V. Bevill in his 1871 *Barkeeper's Ready Reference* instructs that his cocktails be shaken well. Judging by the numerous depictions of bartenders "tossing the foaming cocktail" back and forth in a huge arc, in the 1860s and 1870s consensus favored his method—or perhaps it was just the more picturesque one and hence was noticed more often. In my experience, a stirred plain Cocktail has a transparent silkiness that a shaken one cannot achieve.

Once the mixing is done, however it's done, it's straining time—unless it isn't. Here, again, Thomas differed with himself: His gin and whiskey Cocktails are strained, his brandy Cocktail is not. As often, the *Steward & Barkeeper's Manual* provides some elucidation, noting that, "It is a matter of preference with many to drink the cocktail from the glass in which it is made." As for the twist: It comes in at the end, though some preferred to mix it in with everything else.

FANCY BRANDY, GIN, OR WHISKEY COCKTAIL

The difference between plain and fancy can be as small a thing as a thin cordon of hammer marks around the rim of a silver cup or as large a one as spinning chrome hubcaps, a cushion of ground-effect neon, and woofers the size of garbage cans. In his person, Jerry Thomas favored the latter aesthetic; in his drinks, the former, as one can see by his recipe for the Fancy Brandy Cocktail: "This drink is made the same as the brandy cocktail, except that it is strained in a fancy wine-glass, and a piece of lemon peel thrown on top, and the edge of the glass moistened with lemon." In 1862, there was no such thing as a dedicated Cocktail glass, plain or fancy, so a small wineglass had to do. (By 1876, that situation had been remedied with the adoption of the small, cup-bottomed coupe for Cocktail use.) Other than the glass, there's nothing here to separate the Fancy Cocktail from the plain one besides that genteel lemoning of the rim of the glass; not for Jerry Thomas was the decadent practice of serving a Cocktail "plentifully trimmed with orange, banana and things of that sort," like the house special some wags at the famous Hancock's in Washington slipped in front of Marcus Aurelius Smith, a notoriously crusty Arizona politician, in 1890. "I don't drink slops or eat garbage," Smith announced. "Gimme some of the best whisky." His reply was widely reported enough to enter the language: For at least two generations afterward, a fruit garnish on a Cocktail was known as "the garbage." (For the record, that garbagey Cocktail was the creation of the great black bartender Richard Francis, who served it with a slice of lemon muddled up with some pulverized sugar, dashes of maraschino, Angostura, and raspberry cordial, and a shot of spirits, shaken well, strained and garnished with slices of banana and orange. Hardly disgusting.)

(USE SMALL BAR - GLASS .)

3 OR 4 DASHES [1 TSP] **OF GUM SYRUP**

2 DASHES OF BITTERS

1 WINE-GLASS [2 OZ] **OF** [SPIRITS]

1 OR 2 DASHES [½ TSP] **OF CURAÇOA**

Squeeze lemon peel; fill one-third full of ice, and stir with a spoon. Strain into a fancy wine glass, twist a piece of lemon peel over the top, moisten the rim of the glass with it and throw it in.

SOURCE: JERRY THOMAS, 1862 (COMPOSITE)

NOTES ON INGREDIENTS: As for the Cocktail (Plain), except for the dashes of curaçao. Few things in mixology are as variable as the precise measure of a dash, but in this case a quarter-teaspoon of good-quality imported orange curaçao (such as Marie Brizard) or Grand Marnier will do nicely.

NOTES ON EXECUTION: As for the Cocktail (Plain), Thomas eschewed the bit of decadence described in the *Continental Monthly* in 1864, whereby a Whiskey Cocktail is served in a glass "with the edge . . . previously lemoned and dipped in powdered sugar." But then again, Thomas was conservative, and particularly (and rightly) when it came to Whiskey Cocktails.

If you've got a Fancy Brandy Cocktail all made up and just can't resist the temptation to top it off with a splash of chilled brut champagne, go ahead; at the old Waldorf-Astoria, they called that a **Chicago Cocktail**; elsewhere, it was a **Saratoga Cocktail**. Whatever it was called, it dates to the gaudy years immediately before Prohibition, when Chicago was run by those paragons of the Aldermanly virtues Bath-House John Coughlin and Hinky-Dink McKenna, and Saratoga by the great gambler Richard Canfield.

IMPROVED BRANDY, GIN, OR WHISKEY COCKTAIL

In 1876, when Dick & Fitzgerald got wise and reissued Thomas's book in a format handier for the working bartender, among the drinks tacked on in the Appendix were "Improved" versions of the three standard Cocktails, all sharing the same basic formula. In brief, curaçao was out, maraschino was in, "Bogart's" was corrected to "Boker's," and the option of Angostura was given.

More important, there was a new ingredient: absinthe. As faddish in the 1870s and 1880s as pomegranate and mint are in the 2000s, absinthe was everywhere—when the *New York Tribune* asked "a man with a waxed moustache, a diamond pin and a white linen jacket, who was dispensing fluids behind the bar of a well-known up-town hotel" about it in 1883, while "deftly squeezing a bit of lemon peel into a cocktail as a finishing touch" the bartender—almost certainly Jerry Thomas himself, at the Central Park Hotel—answered, "Much absynthy drunk? Well I should smile. Pretty near every drink I mix has a dash of the green stuff in it." For one thing, the dash of absinthe—first attested to in the 1869 *Steward & Barkeeper's Manual*—helped to polish up the

Cocktail's medicinal luster, although with a hot-rails-to-hell edge that bitters alone could never quite achieve. "Bad for the nerves? I guess not," continued the man uptown, almost defensively. "You jest get up of a mornin' feeling as if yer couldn't part yer hair straight an' see if a cocktail or John Collins dashed with absynthy don't make a new man of yer. Bad for the nerves! Why, you ain't been around much, I guess, young man. . . ."

It didn't hurt, of course, that not only did absinthe carry an aura of danger, but used sparingly it gave the drink an offbeat fragrance that many found mighty pleasing to the palate. In the last decades of the century, bartenders were dashing it into everything in sight, to the point that master mixologist George J. Kappeler felt compelled to warn, "Never serve it in any kind of drink unless called for by the customer."

(USE ORDINARY BAR-GLASS.)

2 DASHES BOKER'S (OR ANGOSTURA) BITTERS

3 DASHES [1 TSP] GUM SYRUP

2 DASHES [½ TSP] MARASCHINO

1 DASH [⅛ TSP] ABSINTHE

1 SMALL PIECE OF THE YELLOW RIND OF A LEMON, TWISTED TO EXPRESS THE OIL

1 SMALL WINE-GLASS [2 OZ] OF [SPIRITS]

Fill glass one-third full of shaved ice, shake well, and strain into a fancy cocktail glass. The flavor is improved by moistening the edge of the cocktail glass with a piece of lemon.

SOURCE: JERRY THOMAS, 1876 (COMPOSITE)

NOTES ON INGREDIENTS: In general, as for the Cocktail (Plain). This drink is particularly good with Holland gin—and, for that matter, cognac and rye. In fact, there's really nothing wrong with it at all. For those who have ever had one, to contemplate it is to desire it. (If ever in New York, it's worth remembering that this formula is known to the sleeve-gartered wizards at the Pegu Club.)

NOTES ON EXECUTION: As for the Cocktail (Fancy). If you'd rather be right and stir, be right and stir. Then smile.

PRINCE OF WALES'S COCKTAIL

The prince was a pup. A gay dog. A letch. A lush. A charming—if stout—son of a bitch, said bitch being Queen Victoria, he watched decade after decade roll by with her grasping the reins of power for dear life and nothing for him to do in the official line but wave to the nice folks. So he did what anybody else would have: He got grumpy and he got loose. Mistresses and mischief ensued. He spent a lot of time at the table, the theater, and the club. Somewhere along there, he learned how to make a pretty fair variation on the Improved Whiskey Cocktail—in fact, one of the sportiest on record. If his circumstances had been different, Albert Edward, Prince of Wales, would've made a hell of a bartender.

The particular sportiness of the prince's brainchild lies in the addition of champagne. This Gilded Age refinement appears to date from the 1880s, when any saloon with pretensions to quality was splashing the bubbly about pretty liberally into anything from a Brandy Punch to a Manhattan Cocktail. It helped that they had special equipment, like the "solid silver champagne case pendant from the ceiling over the bar" installed at the new Palace Exchange in Decatur, Illinois, in 1882. "This novel contrivance is an innovation in Decatur," the local paper explains, "and will be used to 'dash' punches, sours, cocktails, and other fancy drinks." Most bartenders made do with a "champagne tap," a hollow-stemmed gimlet with a tap at the end that you screwed through the cork. The prince, he probably sabered the top off a magnum of Mumm and hosed it about with gayish abandon.

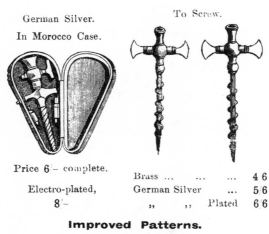

German Silver.

In Morocco Case.

To Screw.

Price 6/- complete.

Electro-plated,
8/-

Brass	...	...	...	4 6
German Silver		...		5 6
,,	,,	Plated		6 6

Improved Patterns.

With removable Pin, Nickel-plated, 2/6 each.

Ditto, with Wood Handle, Nickel-plated, 3/- each.

Champagne taps, circa 1898; handy things and well worth
reviving. (Author's collection)

[The Prince of Wales] **is also credited with having composed an
excellent "cocktail." It consists of a little [1½ oz] rye whisky, crushed
ice, a small square of pineapple, a dash of Angostura bitters, a piece of
lemon peel, a few drops [¼ tsp] of Maraschino, a little [1 oz]
champagne and powdered sugar to taste [1 tsp]. This "short drink" is
often asked for at the clubs which he frequents.**

SOURCE: *PRIVATE LIFE OF KING EDWARD VII*, BY A MEMBER OF THE ROYAL
HOUSEHOLD (LONDON, 1901)

NOTES ON INGREDIENTS: Obviously, for the quantities we must
rely on our judgment. The champagne should be brut, of course,

and no doubt expensive. The pineapple should, preferably, be fresh, but the drink doesn't suffer unduly if you use an eighth or so of a canned pineapple ring; just make sure it's not dripping with syrup.

NOTES ON EXECUTION: Put the sugar in the mixing glass with the bitters and 1/2 teaspoon of water. Stir briefly until it has dissolved. Add the rye, the maraschino, and the pineapple chunk, fill two-thirds full of cracked ice and shake brutally to crush the pineapple. Strain into a chilled cocktail glass, add the cold champagne, and deploy the twist. Then smile.

OLD-FASHIONED WHISKEY, BRANDY, OR HOLLAND GIN COCKTAIL

Everything new always turfs up a few people who liked the old way better. So no one should be surprised that when the plain Cocktail began gathering unto its bosom troubling dashes of curaçoa and absinthe and truly alarming splashes of vermouth, fruit juice, and orgeat syrup, there were those who cried bloody murder. (And to a degree I can see their point: In these days of Apple Pucker Martinis, my sympathies tend to lie with the purists.) For the drinker who resisted change, the 1870s must've been trying times. At some point, this resistance coalesced into a catchphrase. Just as the modern-day fogey has learned that the phrase "gin Martini, straight up" when uttered to a bartender will secure an approximation of a real Martini, his or her Gilded Age counterpart learned that saying "old-fashioned Whiskey [or Gin, or Brandy] Cocktail" would bring forth a drink made with a slug of good (hopefully) booze, lump sugar instead of syrup, ice in the glass, and none of that vulgar shaking and straining and garnishing.

It should come as no surprise that Chicago, that most broad-shouldered of cities, seems to have been one of the main centers of resistance. In fact, discounting an ambiguous newspaper squib from 1869, the earliest clear references to the "Old-Fashioned" way of making cocktails come from the pages of the *Chicago Tribune*. The first is from 1880, when Samuel Tilden, the Al Gore of his age, decided not to run for president again, prompting goal-oriented Democrats to toast his withdrawal with "Hot-whiskies . . . sour mashes and old-fashioned cocktails." (Note that this busts the myth that the drink was invented at the Pendennis Club in Louisville; the club wasn't founded until 1881.) Two years later, when the *Trib* quizzes a prominent local bartender about what the gents are drinking, he replies, "The old-fashioned cocktails [are] still in vogue; cocktails made of loaf-sugar and whisky . . . Rye whiskey [is] called for more than Bourbon."

It wasn't just a Chicago thing, though; the Old-Fashioned also appears in Lafcadio Hearn's seminal 1885 New Orleans cookbook, *La Cuisine Creole*, albeit under the name "spoon cocktail" (the drink was generally served with a smaller version of the barspoon in it, for the customer to stir in any undissolved sugar). By 1895, the old-fashioned way was sufficiently popular for both Chris Lawlor, of the Burnet House hotel in Cincinnati, and George Kappeler, of New York's Holland House, to include it in their books. Both recipes are nearly identical, describing an agriculturally simple drink, just spirits stirred up with sugar, bitters, and a little ice, with a bit of lemon peel for accent—in other words, a Cocktail straight out of the 1850s. In 1895, you can see why that might appeal; why people in the age of the automobile and the electric light might like a liquid look back to the days when the railroad was the latest thing; when Indians still paddled the Mississippi; when the best restaurants served roast bear and the passenger pigeon was a popular game bird; when barrooms were alive with "the merry raps of the toddy stick." The Old-Fashioned was a drinker's plea for a saner, quieter, slower life, one in which a gent could take a drink or two without fear that it would impair his ability to dodge a speeding streetcar or operate a rotary press.

But Americans are a restless people and seldom willing to let well enough alone. In the fullness of time, even the Old-Fashioned, whose very essence was its monolithic plainness, started getting the treatment. In New York, that treatment varied from having both lemon and orange peel slathered onto it and a chunk of pineapple tossed in to boot, as in Times Square bartender Hugo Ensslin's 1916 recipe for an Old-Fashioned Gin Cocktail, to the same plus orange curaçao, to an all-out assault combining rye, Dubonnet, curaçao, absinthe, and so forth. Ensslin called that one an "Old-Fashioned Appetizer"; others might have disagreed on both counts.

Don Marquis, for one. In a series of essays the *New York Sun* writer—and creator of the immortal archy and mehitabel—published in the early days of Prohibition, he has his alter ego, the "Old Soak," utter what amounts to the Old-Fashioned drinker's manifesto: "In the old days when there was barrooms you would go into one . . . and say Ed, mix me one of the old-fashioned whiskey cocktails and don't put too much orange and that kind of damned garbage into it, I want the kick." What he would've made of the version you get today, with muddled orange slice and maraschino cherry and an ocean of seltzer, one shudders to think.

Dissolve a small lump [½ tsp] of sugar with a little [½ tsp] water in a whiskey-glass; add two dashes Angostura bitters, a small piece ice, a piece lemon-peel, one jigger [2 oz] whiskey. Mix with a small barspoon and serve, leaving spoon in the glass.

SOURCE: GEORGE J. KAPPELER, *MODERN AMERICAN DRINKS*
(NEW YORK, 1895)

NOTES ON INGREDIENTS: Kappeler gives recipes for versions with whiskey, brandy, Holland gin, and Old Tom gin. Indeed, anything beyond these has little legitimate claim to the title "Old-Fashioned" (e.g., Ensslin's version, which calls for dry gin—a spirit that wasn't introduced until the 1890s). I prefer lemon peel when using rye, and orange peel when using bourbon.

NOTES ON EXECUTION: Use a muddler to crush the sugar. I like to add the liquor before the ice and give it a quick stir; this leaves less sugar at the bottom of the glass. Some people, though, like that deposit. As for that ice. According to the Chicago *Chronicle*, the customary size of the pieces used was "about as big as a toy rubber ball"—the kind, I assume, you play jacks with. Also according to that same 1899 article, some mixologically ambitious saloons preferred to refrigerate their Old-Fashioned with ice cut into "perfect cubes about two inches on a side"—the idea being, the bigger the ice, the less it would melt and the stronger the Cocktail. There were even some who went so far as to have the ice "frozen to order in balls which fit nicely into the glass." (Interestingly enough, this all-but-lost art still survives in Japan, of all places, where the best Tokyo bartenders are expert at hand-carving ice balls to fit the glass precisely, though molds are also available for he who wieldeth not the Samurai ice pick.) If all that seems like a whole lot of damned bother to you, you've caught the spirit of the drink. Three or four regular home ice-cubes will do just fine.

SAZERAC COCKTAIL

New Orleans' own liquid lagniappe has a way of striking sophisticated tipplers from Basin Street to Bombay in just the exact right place they like to be struck. When William Sydney Porter, alias O. Henry—a man who knew all the cushions and angles when it came to drinks—rhapsodized in one of his stories about New Orleans and "[making] the acquaintance of drinks invented by the Creoles during the period of Louey Cans," it was undoubtedly the Sazerac he had in mind. He often did, you see. In his last years, when he was living at the Caledonia Hotel on Twenty-sixth Street in Manhattan, according to the keeper of the "quiet little bar" down the street, "Sazerac cocktail was his favorite drink." As if to prove it, Porter made a daily practice of dropping in for them "more or less regularly" from ten in the morning until midnight. This may help to explain his confusion regarding the chronology of Cocktails and Kings: The Sazerac, venerable as it may be, postdates the period of Louis Quinze by several generations. But the history of this drink is so intricate and entangled in myth that it requires a monograph of its own. I know this because the untangling of it I was originally planning to include here had already reached some sixteen pages with no sign of wrapping up when my editor wisely suggested I take a different tack. So let me merely state for the record that the Sazerac was in no way the first Cocktail, as has been asserted time and again by its enthusiastic proponents. There is in fact no written record of it before the first decade of the twentieth century, which is perfectly understandable: When all is said and done, the Sazerac is merely a plain Whiskey (or Brandy—see Notes on Ingredients, page 188) Cocktail, made with Peychaud's bitters and finished with a dash of absinthe. A generation earlier, you could have ordered the same thing in any bar in America that served mixed drinks. But once Evolved (page 202) and Vermouth Cocktails became all the rage (page 233), such simple, robust pleasures began to seem rather exotic and worthy of notice.

And so they have remained. Nowadays, just try ordering a Whiskey Cocktail with a dash of absinthe (or legal substitute). Not even in New York, the cradle of fancy drinking in America, can you count on obtaining such a thing. But walk into Tujague's, the Napoleon House, just about any central New Orleans bar save the most egregious Lite beer and Hand-Grenade joint, and moments later you're sipping a drink that's remained unchanged since the 1880s. To paraphrase Norma Desmond, the Sazerac *is* big. It's the other Cocktails that got small.

The recipe below is the first one in print for the modern, whiskey-based version of the drink. The famed Sazerac Bar on Royal Street was the drink's cradle and headquarters until Prohibition shut it down. There's a Walgreens on the site today. So it goes.

From the recipe of the late Tom Handy, ex-manager of the world-renowned Sazerac Bar.

Frappé an old-fashioned flat bar-glass; then take a mixing glass and muddle half a cube [½ tsp] of sugar with a little water; add some ice, a jigger [2 oz] of good whiskey, two dashes of Peychaud bitters, and a piece of twisted lemon peel; stir well until cold, then throw the ice out of the bar-glass, dash several drops of Absinthe into the same, and rinse well with the Absinthe. Now strain the Cocktail into the frozen glass, and serve with ice water on the side.

SOURCE: WILLIAM (COCKTAIL) BOOTHBY, "SOME NEW UP-TO-NOW SEDUCTIVE AMERICAN COCKTAILS" (UNDATED SUPPLEMENT TO THE WORLD'S DRINKS AND HOW TO MIX THEM, 1908)

NOTES ON INGREDIENTS: The sugar cube is traditional (use a whole standard cube). I've always found, though, that this drink responds exceptionally well to a scant teaspoon of real gum syrup (i.e., with the gum Arabic in it; see Chapter 9) instead. Others call for bourbon. Nowadays, nobody in New Orleans who's serious about the Sazerac would make it with anything but rye whiskey. Since the days of the flatboats, New Orleans always was a rye town. The six-year-old rye the Sazerac company is selling at the time of this writing does a fine job, as does the Rittenhouse Bonded rye. In New Orleans, most people use plain old Old Overholt, which makes a perfectly acceptable drink, although not without room for improvement. Or you can go the cognac route: the drink was originally made with Sazerac de Forge et Fils cognac, a brand that perished in the phylloxera epidemic of the 1880s. The occasional bottle of true Sazerac still turns up at auction; good luck. Otherwise, whatever cognac you use, don't skimp on the quality. Perhaps best of all is a combination of cognac and rye, as Dale DeGroff likes to deploy (go with 1½ ounces cognac and ½ ounce rye). If, however, you can get your hands on some good Hollands, be aware that it responds exceptionally well to the Sazerac treatment (the Sazerac House made many a Gin Cocktail, back in the day). Some recipes supplement the Peychaud's with Angostura bitters. Don't; as a side-by-side taste test of this formula made with just Peychaud's, just Angostura, or a mixture of the two will handily prove, the bitters do make a difference. There's just something about the way the Peychaud's interacts with the absinthe that moves the whole shebang from the "excellent" column into the "unforgettable" one, particularly if you're using a good-quality real absinthe. The Herbsaint they use in New Orleans as a substitute isn't bad, by any means, but it's sweeter and less complex than the real McCoy. If used only in Sazeracs, you'll be able to squeeze hundreds of 'em out of one $100 bottle.

NOTES ON EXECUTION: To "frappé" a glass is to fill it with shaved or finely cracked ice. The Sazerac House's technique of stirring this drink in one small bar-glass and straining it into another has become enshrined in tradition, and it's still generally made that way—even though the small bar-glass hasn't been otherwise used for mixing for four or five generations and it's easier to use a regular mixing glass. Which glass you mix it in affects the taste of the drink not a whit, so stir where you like. But whichever you use, give it a good, long stir. How long is enough? In a mixing glass with plenty of cracked ice, twenty seconds will do; in a small bar-glass with less ice, you may need more. Handy's formula deploys the twist before mixing, but if ever there was a drink that cries out for the terminal spray of lemon oil, it's this. As for rinsing the glass with absinthe, Paul Gustings, the best present-day New Orleans Sazerac maker, does a neat little thing where he puts some Herbsaint in the bottom of the chilled glass and then gives it a little toss in the air, with enough English on it for the liqueur to spin up the sides of the glass and coat it. If you can master that . . .

II. EVOLVED COCKTAILS

Judging by their elaborately printed list, the boys behind the bar at Mart Ackermann's Saloon in Toronto sure knew a mess of mixed drinks. One hundred and seven of them, to be precise. All the old favorites, to be sure—the Mint Juleps, Sherry Cobblers, Tom and Jerries, etc. But the boys didn't stop there; they went on beyond zebra with a vengeance. The list, which has the year 1856 written in by hand, is packed with things like the "Canadian Favourite," the "American Standard," the "Silistrian Smash," the "Esplanade Cobbler" and the supremely enigmatic "Maelstrom Tost." The Cobblers number to thirteen, the Smashes to fifteen, the Punches to eighteen. There are even eight Fixes—and eight Cocktails. Gin, Brandy, Whiskey, as you would expect. Champagne, which is novel, but comprehensible. But then there's a "Dublin" Cocktail. An "Ontario" Cocktail. A Cocktail "a la Mode." Even an "Omar Pasha" Cocktail. Now, the Dublin and the Ontario can be tentatively deciphered with the application of reason, Irish whiskey and Canadian whiskey being the likely X-factors. The Cocktail a la Mode? Probably a Fancy Cocktail, as in Jerry Thomas. But the story of the Crimean War hero Omar Pasha, who had recently attained celebrity among the peoples of the British Empire when his Turkish army defeated forty thousand Russians at the battle of Eupatoria, offers few clues as to what might be in a Cocktail bearing his name.

It's a matter of chance that the list at hand, by far the earliest such piece of ephemera I've come across, is from Toronto; if a contemporary one from a drink palace in New York or Cincinnati or Boston or San Francisco or Washington, D.C., were available, it would doubtless show the same thing happening. Whatever went into it, and we have no earthly idea, the Omar Pasha Cocktail marks the beginning of the evolution of "Cocktail" from a term for the Bittered Sling and a few simple variations to a generic term for any short, iced drink. Today, a Cocktail that doesn't telegraph its composition with its name is completely unremarkable; in 1856, it was a novelty (the Omar Pasha is in fact the first on record). It wouldn't remain so for long. As the American bar evolved and mixing drinks became more and more demanding (and lucrative), bartenders began to treat the drinks they made as works of art. Art is no respecter of boundaries, and once the humble Cocktail became a work of art it found itself harboring all kinds of ingredients that it had once rigorously excluded (citrus, eggs), and excluding ones that had once defined it (spirits, bitters). If the Immortal Willard had whipped up a mess of cognac, port, sugar, and egg and tried to palm it off on one of his clients as a Cocktail, that client would have assumed that the master's hand had lost its cunning and removed his business elsewhere. By the time the Civil War broke out, such things were possible.

Much of this artistic impulse was expended in citrusing Cocktails or vermouthing them; you'll find those formulae in the next two sections. Here you'll find the miscellaneous ones, a somewhat motley collection of Cocktails that go beyond the base category in their ingredients, their nomenclature, or both.

CHAMPAGNE COCKTAIL

The first evolved Cocktail on record. The record is silent as to who came up with the idea of replacing the spirits in a Cocktail with champagne, but whoever it was, he knew how to step high, wide, and handsome. The Champagne Cocktail would be a favorite of sporting gentlemen well into the twentieth century. Increasingly, it would also find a home with young ladies who had no fixed bedtime—indeed, it would eventually acquire the evocative nickname "chorus girl's milk." Its first appearance on record, however, is among the easy-come, easy-go Argonauts, whom Frank Marryatt found drinking it in San Francisco in 1850. It is pleasant to imagine the young Jerry Thomas laying

CHAMPAGNE COCKTAIL.

The Champagne Cocktail, Before and After the Bubbly. From Harry Johnson's *New and Improved Illustrated Bartender's Manual*, 1888. (Courtesy Ted Haigh)

out a round of these for some party of black-fingered sons of toil as they pour the gold-dust out on the bar. "More French wines [i.e., champagne] are drank in California, twice over," wrote a visitor to the Golden State a few years later, "than by the same population in the eastern States"—much of it in Cocktail form. Not that they weren't trying, back East: The Champagne Cocktail was to be found everywhere there was money and a desire to spend it and New York and Washington (a notorious champagne town) didn't shirk their duty.

The Champagne Cocktail enjoyed a considerable reputation as a morning "bracer," to the point that bleary-eyed wags wrote verses about it; one set, from 1859, runs to eleven stanzas, ending with the peroration,

And the morn shall be filled with cocktail,
And the cares of the early day,
Like disappointed collectors,
Shall silently slip away.

But the Champagne Cocktail's usefulness didn't end there. Many a jittery gent began his day with Cocktails of "wine," as champagne was simply called in sporting circles (because really, is there any other kind worth bothering with?)—saw out the morning with them—lunched on "chicken and wine"—sailed through the midafternoon doldrums with more Cocktails— supped with a foaming bottle at hand—Cocktailed at cards— watered the long-stemmed chorine with frequent sprinklings—tucked the boys on Broadway in with another— took one more for the road and another to greet the dawn.

All this wine-drinking adds up, especially when a Champagne Cocktail made with the real stuff cost three or four times what a regular Whiskey Cocktail did. When Jerry Thomas's bar was at its highest ebb, between Cocktails and just plain guzzling, the place nonetheless went through enough fizz for him and George to "sometimes buy a hundred baskets of one brand at a time." (A basket of champagne held a dozen bottles, or two dozen splits.) They kept at least seven premium brands on hand, including such modern icons as Veuve Cliquot, Moet & Chandon, Heidsieck & Co., and Roederer. No wonder they called it the Gilded Age.

(ONE BOTTLE OF WINE TO EVERY SIX LARGE GLASSES.)

(PER GLASS.)

½ TEASPOONFUL OF SUGAR

1 OR 2 DASHES OF BITTERS

1 PIECE OF LEMON PEEL

Fill tumbler one-third full of broken ice, and fill balance with wine. Shake well and serve.

NOTES ON INGREDIENTS: In the latter years of the century, it was discovered that a cube or lump of sugar in the bottom of the glass, saturated with the bitters, will dissolve slowly, infusing the drink as it does; the standard Domino Dot works perfectly for this, holding as it does ½ teaspoon of sugar. In 1895, George Kappeler suggested Peychaud's bitters as an alternative to the traditional Angostura. I find them particularly effective if I'm adding brandy, which I'll get to in a moment.

Jerry Thomas and his contemporaries preferred broken or cracked ice in their Champagne Cocktails, doubtlessly because they disappeared them so fast there was little danger of dilution. Later in the century, when giants ceased to walk the land, the Cocktails were smaller, dryer, and used a single lump of ice, which was far less likely to water down the champagne.

As for the wine. If complete authenticity is a priority, a (sweeter) sec or even a demi-sec should be used. On the other hand, the brut champagne that came in late in the century (famed "King of the Dudes" Evander Berry Wall claims it was his exquisite taste responsible for this, and it may well have been) makes for a better Cocktail. In any case, one bottle of champagne will yield six small Cocktails, not large ones. Some—the *Steward & Barkeeper's Manual*, anyway—liked to disburse the stuff with a heavier hand: "One quart bottle," its author notes, "will make a little over four large cocktails." To me, this is more like it, but you must of course follow the dictates of your conscience.

There are, of course, variations and refinements. I must confess that I'm shamefully partial to the hot-rails-to-hell practice Delaware mixologist Joseph Haywood recorded in 1898 of adding "one-half glass of brandy," although I usually settle with one-quarter glass, or $\frac{1}{2}$ ounce, of VSOP cognac or better.

NOTES ON EXECUTION: By "shake," Thomas here clearly means "pour back and forth." This makes for a cold and foamy drink, but one that flattens quickly; better have another lined up. Before long, the accepted practice was, as the *Steward & Barkeeper's Manual* instructed, to "agitate well with a spoon." Later, once the bittered sugar cube became standard, even this was felt to be too much for the drink. The admonition in Boothby's *World's Drinks* from 1908 was typical: "Never stir . . . this beverage." This was calculated to keep the bubbles streaming up from the cube as long as possible and the drink almost as dry as naked champagne.

BUCK AND BRECK

When Alan Dale got Jerry Thomas to talk about the famous drinks he had invented, that Sunday afternoon in 1883 or 1884, the Professor owned up to five: the **Tom & Jerry**, the **Blue Blazer**, the Champarelle, Lamb's Wool, and the "Buck and Brick" [sic]. The first two we have discussed in detail. Champarelle is both confusing—he described it one way to Dale and another way in his book, and there were other versions out there—and not particularly interesting, so I will skip over it. About Lamb's Wool, which in Thomas's seems to have been nothing more than a flaming Hot Buttered Rum flavored with curaçao, we have too little information to comment further. That leaves the "Buck and Brick," which Thomas describes as a mixture of brandy and champagne served in a sugar-coated glass.

At first glance, it doesn't seem like much to claim—an oddly named drink that appears in none of the standard compendia of drink. But not so fast. If you trace back the lineage of the standard works of drink history, most of them go back to a handful of books by New York bartenders, and—as it turns out—the Buck and Breck, as the drink's name must be spelled ("Buck and Breck" was the popular nickname for the winning 1856 Democratic ticket, James Buchanan and John C. Breckenridge)—was a West Coast drink. It pops up here and there in California and Nevada newspapers of the 1860s and '70s, and even appears under a garbled name in the classic record of California mixology, Bill Boothby's 1900 *American Bartender* (that garbling is understandable: until very recent times, Buchanan was a candidate for worst president in American history).

Did Jerry Thomas actually invent the Buck and Breck? In 1856, he was nowhere near California. But the drink doesn't actually appear in print until early 1864, when it turns up in the pages of the San Francisco *Daily Alta* as a specialty of the Bank Exchange (for which see **Pisco Punch**, page 73). The Professor having recently been in town and made rather a big splash, what with his diamonds and his recent literary celebrity, it seems more than likely that one or another of his signature concoctions would have caught on. And if one's going to catch on, it might as well be this—to taste it made properly, with a couple of touches that the Professor neglected to pass on to Alan Dale (for which see below), is to agree with the *Daily Alta* reporter, who dubbed it "Bully! Pleasant to the taste and mild as a zephyr." It is, however, rather intoxicating, so tread lightly.

Fill a small bar-glass with water and throw it out again, then fill the glass with bar sugar and throw that out, leaving the glass apparently frosted inside. Pour in a jigger [1½ oz] of cognac [and a dash of

absinthe and two of Angostura bitters] **and fill the glass with cold champagne. Then smile.**

SOURCE: COCKTAIL BOOTHBY'S *AMERICAN BARTENDER*, 1900
(BOOTHBY CALLS IT THE "BRECK AND BRACE")

NOTES ON INGREDIENTS: According to that San Francisco reporter, the Bank Exchange's bartender "put in something that looked like a solution of verdigris [and] added a bright crimson liquid." The only green and crimson ingredients in general bar use in 1864 were absinthe and bitters, both of which were used in dashes. Since dashes are the kinds of things that people tend to omit when describing a drink, it seems entirely reasonable to restore these—besides, they make for a far more bewitching beverage. If you want to use lemon juice to wet the inside of the glass, that's an old San Francisco bartender's bit of fanciness for this sort of drink (there were others like it: Omit the dashes, do the lemon juice thing, and replace half the brandy with kümmel, and you have Ernest Rawling's equally stupendous **Russian Cocktail**). Use a VSOP or better for the cognac.

NOTES ON EXECUTION: A champagne flute makes a good substitute for the bar-glass here.

JERSEY COCKTAIL

Unbeknownst to its consumer, many a Champagne Cocktail was actually a Jersey Cocktail. Much more French champagne was consumed in America than was shipped here from France, and the "apple-knockers" of New Jersey were more than ready to make up the deficit. In an age of "compound" or "artificial" beverages—we would say "adulterate," "fraudulent," or "recklessly toxic"—few were so voluminously and openly counterfeited as champagne. If you were lucky, you'd get good Garden State hard cider, pressurized with CO_2 (preferably without too much residual carbonic acid) and bottled in a Frenchy-looking bottle. If you were unlucky . . . processed beet juice. Better to simply call a spade a spade and enjoy your cider for what it is.

The Jersey Cocktail doesn't turn up often outside of bartenders' guides, but in Thomas's formulation it's an honest, straightforward drink. Let that be its recommendation.

(USE SMALL BAR-GLASS.)

1 TEASPOONFUL OF SUGAR

2 DASHES OF BITTERS

Fill tumbler with cider, and mix well, with lemon peel on top.

SOURCE: JERRY THOMAS, 1862

NOTES ON INGREDIENTS: The sugar, as always, is a matter of preference; some add another 1/2 teaspoon. Use a good, filtered hard cider. In 1908, Boothby suggested that one "flavor" the drink with applejack. He's not wrong: 1/2 ounce or so of bonded Laird's does wonders for its oomph. For Jerry Thomas's **Soda Cocktail**, replace the cider with soda water (use ice and the large glass). This formula was, and still is, much appreciated by the hungover.

NOTES ON EXECUTION: Thomas's 1862 version is made without ice; presumably, the cider is chilled. Others built it on the rocks, or even shook it and strained it.

EAST INDIA COCKTAIL

A favorite of mine for its mellow richness, the East India was, according to Harry Johnson, also "a great favorite with the English living in the different parts of East India" (for more on Mr. Johnson, see the Bijou Cocktail, page 256). In its composition nothing more than a particularly fancy Brandy Cocktail, the East India finds itself among the Evolved Cocktails chiefly by virtue of its name. If the Jersey Cocktail illustrates one of the most common and productive strategies for drink nomenclature, which is to simply name it after whence its most prominent ingredient hails (cf. the White Russian), the East India—alias the Bengal—illustrates another, which is to tag it with the name of wherever they're drinking 'em.

Beyond Johnson's statement, we have very little hard information about the East India. But there were American bars aplenty in the grand new hotels that dotted the Eastern reaches of Queen Victoria's empire, and many an American bartender to tend them. Judging by the basic soundness of this formula, which first appears (with a slightly different—and inferior—formula) in Johnson's 1882 *New and Improved Bartender's Manual*, the East India may well have been the work of one of these wandering Yankees.

(USE LARGE BAR-GLASS.)

FILL THE GLASS WITH SHAVED ICE

1 TEASPOONFUL OF CURAÇOA (RED)

1 TEASPOONFUL OF PINEAPPLE SYRUP

2 OR 3 DASHES OF BITTERS (BOKER'S GENUINE ONLY)

2 DASHES [¼ TSP] OF MARASCHINO

1 WINE GLASS FULL [2 OZ] OF BRANDY (MARTELL)

Stir up with a spoon, strain into a cocktail glass, putting in a cherry or medium-sized olive, twist a piece of lemon peel on top, and serve.

SOURCE: HARRY JOHNSON, *NEW AND IMPROVED BARTENDER'S MANUAL*, 1900 EDITION

NOTES ON INGREDIENTS: For red curaçoa, use orange. The pineapple syrup, which makes this drink, can easily be prepared at home; see Chapter 9. For Boker's bitters, Byron and others suggest Angostura, which is fine, although I find Peychaud's gives it a lovely, soft edge. And you can of course use cognacs other than Martell, although there's absolutely nothing wrong with Martell (as always, use a VSOP or better for best Epicurean effect). The cherry can be omitted, and the olive should be avoided at all costs.

JAPANESE COCKTAIL

Quoth the *Minneapolis Tribune* in early 1885: "The Japanese cocktail is [a] liquid attack of spinal meningitis. It is loaded with knock-kneed mental ceramics, and is apt to make a man throw stones at his grandfather." It's hard to think of a drink less worthy of such vitriol than the Japanese Cocktail. Perhaps the only drink in Jerry Thomas's *How to Mix Drinks* actually invented by him, this suave and sweet social surfactant is many things, but a haven for "knock-kneed mental ceramics" isn't one of them. Nor did it come from Japan. There's nothing Japanese in it. In fact, as well as can be determined, the Japanese Cocktail is a fine example of yet another Cocktail-naming gambit, the commemorative Cocktail.

In June 1860, the first Japanese legation to the United States finished up their sensational tour with a few weeks in New York. A bunch of dignified, reserved, non-English-speaking Samurai, plus Tommy—well, Tateishi Onojirou Noriyuki, but nobody called him that. A young, frisky English speaker, Tommy was the legation's legman—in both senses of the word: He had a decided interest in flirting with the ladies (and they with him).

If the American journalist who accompanied the legation on the long voyage home is to be believed, Tommy was interested in another American social custom as well, and in this his comrades joined him: "From breakfast to supper, they . . . [kept] the toddy-sticks going with much vivacity." Their preferred poison? Cocktails. Small wonder: Their New York residence had been the Metropolitan Hotel, just a block away from Jerry Thomas's "palace" bar at 622 Broadway. I can't imagine that in their strolls around the neighborhood, they wouldn't have stopped in to see the Professor for a quick one. And if you were Jerry Thomas, wouldn't you come up with something special to mark the occasion?

The *Minneapolis Tribune* notwithstanding, the Japanese Cocktail remained in the current rotation, if not at the top of the list, until Prohibition, albeit often under the monickers "Mikado Cocktail" or "Chinese Cocktail" (let's not go there).

(USE SMALL BAR-GLASS.)

1 TABLE-SPOONFUL OF ORGEAT SYRUP

½ TEASPOONFUL OF BOGART'S BITTERS

1 WINE-GLASS [2 OZ] OF BRANDY

1 OR 2 PIECES OF LEMON PEEL

Fill the tumbler one-third with ice, and stir well with a spoon.

SOURCE: JERRY THOMAS, 1862

NOTES ON INGREDIENTS: Note the unusual amount of bitters, suggested no doubt to counteract the thick sweetness of the orgeat (which probably also explains the extra piece of lemon peel). If proceeding this way—and it's well worth trying, yielding a fragrant and delightful drink—you'll have to use Fee's Aromatic Bitters or your own homemade Boker's (see Chapter 9); Angostura and Peychaud's are too concentrated to be used in this quantity. Otherwise follow the 1887 *Bar-Tender's Guide* and go with 2 dashes of Angostura. Worthy of note is the *Steward & Barkeeper's Manual*'s idiosyncratic suggestion that this can also be made with gin (Hollands, of course) and curaçao or maraschino instead of the orgeat.

NOTES ON EXECUTION: As for a regular Cocktail. By the time the *Minneapolis Tribune* had taken to calling it "liquid spinal meningitis," the Japanese Cocktail was no longer a rocks drink, but was strained into a Cocktail glass, like just about everything else. In this case, it's an improvement.

MORNING GLORY COCKTAIL

As we have seen, much of the Cocktail's development was intimately connected to the search for a better hangover cure. In an
age before aspirin, Advil, or morphine, an age without Alka-
Seltzer, Pepto-Bismol, or Starbucks' bottled Frappucino, this
quest was not an unreasonable one, particularly for the sports
who were ordering champagne by the basket. When confronted
by the "cold grey light of dawn" (a phrase coined by humorist
George Ade for just this situation), the toper recognized it as
"the great necessity of the age" (to quote the *Brooklyn Eagle*)
that he should at once take some sort of "anti-fogmatic" (attested as early as 1808), "eye-opener" (1818), "bracer" (1829),
"corpse reviver," or "morning glory" (both 1862).

Which brings us to the Morning Glory Cocktail (which is to
be distinguished from the Morning Glory Fizz). The plain Cocktail was clearly considered to be a pretty fair tonic—as well it
should be, that function having been bred into it from the very
beginning. But by the 1880s the original Cocktail was something
like a hundred years old, and the antifogmatic arts had made
some important advances. Perhaps a Cocktail could be produced
to reflect this progress? That, at any rate, seems to be the con-
sideration driving this formula, which first appeared in the 1887
rewrite of Thomas's book. It's got every key eye-opening ingredient, beginning with brandy and whiskey, running through bitters and absinthe, with a little curaçao to take the edge off and a
healthy tot of soda or seltzer to provide hydration. Not surprisingly to one who has drunk of the Sazerac and the Improved
Cocktail, which it closely resembles, it also tastes pretty fine.

(USE MEDIUM BAR-GLASS.)

TAKE 3 DASHES [1 TSP] **OF GUM SYRUP**

2 DASHES [½ TSP] **OF CURAÇOA**

2 DASHES OF BOKER'S BITTERS

1 DASH OF ABSINTHE

1 PONY [1 OZ] OF BRANDY

1 PONY [1 OZ] OF WHISKEY

1 PIECE OF LEMON PEEL, TWISTED TO EXPRESS THE OIL

2 SMALL PIECES OF ICE

Stir thoroughly and remove the ice. Fill the glass with Seltzer water or plain soda, and stir with a teaspoon having a little sugar in it.

SOURCE: *JERRY THOMAS'S BAR-TENDER'S GUIDE,* 1887

NOTES ON INGREDIENTS: For the bitters, use Angostura (it's the purest and most medicinal). The brandy should be a VSOP cognac (at this crucial time of day, it's especially important to use a mild and mellow product). Cognac mixes particularly well with rye whiskey, so that choice is made. And use more ice than the book calls for. Oh, and if you're like me, you'll have an anarchic little voice in your head that suggests substituting champagne for the seltzer. Listen to it at your peril.

NOTES ON EXECUTION: This hybrid Cocktail-Fizz should be stirred in the mixing glass and strained into a chilled small highball glass, with fizz water to follow. The trick with the teaspoon will raise a nice head; see the Gin Fizz (page 111) for details.

ABSINTHE COCKTAIL AND ABSINTHE FRAPPÉ

Although absinthe was sold in New Orleans by 1837 and New York by 1843, it took a while for anyone to get around to making an actual according-to-Hoyle Cocktail out of it. In part, this is understandable. Absinthe was something that you dashed into Cocktails, not something you built a drink around. Eventually, though, someone saw the light, *et voila!* the Absinthe Cocktail. By the late 1870s, anyway, for the bartenders on Park Row, where New York's newspapers kept their headquarters, making Absinthe Cocktails was "child's play."

Before long, though, American absinthe drinkers began to feel that the best thing about the Absinthe Cocktail was the absinthe itself, with the ice running a very close second and the anisette and the bitters lagging by several lengths. And thus the Absinthe Cocktail begat the Absinthe Frappé, which was simply ingredient *a* shaken up with lots of ice and strained into a Cocktail glass, which may or may not have been packed with shaved ice. These "clouded green ones" were regarded by the Sporting Fraternity as (what else) just the thing to ring for first thing in the morning when you had a "head the size of a birdcage" and a taste in your mouth "like a motorman's glove" (as Clarence Louis Cullen of the *New York Sun* delineated the condition). Then, in 1904—ten years after the frappé starts turning up in sporting circles—Victor Herbert and Glen Macdonough included an ode to the Absinthe Frappé and its remarkable curative powers in their new show, *It Happened in Nordland*. With "Absinthe Frappé" spreading throughout the land in sheet music and recorded on Edison cylinder, suddenly the clouded green one found itself a white-hot drink, consumed by anyone, male or female, with pretensions to pretentiousness. This was akin to someone with an outstanding felony warrant going on *American Idol*. If absinthe had kept to its place among the sports and bohemians, it would have gone quietly to Prohibition with all the other spirits, and perhaps come out the other end with them as well. But given the stuff's fearsome reputation, when the folks who live out where the bullfrogs croak saw their sons and daughters recreating on it, they took firm action. Absinthe was granted a special Prohibition all its own in 1912.

(USE SMALL BAR-GLASS.)

   TAKE 2 DASHES [½ TSP] OF ANISETTE

   1 DASH OF ANGOSTURA BITTERS

   1 PONY-GLASS [1 OZ] OF ABSINTHE

Pour about one wine-glass [2 oz] of water into the tumbler in a small stream from the ice pitcher, or preferably from an absinthe glass. Shake up very thoroughly with ice, and strain into a claret glass.

SOURCE: *JERRY THOMAS'S BAR-TENDER'S GUIDE*, 1887

NOTES ON INGREDIENTS: If you can find the Spanish Anis del Mono brand, get it—it's historic, and excellent. The absinthe is dealt out in ponies rather than wineglasses because it was, and still is, between 120- and 140-proof. For a **Frappé**, simply omit the anisette and bitters and, depending on whether you're going for the simpler Eastern style or the more baroque California style, half or all of the water.

NOTES ON EXECUTION: The water is trickled in so the customer can watch the absinthe louche up. Once you've seen the show a couple of times, you can speed things up. For a Frappé, there are two ways to go. The Eastern style is basically as above, sometimes without the water and with the receiving glass packed with shaved ice. The California style, according to Bill Boothby of the Palace in San Francisco, is to shake a pony of absinthe well with plenty of ice and no water and then pour it and the ice into a Julep strainer perched atop a highball-glass, topping it off with seltzer slowly squirted over the ice resting in the strainer. Odd, but fun to watch.

COFFEE COCKTAIL

Rumor had it that this suave and rich concoction came from New Orleans. I shouldn't wonder. In any case, it clearly pushes the Cocktail envelope, as the anonymous compiler of the 1887 edition of Thomas's book noted: "The name of this drink is a misnomer, as coffee and bitters are not to be found among its ingredients, but it looks like coffee when it has been properly concocted, and hence probably its name."

(USE LARGE BAR-GLASS.)

TAKE 1 TEA-SPOONFUL POWDERED WHITE SUGAR

1 FRESH EGG

1 LARGE WINE-GLASS [2 OZ] OF PORT WINE

1 PONY [1 OZ] OF BRANDY

2 OR 3 LUMPS OF ICE

Break the egg into the glass, put in the sugar, and lastly the port wine, brandy and ice. Shake up very thoroughly, and strain into a medium bar goblet. Grate a little nutmeg on top before serving.

SOURCE: *JERRY THOMAS'S BAR-TENDER'S GUIDE*, 1887

NOTES ON INGREDIENTS: Use a decent ruby port and a lot more ice.

WIDOW'S KISS

Back when Fifth Avenue was still lined by millionaires' mansions, George J. Kappeler was head bartender at the Holland House hotel, at Fifth Avenue and Thirtieth Street. A German like so many who inhabited the highest reaches of turn-of-the-century mixology (e.g., William Schmidt, Hugo Ensslin, Leo Engel, Louis Eppinger, Louis Muckensturm, and even the great Harry Johnson, who retired to Berlin), Kappeler had a true artist's combination of effortless command of detail and willingness to transcend petty rules. A less elevated soul would have pondered the combination of apple brandy, Benedictine, yellow Chartreuse, and bitters and said, "No, too much!" With three out of the four ingredients being highly pungent and aromatic herbal tonics, that's only sensible. But Kappeler said—well, we don't know what he said, but he put the combination on his list, under the somehow bewitching name "Widow's Kiss." It made it into all the standard Cocktail books.

We don't know if Kappeler had any particular widow in mind. If he did, she must have been something. As the *New York Herald* observed in 1897, "The combination, if taken in rapidly repeating doses, is said to be intoxicating"—and well it should: The drink is essentially all booze, with nothing in it weighing in at less than 80 proof except the ice. Now, the *Herald* claimed that "This fact is pointed to with pride by those who champion the fitness" of the drink. There were plenty of others who would've begged to differ. Not only because of its alcoholic strength, but also because of how that strength was imparted: "Properly made," opined the *New York Sun* in 1900, "a cocktail should be a mild and harmless stimulant, but when cordials are added it is a thing to shun."

In part, the *Sun* can be excused by the novelty of the cordial Cocktail; aside from maraschino, curaçao, and perhaps a little crème de noyeaux, cordials were little used in American mixed drinks until the 1880s, when mixologists, seeking to expand their palettes of flavor, began little by little incorporating the more complex herbal liqueurs into their drinks. But I like to think the *Sun*'s man (perhaps Don Marquis or Clarence Louis Cullen, both adepts who knew their tipples), had he tasted one of Kappeler's Widow's Kisses, would've made an exception: an astonishingly harmonious and yet intriguing drink, wherein all the usually warring ingredients are somehow held in a state of détente.

A mixing-glass half-full of fine ice, two dashes Angostura bitters, one-half a pony [½ oz] yellow chartreuse, one-half a pony [½ oz] Benedictine, one pony [1 oz] of apple brandy; shake well, strain into a fancy cocktail-glass, and serve.

SOURCE: GEORGE J. KAPPELER, *MODERN AMERICAN DRINKS*, 1895

NOTES ON INGREDIENTS: For the apple brandy, see under the Jack Rose (page 225). If you can only get the green Chartreuse, make something else: The green is an entirely different product, and far too concentrated to work here. Do not substitute B&B for Benedictine. This drink is a balancing act, and if one thing is out of whack, everything is.

NOTES ON EXECUTION: Normally, a drink like this should be stirred. But Kappeler says to shake, and since he's not one of those "I shake everything" types, I'm inclined to follow his advice.

III. CRUSTAS AND COCKTAIL PUNCHES

You know how hard it is in America to keep things apart that belong apart. If it's not churches running political campaigns, it's peanut-butter-and-bacon sandwiches; if it's not hillbilly rhythm-and-blues, it's reality television. Establish a boundary, and we just want to cross it. This holds as true in the field of mixology as it does everywhere else. Cocktails were short drinks with bitters, Punches were long drinks with citrus. Shouldn't be too hard to keep them apart, if you wanted to. But really the only surprising thing is that it took so long for them to get naked with each other.

BRANDY, WHISKEY, OR GIN CRUSTA

Just like drinkers of the 1990s who liked the Martini more for its glass than for the strongly alcoholic mixture of gin and vermouth that it contained, there were plenty of drinkers in the middle of the nineteenth century who appreciated the newly popular iced Cocktail more for the idea of a quick, short blast of something cold than for the strongly alcoholic mixture of spirits, bitters, and sugar that made it flesh. Some thought that perhaps a little lemon juice in that Cocktail might be just the thing; who cares if, by some arbitrary system, that kind of makes the drink a Punch. Some might kick about it, but it's a free country, so it's really none of their business, right?

It wasn't the hard-drinking Yankees who first crossed that line. Not surprisingly, as far as we can tell it was the Epicurean Creoles, to whom "the fiery cocktail" had always been a little suspect. Sometime around 1850, one Joseph Santini took over management of the bar and restaurant at New Orleans' City Exchange, right in the heart of the French Quarter. There he invented the Crusta, a fancy variation on the Cocktail that introduced citrus juice into the list of things that could go into the drink. This was purely a local drink until Jerry Thomas, who must have met Santini and/or had his drinks when he was in the Crescent City in the 1850s, put the Crusta in his book. This isn't to say that the Crusta was a huge hit; it was always a cult

The proper way to present a Crusta. From *The Bon Vivant's Companion*, 1862. (Author's collection)

drink, one with few but fanatic devotés. But it planted a seed. That seed would remain dormant until the 1890s, when suddenly everyone stared putting lemon juice, lime juice, even orange juice into their Cocktails. From the Crusta, evolution brings us the Sidecar, and life without Sidecars would be very dreary indeed. If Santini hadn't done it first, they still might have done that anyway, but at least they had someone in the dark backward of time shining a flashlight for them to show them the way. Mr. Santini, we salute you. (And besides, there are few drinks as purely delightful as a properly assembled Brandy Crusta.)

(U S E   S M A L L   B A R - G L A S S .)

Crusta is made the same as a fancy cocktail, with a little lemon juice and a small lump of ice added. First, mix the ingredients [1 tsp gum syrup, 2 dashes bitters, 2 oz spirits, ½ tsp orange curaçao, 1 tsp lemon juice] in a small tumbler, then take a fancy red wine-glass, rub a sliced lemon around the rim of the same, and dip it in pulverized white sugar, so that the sugar will adhere to the edge of the glass. Pare half a lemon the same as you would an apple (all in one piece) so

that the paring will fit in the wine-glass, as shown in the cut, and strain the crusta from the tumbler into it. Then smile.

SOURCE: JERRY THOMAS, 1862

NOTES ON INGREDIENTS: Although Thomas also includes a gin version (use Hollands, of course) and a whiskey one, the only Crusta one actually hears of people drinking is the brandy version. Later in the classic period, the curaçao got displaced by maraschino liqueur, which works quite as well. But let's talk lemon juice. How much is "a little"? Thomas's indeterminacy left a good deal of room for interpretation, and mixologists are all over the map on the question. Modern drink-mixers—well, the few who bother with things like Crustas—tend to splash the stuff around pretty liberally, going so far as the juice of half a lemon. Back in the day, though, it's clear that the drink was conceived differently—not as a Sour, but a true Cocktail, with the lemon juice serving as merely an accent. Thus the experts of the period suggest everything from no lemon at all to a quarter of a lemon (about ⅓ of an ounce), with a decided preference for less rather than more. In my view, 1 teaspoon will do it.

NOTES ON EXECUTION: Use a vegetable peeler on the lemon; your life will be easier. For the business with the peel to work, you really need a shallow, 3- to 4-ounce small wineglass. A visit to the thrift store might be in order.

BRONX COCKTAIL

If, at the very end of the twentieth century, the Cosmopolitan made it safe for a nice, middle-class person to have a cocktail before a meal, it was just repeating what the Bronx Cocktail did at the century's very beginning. Either unknown or practically so in 1900, by 1910 this simple mixture of gin, fresh orange juice, and two kinds of vermouth was being served at charity dinners and banquets of state.

As with most famous drinks, its origin is unclear. In 1931, Albert Stevens Crockett, former press agent of the Waldorf-Astoria Hotel, claimed that Johnnie Solon, one of the hotel's bartenders, threw it together for a customer and named it to honor both the famous zoo and the "strange animals [the customers] saw after a lot of mixed drinks." On the other hand, in 1921 the *New York Times* reported on the closing of one Peter Sellers's café on Brook Avenue in the Bronx, noting that "it was said to be the place where the Bronx Cocktail had its inception" and that Billy Gibson's Criterion Restaurant, another Bronx bar, "also claims that distinction." We may never know.

Whoever concocted it, the Bronx was certainly in existence by 1904, when the *Police Gazette* included it in a list of new Cocktails, and perhaps four or five years earlier, since it also appeared in a menu in the collection of the New York Historical Society from around 1900.* As usual with new drinks, it took a couple of years to reach general popularity. Its breakthrough came in 1907, when suddenly the Bronx Cocktail was everywhere. That didn't mean everybody was satisfied with it, though. The most common criticism was encapsulated in this zinger from Zoe Atkins in her 1913 play *Papa: An Immorality in Three Acts* (don't ask): "He looks as weak as a Bronx cocktail." The problem wasn't the gin, or even the vermouth. It was—you guessed it—that damned orange juice. Put enough in that you can taste it, and the drink is weak; leave it out, and you've got nothing more than a Perfect Martini. People tried everything in the way of dashes of juice, orange bitters, and orange peel to effect a compromise, but ultimately it was a case of you pays your money and you takes your choice. Myself, I like my Bronx with a fair amount of Florida sunshine in it, accepting the weakness—which is, after all, relative: The drink is no weaker than, say, an Aviation. But people were used to lemon juice in their drinks. Orange juice, however, was a different story. Before

* This is dated in pencil as "about 1895," but this cannot be as it lists the "Zaza Cocktail," christened after the Broadway play that opened in January 1899.

the Bronx, it was not an acceptable Cocktail ingredient; after, it was, although there were still dissenters well into the twentieth century who could be called upon to rant and rave about kiddie drinks and fruit punch and what the hell is the world coming to when a perfectly good Martini is going around with breakfast squeezings in it (the story is much the same with cranberry juice and the Cosmopolitan).

A la Billy Malloy, Pittsburgh, PA

One-third [1 oz] Plymouth gin, one-third [1 oz] French vermouth and one-third [1 oz] Italian vermouth, flavored with two dashes of Orange bitters, about a barspoonful of orange juice and a squeeze of orange peel. Serve very cold.

SOURCE: WILLIAM T. "BILL" BOOTHBY, *WORLD DRINKS AND HOW TO MIX THEM* (1908)

NOTES ON INGREDIENTS: It should be noted that Plymouth Gin was an advertiser in Boothby's book, although it does indeed make a toothsome Bronx. But so does Tanqueray, or Beefeater, or any other good London dry gin. As for the proportions: Mr. Malloy is a trimmer, trying to have both the orange and the strength. His recipe—the first on record—is not a bad drink, but for the full Bronx experience I suggest waiting for a very hot day and then mixing 'em up as Johnny Solon of the old Waldorf bar did: 1½ ounces of gin, half that of orange juice, and 1 teaspoon each of French and Italian vermouth. No garnish. When I want a stronger drink, I'll fix myself a Sazerac and be happy. But when the heat is oppressive, a nice, cold Bronx prepared thus is a fine thing.

NOTES ON EXECUTION: Shake well with cracked ice; strain and serve.

JACK ROSE COCKTAIL

I spent many years believing that this drink, one of only two classic applejack cocktails (for the other, see the Star, page 253), was named after "Bald Jack" Rose, one of the yeggs involved in the notorious 1912 Becker-Rosenthal case (in which Police Lieutenant Becker eventually went to the chair—probably wrongly—for hiring Rose to put out a hit on gambler "Beansy" Rosenthal; see the Metropole, page 249). In part, this belief was wishful thinking of the kind all mixographers indulge in. Alas, the facts say different, or at least the *Police Gazette* does, which is not always the same thing. In this case, however, the evidence seems pretty straightforward: According to a squib the *Gazette* published in 1905, "Frank J. May, better known as Jack Rose, is the inventor of a very popular cocktail by that name, which has made him famous as a mixologist." This May/Rose fellow was apparently employed at Gene Sullivan's Café on Pavonia Avenue in Jersey City—and indeed, it's worth noting that applejack is the state spirit of New Jersey. A less glamorous back story, to be sure, but most likely a factual one. As for Bald Jack, according to a widely reprinted newspaper squib from the end of 1912, his notoriety put such a dent in the drink's popularity that some bartenders took to calling it a "Royal Smile" instead. Perhaps.

1 JIGGER [2 OZ] APPLEJACK

[JUICE OF] ½ LIME

¼ JIGGER [½ OZ] GRENADINE SYRUP

Shake well.

SOURCE: JACQUES STRAUB, *DRINKS* (1914)

NOTES ON INGREDIENTS: The Jack Rose's basic formula was definitely open to debate. Some early recipes, such as the one downtown New York bartender R. H. Townes gave Bill Boothby some time around 1905 (the first in print), call for lemon juice. Others agree with Straub. Personally, I prefer lime juice in this; its sharp fragrance helps cut the thickness of the grenadine. For the apple-jack, see Chapter 2. Try to use real grenadine, if possible. Some used to make this drink with a little French vermouth, say ¾ of an ounce, to twice that of applejack, plus the lime and the grenadine to 1½ ounces applejack (thus veteran East Coast "wine clerk" Jere Sullivan, writing during Prohibition). Straub prints this, too—but as that **Royal Smile** . . .

CLOVER CLUB COCKTAIL

The Clover Club was a rather riotous Philadelphia organiza-tion that met at the Bellevue Stratford hotel in that city from the late 1880s until at least the First World War. Dedicated to raillery and refreshment, it was the Friar's Club of its day, although with more lawyers and fewer professional comics. We don't know exactly when it was fitted out with a Cocktail of its very own, but it appears to have been rather late in the club's history. At any rate, if we're to believe the *Phil-adelphia Inquirer*'s "Clubs and Clubmen" column, written by a certain A. Jin Rickki, the drink didn't break out of Philadelphia until 1910. "The 'Clover Club cocktail' is fast becoming the rage in New York," wrote Mr. Rickki. "All of the actors drink it now and the bartenders of the Plaza can teach the man who invented them"—sadly unidentified—"the art of mixing."

This recipe comes from the bar-book of the old Waldorf-Astoria, where in 1911 William Butler Yeats, in town with his Irish Players, found the Clover Clubs shaken up by Michael J. Killackey, then the hotel's head bartender, so seductive that he drank three in a row. There are some who even say he kept at them right through dinner. While I might not go that far, a properly assembled Clover Club is a powerful argument that the center might just hold after all.

JUICE ½ LEMON

½ SPOON [⅛ OZ] SUGAR

½ PONY [2 TSP] RASPBERRY [I.E., SYRUP]

¼ PONY [¼ OZ] WHITE OF EGG

1 JIGGER [2 OZ] GIN

Shake well. Strain.

SOURCE: ALBERT STEVENS CROCKETT, *OLD WALDORF BAR DAYS* (1931; CROCKETT WAS PRESS AGENT FOR THE "HYPHEN," AS THE HOTEL WAS KNOWN AMONG THE SPORTS, AND WHEN PROHIBITION CLOSED ITS BAR, HE RECEIVED CUSTODY OF ITS HANDWRITTEN BAR-BOOK)

NOTES ON INGREDIENTS: Harry MacElhone, who worked at the Plaza in the early 1910s, suggests lime juice instead of lemon; in either case, ½ ounce should do. *Beverages De Luxe*, a 1911 drink book that prints a Clover Club recipe its authors picked up from the Hotel Belvedere in Baltimore, agrees about the lime and suggests replacing the raspberry syrup with actual raspberries, if in season. This is a fine suggestion, but if adopted, it will require more sugar: say, half a dozen berries and 1½ teaspoons of superfine sugar, depending on the tartness of the raspberries. If you lightly whip the egg white—here to add froth and body—with a fork, you can divide it; otherwise, use 1 white for every two or three drinks.

Both the Belvedere's recipe and MacElhone's (which was presumably the Plaza's) cut back on the gin and added some vermouth. The Waldorf's is brighter tasting and simpler (and stronger), but the Plaza-Belvedere school's is rather more interesting. If you like interesting, I suggest using 1½ ounces of gin (London dry or Plymouth) and 2 teaspoons each of Noilly Prat white and Martini & Rossi red vermouths. Whichever formula you use, float a leaf of mint on top and you've got a **Clover Leaf.**

NOTES ON EXECUTION: If you use fresh raspberries, muddle them with the sugar and the citrus and double-strain the drink—i.e., use the Hawthorne strainer in the shaker and put a Julep strainer over the glass to catch the raspberry seeds. Like all drinks using eggs, this one will have to be shaken extra hard.

DAIQUIRI COCKTAIL

The first true classic cocktail to be invented outside the United States. I'm going to take advantage of that fact and ignore the whole Cuban part of its history, whatever that might be (let's just say it's one of mixology's great open questions), and focus briefly on its early fortunes stateside. Although the Americans who in 1898 suddenly found themselves in Cuba in great numbers took to Bacardi's exceptionally smooth, light rum pretty much instantly, it needed about ten years for it to filter across the Florida Straits and invade the invader. After a couple of years of percolating, in the mid-1910s it suddenly became a sensation. The usual mixological capers ensued. New Cocktails were mixed, with racy new names (the September Morn, named after a famous painting of a naked chick; the Jazz, named after a music that was considered to be a concatenation of vulgarity). Old Cocktails were dug up and rebored to fit the new spirit, and everybody ran around trying to figure out how to make 'em all.

1 JIGGER [2 OZ] BACARDI RUM

2 DASHES [1 TSP] GUM SYRUP

JUICE OF ½ LIME

Shake well in a mixing glass with cracked ice, strain and serve.

SOURCE: HUGO ENSSLIN, *RECIPES FOR MIXED DRINKS*
(1916; ENSSLIN ACTUALLY CALLS THIS THE "CUBAN COCKTAIL," BUT HE
CORRECTS IT IN A LATER EDITION. JACQUES STRAUB HAD
ALREADY PUBLISHED A FORMULA IN 1914, BUT IT WAS GARBLED)

NOTES ON INGREDIENTS: In the absence of true Cuban Bacardi, one is reduced to finding a substitute or smuggling Havana Club in from abroad (the Cuban H. C. is made in part in the old Bacardi plant). This is of course illegal (but get the three-year-old). The Flor de Caña from Nicaragua is a fine and economical substitute, but many other white rums will work as well. Alas, the modern Bacardi is not among them—it's just too light (10 Cane, from Trinidad, is another favorite). Some Progressive Era American bartenders took to sweetening their Daiquiris—aka "Bacardi Cocktails"—with grenadine. This makes for a nice pink drink, but it muddies up the clean flavor of the original. A better option is to make it the Cuban way, with ½ teaspoon of superfine sugar as the only sweetener.

NOTES ON EXECUTION: If you make this with superfine sugar, dissolve it in the lime juice before adding the rum and ice. Daiquiris were often served frappé, which is to say poured into a Cocktail glass full of finely shaved ice. Save this option for days when it's 100 degrees with 100 percent humidity.

AVIATION COCKTAIL

One of the last truly great Cocktails to be invented before Prohibition. In recent years, this once-obscure combination of gin, lemon juice, and maraschino liqueur has become a favorite of true Cocktail fiends everywhere. It is generally considered to be a London drink, since its most prominent early appearance was in Harry Craddock's classic *Savoy Cocktail Book*, published in 1930. In fact, its origins lie in pre-Prohibition New York, for it is among the formulae found in the last serious Cocktail book published in Gotham before the great drought—the 1916 *Recipes for Mixed Drinks*, by the thirty-year-old German-born head bartender at the Wallick House Hotel in Times Square, Hugo Ensslin. Although Ensslin's book was one of the prime sources for both Craddock (who nicked from it such Savoy favorites as the Affinity, the Fair

Lemon Squeezers.

No. D 371. The Rapid Lemon Squeezer.

Is made to clamp to Bar. The Cup and Cone between which lemon is placed are of Solid Aluminum, thus avoiding all danger of corrosion. When handle is lowered, the plunger not only presses down on lemon, but also rotates, thus securing every drop of juice. This lemon squeezer is "rapid" in its operation and is especially valuable where a large number of lemons are used. A whole day's supply can be prepared in a few moments. The Cup catches both seed and pulp so that you secure the pure juice.

Price...........$2.45 each.

For the citrus-heavy Cocktails fashionable in the years before Prohibition, bartenders rolled out the heavy artillery. (Author's collection)

and Warmer, the Fluffy Ruffles, and the Raymond Hitchcocktail) and Patrick Gavin Duffy, whose classic *Official Mixer's Manual* plundered it wholesale, the extreme rarity of *Recipes for Mixed Drinks* has prevented its author from getting credit where it is due.

Of course, just because Ensslin printed the first recipe for the Aviation, that doesn't mean he invented it—the only notice of the drink I've been able to find in the contemporary press, a 1911 three-liner from the pages of the Albany, New York, *Knickerbocker Press*, merely notes that "The 'aviation cocktail' is the latest," with no clue as to its origin. The new sport of aviation was much in the news at the time, and there were two other drinks of the same name floating around (one merely a Jack Rose with a dash of absinthe, the other a rather unimpressive fifty-fifty mix of Dubonnet and dry sherry with an orange twist)—and no hint of who might be responsible for them, either.

One thing that has always puzzled the drink's aficionados:

Whence the name? Here, too, Ensslin makes himself useful. His Aviation recipe calls for one additional ingredient that didn't make it into Craddock's final recipe: Besides the maraschino, there's also a bit of crème de violette, a violet-flavored liqueur that tints the drink a pale sky blue and, incidentally, explains its name.

⅓ [¾ OZ] **LEMON JUICE**

⅔ [1½ OZ] **EL BART GIN**

2 DASHES [1½ TSP] **MARASCHINO**

2 DASHES [1 TSP] **CRÈME DE VIOLETTE**

Shake well in a mixing glass with cracked ice, and serve.

SOURCE: HUGO ENSSLIN, *RECIPES FOR MIXED DRINKS* (1916)

NOTES ON INGREDIENTS: El Bart has gone to that happy land far, far away where Crazy Eddie zooms around in his Kaiser-Frazer with his arm around Virginia Dare and Burma Shave loafing in the backseat. No matter; since El Bart was a sponsor of Ensslin's book, we can assume that its selection here was driven by other than gustatory necessity. In other words, use the (dry) gin you like. To my palate, Ensslin's equilibrium between the maraschino and crème de violette produces a drink that tastes like hand soap; I prefer more maraschino and less of the blue stuff—just enough to produce the requisite color, but not so much as to shoot the drink down. If you like it sweeter, it's better to round the drink out with a touch of simple syrup rather than adding more of the liqueurs, as they have a tendency to hijack the drink.

WARD EIGHT

The Ward Eight looms large in the mythical history of mixology, wherein it stands tall as the Champion of the Hub, proving to one and all that when Boston was called upon to contribute a Cocktail to the great pageant of American intoxication, it did not say "I shall not serve." The story goes—well, if I may quote myself, here's what I said in *Esquire Drinks*: "They say this old smoothie was inaugurated at Boston's ancient Locke-Ober restaurant, at the victory supper (held the night *before* the election, naturally) for Martin 'the Mahatma' Lomasney, running for something or other from Boston's Ward Eight." All well and good, but try documenting it. Other than a garbled description—as "what the Irish drink in Boston"—in a 1918 novel (which, truth be told, does add that after one "you're ready to vote right," which may be a jab at its origin) and a passing reference in a 1920 *New York Times* article about the dawn of Prohibition in Massachusetts, the newspapers and history books are of no assistance. Considered from a mixological point of view, the presence of grenadine in the drink makes it somewhat unlikely that it goes all the way back to 1898, when the little drama in question supposedly took place; grenadine was the hot ingredient of the 1910s, and very rare before that. But we may never know.

The only pre-Prohibition recipe for the drink is a rather lackluster affair, so I've taken the liberty of substituting one a reader sent to G. Selmer Fougner of the *New York Sun* when he called for information on the drink, right after repeal. "The basis of a 'Ward 8' was a whisky sour," the reader wrote with unmistakable authority, "the idea being to eliminate certain objectionable features of that drink. The Ward 8 was distinctly a warm weather drink, and should be so considered. It was always served in a large, heavy glass of the type generally used for beer—that is, with a large round bowl." His recipe is equally precise.

[NOTE: FOR QUANTITIES, SEE NOTES ON EXECUTION, BELOW.]

Juice of one lemon, one barspoon of powdered sugar, a large whisky glass three-quarters full of Bourbon (dissolve the sugar in the juice and whisky), place a rather large piece of ice, in the glass, pour in glass, add three or four dashes of orange bitters, three dashes of crème de menthe, one-half jigger grenadine, fill glass with either plain water or seltzer, add two half slices orange, piece of pineapple and one or two cherries.

When fresh mint is available the crème de menthe is omitted, and a slightly bruised sprig of mint added with the slices of orange, &c. This is an improvement.

Many prefer the juice of half an orange instead of the orange bitters.

The amount of sugar should be regulated to taste, and likewise the grenadine. The important factors are good liquor and care in mixing. Properly made, the drink is very pleasant, although highly potent.

SOURCE: G. SELMER FOUGNER, *ALONG THE WINE TRAIL* (1934)

NOTES ON INGREDIENTS: This is always considered to be a rye drink, and is described as such in that sole pre-Prohibition recipe, from *The Cocktail Book: A Sideboard Manual for Gentlemen* (numerous editions from 1900 through the 1910s; the early ones don't have the Ward Eight, though). I say use the fresh mint instead of the crème de menthe and the orange juice instead of the orange bitters.

NOTES ON EXECUTION: The man knows what he's talking about, but it's a little hard to untangle what he's saying. I offer this as an aide to construction:

Combine in mixing glass,

JUICE OF 1 LEMON

JUICE OF ½ ORANGE

1 BARSPOON SUPERFINE SUGAR

Stir until sugar dissolves, and add:

3 OZ RYE WHISKEY

1 SPRIG OF MINT

Add ice, shake gently so as not to brutalize the mint and strain into a large beer-goblet containing 1 or 2 large ice cubes. Add grenadine to taste (a half-ounce should be plenty) and fill with chilled seltzer. Fruit as above.

IV. ENTER VERMOUTH

Until 1880 or so, all Cocktails, be they basic, Fancy, Improved, Evolved, or Crusta, shared a basic philosophy. Unlike Punches, which always sought to be a blend of flavors without one dominating, Cocktails were built to point up or accent the flavor of their base liquor without disguising it. With rare exception (i.e., the Japanese Cocktail), the other ingredients were measured in dashes or spoonfuls, not ounces or glassfuls. The resulting drinks were pungent, boozy, and strong. They were also delicious, but they demanded a consumer who was acclimatized to the taste of liquor and knew how to stow it away.

As the Gilded Age unfolded, cutting-edge Cocktail drinkers began to look for something lighter and more urbane than a shot of bittered booze; something more refined and Epicurean and with less savor of riverboat bars and tobacco chaws, bare-knuckle bouts and faro dens. One result was the birth of the Cocktail Punch (and no surprise that it was born in Creole New Orleans). When that was still in its infancy, though, another path suddenly suggested itself. In 1871, Bonfort's *Wine and Liquor Circular* was already on it:

> If we must have an appetizer before dinner, Absinthe or Vermouth deserve the preference over the antiquated and fiery cocktail; and of the two we consider the Vermouth the more desirable beverage. If it is of good Italian origin and properly cooled . . . it is a decidedly good thing.

Vermouth had been known in America for some time. Its Italian and French makers had made several attempts to penetrate the bibulous American market. The precursor to Martini & Rossi may have tried as early as 1836, and Noilly Prat was shipping its dry vermouth to New Orleans in 1851 and San Francisco in 1853; for the rest of the decade, it turns up in liquor ads in gold-country newspapers, so somebody up in the hills must've been drinking it (there were lots of French miners and whores up in those hills).

In any case, as the passage from Bonfort's suggests, it was the Italian stuff—the red, sweet kind—that was getting the traction. By the 1860s, anyway, it was pretty well established in New York and had even reached places like Galveston, Texas, and Dubuque, Iowa. If not exactly a sensation, this "vino vermouth," as it was known, enjoyed enough of a reputation for Delmonico's and the

Metropolitan Hotel to carry it on their wine lists, the latter selling it for a respectable $3 a quart (its best cognac was only $8). It wasn't until the 1880s, though, that it took off, first with the help of the Manhattan, then, in the 1890s, with the Martini, and then, as the new century opened, with, well, just about everything.

VERMOUTH COCKTAIL

Once people noticed vermouth and began poking at it, it was inevitable that sooner or later somebody was going to try to make a Cocktail out of it. After all, this was America, and Cocktails were what we drank. We don't know who served as guinea pig or where the experiment was conducted or, for that matter, who conducted it, but its protocol was recorded in 1869, in the invaluable *Steward & Barkeeper's Manual*. While not a world-beater, for a number of years after that the Vermouth Cocktail maintained its place in the pharmacopoeia. In the field, it was most commonly prescribed as—what else?—a hangover cure. But its use wasn't limited to that; there were plenty who appreciated its gentle touch. As an 1885 newspaper squib noted, "James R. Keene [Robber Baron and horseman extraordinaire] cheers himself to vermouth cocktails because 'they don't break you up.'" If, by the turn of the century, it was getting pretty old-fashioned, the anonymous author of *The Banquet Book* (1902) could still note that "This cocktail is liked by not a few and generally secures constant advocates." After that, while we still hear of the Vermouth Cocktail here and there until Prohibition, it's rarely spoken of with much affection and one gets the impression that the people who ordered it secretly in their hearts of hearts lusted after something with just a little more, well, alcohol in it.

The first recipe for a "Vermuth [sic] Cocktail" is a simple affair, but then again, it's not a drink that needs a lot of looking after.

One wine glass [2 oz] of vermuth; one very small piece of ice; one small piece of lemon peel. Serve in a thin stemmed glass with curved lip.

SOURCE: *STEWARD & BARKEEPER'S MANUAL*, 1869

NOTES ON INGREDIENTS: This drink will work just fine with the standard red Martini & Rossi or Cinzano. If, however, you can find the Carpano Formula Antica, all of the sudden you've got a real drink on your hands. The tiny piece of ice is to avoid dilution; if you keep the vermouth refrigerated, you'll be able to use more ice, and you should. Some later recipes specify bitters; depending on the vermouth you use, this may or may not be an enhancement. With the heavily aromatized Carpano, they're superfluous. In 1884, O. H. Byron printed a version of the Vermouth Cocktail made with 1½ ounces of French vermouth, 3 dashes of Angostura bitters, and ½ teaspoon or so of gum syrup. This is a most pleasant tipple, particularly in summer. For a **Fancy Vermouth Cocktail**, as delineated in the 1887 edition of Thomas's book, use a couple dashes of Angostura and 1 teaspoon of maraschino and replace the twist with a quarter-wheel of lemon, which can be perched on the rim or floated on top. What the hell.

NOTES ON EXECUTION: The 1887 edition of Thomas's book recommends that this drink be shaken and strained; again, overdilution is a concern here—which way to go depends on if you prefer a very cold drink or a concentrated one.

MANHATTAN COCKTAIL

The Vermouth Cocktail is no doubt a fine thing, offering as it does a bold presence on the palate while still being low in impact—perhaps too low. You go to all the trouble of hitching your foot up on the rail, engaging Ed in conversation, supervising his movements as he dashes and splashes and waltzes everything around with ice, and the straining, and the twisting, and the sliding, and the paying, and what do you get for your fifteen cents? Something with no more kick to it than the little glass of sherry your maiden aunt takes when the fantods have got her. But what if you put a stick in it?

Rye, gin, brandy, it doesn't matter. Just a little something to make you feel like you've had a drink.

That's one possibility. On the other hand there's this one. The Whiskey—or Gin, or Brandy—Cocktail is no doubt a fine thing, offering as it does a smooth presence on the palate while still being high in impact—perhaps too high. You go to all the trouble of hitching your foot up on the rail and all the rest, and what do you get for your fifteen cents? Drunk, that's what. The problem with these things is they go down so easy that you want to treat your throat to a couple or three just to show your appreciation for the fine job it's been doing you, but next thing you know it's next Thursday and you're in Oakland with what feels like three black eyes and an anchor tattooed on your arm. But what if you turned the damper down a little, took that new vermouth stuff—plenty flavorful but no John L. Sullivan—and replaced some of the booze with it? Maybe you could have a drink or two without all the vaudeville.

These, then, are the two mixological theories on the origin of the Manhattan and, by extension, the Martini. The earliest recipes provide support for both. However spirits and vermouth first came together, once joined they quickly demonstrated that drinks as complex and subtle in flavor as the most baroque Regency-era Punches could be turned out over the bar as quickly as Stone Fences or Black Strap. The author of the anonymous 1898 *Cocktails: How to Make Them* nailed it when he wrote, "The addition of Vermouth was the first move toward the blending of cocktails." The Martini would ultimately be this new movement's standard bearer, but it was the Manhattan that was the first out of the trenches.

The Manhattan Cocktail is a New York native. That much everybody agrees on. Things begin to come apart a bit in the details, though—specifically, in the universally repeated story that it was invented for a banquet hosted by Jennie Jerome, Winston Churchill's mother, at New York's Manhattan Club to celebrate Samuel J. Tilden's election as governor. This story, one of the most widely propagated of all drink myths, could hold up, except for the fact that the inaugural celebrations happened to coincide with

Lady Winston's delivery and christening of baby Winston—in Oxfordshire. And no, he wasn't christened with Manhattan Cocktails. Having sloughed off Mr. Tilden and Ms. Jerome,* must we also slough off the Manhattan Club itself? According to William F. Mulhall, bartender at the Hoffman House from 1882 until it closed in 1915, we must: "The Manhattan cocktail was invented by a man named Black, who kept a place ten doors below Houston Street on Broadway in the sixties." There may be some truth in this: City directories from the 1870s do show one William Black operating a saloon on Bowery, although above Houston, not below. On the other hand, there's significant evidence for the Manhattan Club's ownership of the drink as well. For one thing, there's the Boston bartender who stated that "the Manhattan cocktail originated in the mind of the drink mixer at the Manhattan Club's rooms in New York." He was interviewed in 1889, thirty-three years before Mulhall's recollections saw print. This theory was seconded in the pages of the *New York Times* in 1902 when "Bobbie," who wrote the "With the Clubmen" column, tossed off as a passing remark that "legend" had it "the Manhattan Club . . . first gave birth to the Manhattan Cocktail."

The club's 1915 official history confirms this, stating simply that "The celebrated Manhattan cocktail was inaugurated at the club." Unfortunately, none of the multitudinous pre-Prohibition references to the Manhattan that I've examined indicate what circumstances attended its inauguration. There is, however, the rumor Carol Truax printed in the April 1963 issue of *Gourmet*, to the effect that the drink was invented by "some anonymous genius" during August Belmont's presidency of the club, which ran from 1874 to 1879. Since her father had been president of the club himself, in the 1890s, this may have some weight. But it may have even predated Belmont's presidency. Consider this little item from the *Galveston Daily News*:

---

* The Jerome part of the story probably comes from the fact that the Manhattan Club later occupied a house once owned by Leonard Jerome, Jennie's father (the same building, in fact, that had housed the Turf Club; see Appendix III).

The New York Club has a peculiar cocktail. It is made of the best brandy and several different kinds of bitters, and they always want it shaken in ice, not stirred. The Amaranth Club has a cocktail made with seltzer, and the Manhattan Club has invented another.

That was published in September 1873. Now, there's no guarantee that this Manhattan Club invention is the drink we all know and love, but there's nothing here to say it isn't. If so, it's extraordinarily early for a Cocktail mixed with vermouth; it would be almost a decade before such things reached general acceptance.

By the mid-1880s, anyway, the Manhattan was common property. Some indications of its progress: On September 5, 1882, the Manhattan made its first appearance in print, in the pages of the *Olean (NY) Democrat*: "It is but a short time ago that a mixture of whiskey, vermouth and bitters came into vogue," notes the paper's "New York Letter." "It went under various names—Manhattan cocktail, Turf Club cocktail, and Jockey Club cocktail. Bartenders at first were sorely puzzled what was wanted when it was demanded. But now they are fully cognizant of its various aliases and no difficulty is encountered." By 1884, the Manhattan had made its way into the bartender's guides. In 1885, the *New Orleans Times-Democrat* pronounced it "a juicy and delicious compound" while the *Brooklyn Eagle* had a "solitary, discontented and rocky specimen" of the New York bachelor walking into a swank Broadway restaurant at breakfast time and addressing the waiter with considerable irritation: "Stand still, can't you? You make a man's head swim bobbing around so. What I want is a Manhattan cocktail with absinthe, frozen [i.e., with shaved ice in the glass]." The Ranch saloon in Albuquerque was proudly offering it to all and sundry in 1886, with a splash of Mumm's champagne to boot. The first recipe for a Dry Manhattan turned up in 1891, in the second edition of O. H. Byron's *Modern Bartender's Guide*. The Cleveland *Leader* dubbed it the "seductive and unconquerable Manhattan Cocktail" in 1892. In the 1894 obituary of Gen. Jubal Early, the most unreconstructed of Confederate generals, it was noted that in recent years "his headquarters for ordinary friends were at the Norvall-Arlington saloon at Lynchburg [Virginia], where his favorite tipple was a Manhattan Cocktail." Since that's like Pat Robertson listening to Boy George, it's a good place to leave things.

Rather than provide a single recipe, I've provided three, each illustrating a different school of Manhattanistics.

FORMULA #1 (OLD STANDARD)

These proportions, the same used at the Manhattan Club, were by far the most popular for the first twenty years or so of the drink's existence. They yield what is essentially a Whiskey Cocktail lightened with vermouth.

(USE LARGE BAR-GLASS.)

TWO OR THREE DASHES OF PERUVIAN BITTERS

ONE TO TWO DASHES [½ TSP] OF GUM SYRUP

ONE-HALF WINE GLASS [1½ OZ] OF WHISKEY

ONE-HALF WINE GLASS [1½ OZ] OF VERMOUTH

Fill glass three-quarters full of fine shaved ice, mix well with a spoon, strain in fancy cocktail glass and serve.

SOURCE: *HOW TO MIX DRINKS—BAR KEEPER'S HANDBOOK*, 1884

NOTES ON INGREDIENTS: Peruvian bitters were an advertiser in the little bar manual put out by New York's G. Winter Brewing Co., from which this recipe hails, and must be evaluated as such. Angostura bitters, Abbott's bitters, and Peychaud's bitters appear in other early Manhattan recipes, though according to its official history the Manhattan Club made them with orange bitters, which are a nice touch (and endorsed by Harry Johnson, whose opinion is not to be taken lightly). The gum can be dispensed with, without affecting the drink's allure in any way.

The Manhattan has been enshrined in tradition as a rye drink, but this recipe isn't alone in calling for plain "whiskey," which could mean rye, but also bourbon or even a blended whiskey. Out of twenty-odd pre-Prohibition recipes consulted, only four specified which kind of whiskey should be used, and two of those went with bourbon. In the northeast, anyway, that generic "whiskey" would generally be taken as rye, but not always. As much of a rye partisan as I am, I've nonetheless found that the choice of rye or bourbon is less important than the choice of 80- or 100-proof whiskey. All things being equal, a 100-proof rye will make the best Manhattan, but a 100-proof bourbon will make a more incisive and balanced drink than an 80-proof rye. This holds particularly true when mixing them fifty-fifty, like this version calls for.

The earliest recipes mention no garnish for this drink—no cherry, no twist. Before long, both found their way in there. Personally, I prefer the twist.

FORMULA #2 (REVERSE)

The one-to-two "reverse" ratio here—essentially, a Vermouth Cocktail with a stick—makes for a light and aromatic drink, if somewhat deficient in Manhattanness (to coin a word). In any case, it was copied a few times by plagiaristic mixographers but had no legs in the marketplace.

(USE SMALL BAR-GLASS.)

TAKE 2 [1 TSP] DASHES OF CURAÇOA OR MARASCHINO

1 PONY [1 OZ] OF RYE WHISKEY

1 WINE-GLASS [2 OZ] OF VERMOUTH

3 DASHES OF BOKER'S BITTERS

2 SMALL LUMPS OF ICE

Shake up well, and strain into a claret glass. Put a quarter of a slice of lemon in the glass and serve. If the customer prefers it very sweet use also two dashes [1 tsp] of gum syrup.

SOURCE: *JERRY THOMAS'S BAR-TENDER'S GUIDE*, 1887

NOTES ON INGREDIENTS: The maraschino makes for a more interesting drink. This is the earliest Manhattan recipe to specify rye, which should again be 100-proof. In place of Boker's, Fee's Aromatic bitters work well in this one. The small amount of ice here is a holdover from the Vermouth Cocktail, and indicates a desire to avoid overdilution. A century and a quarter of experience with vermouth in Cocktails has taught us that this need not be a concern, so feel free to ice con brio.

NOTES ON EXECUTION: Some mixologists are just shaker-happy, and the guy who revised Jerry Thomas's book is one of them. Stir. The claret glass is specified because at 3 ounces before shaking, this drink is bigger than the standard Cocktail glass of the day would safely accommodate; our Cocktail glasses are bigger, so use one. For what to do with the lemon, see the Fancy Vermouth Cocktail (page 236).

FORMULA #3 (NEW STANDARD)

By adjusting the whiskey so that it outweighs the vermouth, this version turns a pleasant, avuncular drink into an incisive, modern one. Kudos to the Only William.

HALF A TUMBLERFUL OF CRACKED ICE

2 DASHES [½ TSP] OF GUM

2 DASHES OF BITTERS

1 DASH OF ABSINTHE

⅔ DRINK [2 OZ] OF WHISKEY

⅓ DRINK [1 OZ] OF VINO VERMOUTH

(A LITTLE [¼ TSP] MARASCHINO MAY BE ADDED.)

Stir this well, strain and serve.

SOURCE: WILLIAM "THE ONLY WILLIAM" SCHMIDT, *THE FLOWING BOWL*, 1892

NOTES ON INGREDIENTS: Be sure to use the right whiskey, as specified above. The gum is eminently dispensable. As for the bitters: Angostura is the modern choice, and has always worked fabulously well in this drink. In the Manhattan's youth, many of its communicants liked the dash of absinthe in theirs, and it does make for a fragrant drink. In fact, if you follow the skilled, creative, and popular bartender William Schmidt's formula to a T, maraschino and all, you've got a drink that is a perfect metaphor for the 1890s, a decade of top hats and electric lights, automobiles and buggy whips. A final twist of lemon peel will do the drink, or you, no harm.

MARTINI COCKTAIL

Whiskey and vermouth having proved itself to be a successful combination, it didn't take long for the bartenders to fall back on standard procedure and try the red stuff out with brandy (see the Metropole, page 249) and gin—indeed, one or both of these combinations may even have come first. It really doesn't matter—the way mixology was practiced in the Gilded Age, to try one combination was to try them all. The whiskey version was merely the most successful—at first, anyway: While the brandy one never amounted to much

MARTINE COCKTAIL.
Copyrighted, 1888.

The Martine, Martinez, Martini or Turf Club, as Mixed (left) and Served (right). From Harry Johnson's *New and Improved Illustrated Bartender's Manual*, 1888. (Courtesy Gary Regan)

with the general tippling public, the gin one, after some tinkering to be sure, would eventually eclipse them all.

The Origin of the Martini is one of those topics that is too large for a headnote; you'll find my thoughts on it in Appendix III. Suffice it to say that it appears close on the heels of the Manhattan, in the same precincts. Here, I'll confine my remarks to matters mixological. The early recipes for the Martini (or Martinez, or Martine, or Turf Club) all called for sweet vermouth and Old Tom gin, which was lighter and more mixable than the old-school Hollands that worked so well in the Gin Cocktail. (Hollands combines poorly with vermouth, as the bartenders discovered for themselves—their unanimity in avoiding it in the Martini was no doubt born of experience.) As with the Manhattan, I've given three recipes, a Turf Club from 1884, to show the drink in its infancy; a Martinez from 1887, to show the reverse option; and a Fourth Degree, from the old Waldorf-Astoria's bar book (so circa 1915), to show it in its maturity. ("Origin somewhat mixed," says the Waldorf-Astoria's chronicler about the last, "but traceable to patrons of the bar who belonged to some secret society or other.") I can vouch for the extraordinary palatability of all three.

FORMULA #1 (TURF CLUB)

TWO OR THREE DASHES OF PERUVIAN BITTERS

ONE-HALF WINE GLASS [1½ OZ] OF TOM GIN

ONE-HALF WINE GLASS [1½ OZ] OF ITALIAN VERMOUTH

Fill glass three quarters full of fine ice, stir well with spoon and strain in fancy cocktail glass, then serve.

SOURCE: *HOW TO MIX DRINKS—BAR-KEEPER'S HANDBOOK*, 1884

NOTES ON INGREDIENTS: For the bitters, see Manhattan Formula #1 (page 240); although for something a bit more integrated in flavor, use Angostura. The loss of Old Tom gin is irreparable, although if you can get your hands on a bottle of the discontinued Tanqueray Malacca you'll come pretty close. Otherwise, Damrak or Junipero are good, thicker-bodied gins to try. If you want maximum authenticity, add a dash—say, ¼ teaspoon—of gum. As with the early Manhattan recipes, this one specifies no garnish. A twist of lemon peel is always welcome, though. Most early recipes for the Martini/Martinez include a couple of dashes of gum on top of the (sweet) Tom gin and the (sweet) Vermouth. For the modern palate, this is entirely unnecessary—and not just the modern palate: As "Cocktail" Boothby noted in 1891, "The Old Tom Cordial gin and Italian vermouth of which the [Martini] are composed are both sweet enough."

FORMULA #2:
MARTINEZ COCKTAIL

(USE SMALL BAR-GLASS.)

TAKE 1 DASH OF BOKER'S BITTERS

2 DASHES [1 TSP] OF MARASCHINO

1 PONY [1 OZ] OF OLD TOM GIN

1 WINE-GLASS [2 OZ] OF VERMOUTH

2 SMALL LUMPS OF ICE

Shake up thoroughly, and strain into a large cocktail glass. Put a quarter of a slice of lemon in the glass, and serve. If the guest prefers it very sweet, add two dashes [½ tsp] of gum syrup.

SOURCE: *JERRY THOMAS'S BAR-TENDERS' GUIDE*, 1887

NOTES ON INGREDIENTS: For the bitters and gin, see Formula #1 (page 244). Maraschino and gin have a particular affinity for each other, and even though the gin is the junior partner in this reverse-proportion Martini, the pairing shines through. For the ice, see Manhattan Formula #2 (page 241).

NOTES ON EXECUTION: Don't shake, stir!

FORMULA #3:
FOURTH DEGREE

ONE-THIRD [1 OZ] **ITALIAN VERMOUTH**

TWO-THIRDS [2 OZ] **PLYMOUTH GIN**

DASH OF ABSINTHE

SOURCE: ALBERT STEVENS CROCKETT, *OLD WALDORF BAR DAYS* (1931)

NOTES ON INGREDIENTS: Self-explanatory. A very simple drink. For an old-school drink, use 1½ ounces of gin to ¾ ounce of vermouth. For a more modern one, go with what's sugested. As always with a vermouth drink, lemon peel is nice.

NOTES ON EXECUTION: Stir with plenty of cracked ice and strain.

DRY MARTINI COCKTAIL

The Martini, when it hit its stride in the late 1880s, brought a new interest to gin drinks. At the same time, there were new gins coming into the market. Dry, unsweetened gins. In fact, the whole tenor of the age was dry (ironically, since in a few years it would be Dry)—dry champagne, dry gin, dry Cocktails. When, in 1897, the *New York Herald* asked "the proprietor of a fashionable drinking place" about this, he gave vent to the following:

> When a customer comes in and orders a sweet drink, . . . I know at once that he's from the country. In all my acquaintance with city men, I know not more than half a dozen who can stand drinking sweet things. It is only the young fellows from the farm, with their rosy cheeks and sound stomachs, who can stand a course of sugary drinks. The reason for this is obvious. The more

sugar a man takes into his stomach the less he can stand of liquors. A year ago I used a quart a day of 'gum,' which is the general term applied to all the syrups used to sweeten whiskies and mixtures. Today I use barely a whisky glass of gum, and my business has increased, too. People are beginning to realize that their stomachs are not of cast iron. They want everything dry, the drier the better.

We don't know who poured the very first true Dry Martini—that is, Plymouth or London dry gin mixed with French vermouth and no syrup—but clearly it was in the air. The *Herald* piece, anyway, gives three separate versions of the drink, under different names. Here's the one from the Hoffman House; head bartender Charlie Mahoney called it the "Mahoney Cocktail," but it's really just a standard, turn-of-the-last-century Dry Martini.

That is nothing to be sneezed at. Mixed like this, with half gin and half vermouth and a dash of orange bitters, the Martini is an entirely different drink from the one we know and, as many still believe, a superior one. For those who have learned the Dry Martini as a fiery chalice of unmixed tanglefoot, it will come as a revelation. A gentleman among Cocktails.

Use mixing glass full of shaved ice.

Add one-half jigger [1½ oz] of Nicholson gin, one-half jigger [1½ oz] French Vermouth and dash Orange bitters; shake well. Pour into cocktail glass and squeeze orange peel on top.

SOURCE: CHARLIE MAHONEY, *HOFFMAN HOUSE BARTENDER'S GUIDE* (1906)

NOTES ON INGREDIENTS: For the vanished Nicholson, use Tanqueray or Beefeater. The gin must be strong and aromatic if it's to stand up to this much vermouth (which should be Noilly Prat). The orange bitters are essential, but lemon peel will work as well as orange peel here. By 1900, an order like the one in Lilian Bell's novel, *The Expatriates*, for "Dry Martini . . . with an olive in it" would be understood at any fancy bar in the country.

NOTES ON EXECUTION: Probably better to stir this one, if you want that thick, silky Martini texture.

GIBSON COCKTAIL

If the paternity of the Martinez rests on shaky ground, California's contribution to the art and evolution of the Dry Martini is far more firmly anchored. "The Gibson," wrote the *Oakland Tribune* in 1915, "is a blend peculiar to San Francisco. Since its introduction along the cocktail route in this town, it has become known over the two great divides, across the rivers and valleys and in the cavernous canyons of a metropolis just beyond Jersey City." If, as San Francisco's own Bill Boothby asserted, it was named after (and presumably championed by) Charles Dana Gibson, that couldn't have hurt its distribution—Gibson was just about the most popular artist in America. On the other hand, it may very well have been named after San Francisco financier and Bohemian Club member Walter D. K. Gibson, whose family maintains that the club's bartender made the drink under his instructions in 1898 or thereabouts. Whichever Gibson it was, the drink was nationwide by 1904.

None of the early mentions of the Gibson include the now-iconic pickled onion. I suspect that the onion was added in later years as an attribute by which to distinguish the Gibson from the Dry Martini, once the latter had sloughed off the dashes of bitters that had been the distinguishing mark between them.

A la Charles Dana Gibson, Bohemian Club, San Francisco

Equal parts [1½ oz each] **of French Vermouth and Coates Plymouth Gin, thoroughly chilled, is called a Gibson Cocktail. No decorations, bitters or citron fruit rind permissible in this famous appetizer.**

SOURCE: WILLIAM "COCKTAIL" BOOTHBY, "SOME NEW UP-TO-NOW SEDUCTIVE AMERICAN COCKTAILS" (UNDATED SUPPLEMENT TO *THE WORLD'S DRINKS AND HOW TO MIX THEM*, 1908)

NOTES ON INGREDIENTS: The *Tribune* indicated that the drink was made with one particular brand of gin and one particular brand of vermouth, but coyly refused to name either. It did, however, give the proportions as "60-40" dry gin to vermouth. If made thus, I find Plymouth works swimmingly; if mixed 50-50, I prefer the more assertive Tanqueray. N.P. for the vermouth, as usual. As for garnish. In the exceedingly rare *Rawling's Book of Mixed Drinks*, from 1914, San Francisco mixologist Ernest P. Rawling, who knew his onions, noted that "a hazelnut [presumably pickled] is generally added." Beyond that, the early recipes are unadorned.

NOTES ON EXECUTION: Stir with plenty of cracked ice.

V. OTHER VERMOUTH COCKTAILS

In the first two decades of the twentieth century, vermouth Cocktails multiplied like listeria in warm egg salad. The bar-book of the Old Waldorf-Astoria, just for example, had 174 of them. I shall restrain myself and offer only another 5 percent or so of that number (you're not necessarily missing much—something like two-thirds of those 174 recipes were for variations on the gin-and-vermouth Martini).

METROPOLE COCKTAIL

If there's a Cocktail with whiskey and vermouth and one with gin and vermouth, could one with brandy and vermouth be far behind? The question is of course rhetorical. In 1884, the *London Telegraph* was already talking about American bartenders considering "a vermouth cocktail with a dash of brandy in it" to be "de rigeur, just before lunch." And indeed, that same year O. H. Byron included a brandy-and-vermouth "Metropolitan Cocktail" in his *Modern Bartender's Guide*. Unfortunately, he neglects to indicate precisely which Metropolitan it hailed from. At the time, there were various Metropolitan Clubs, Metropolitan

Saloons, and Metropolitan Hotels scattered throughout the country, from the largest cities to the wildest mining camps. Nor is there anything to be deduced from the author's biography: Byron, alas, is a man of mystery. Extensive digging through newspaper archives, city directories, and census records has failed to reveal exactly who the hell he was. I don't even know what city he worked in, let alone what establishment, if any: For all I know, "O. H. Byron" may be the Excelsior Publishing House of New York's nom de plume for some lawyer's clerk hired to scrape together a ream of drink recipes. But whoever collected them, the recipes—at least, the few that weren't directly poached from Jerry Thomas—are well chosen. What's more, considered closely they display an insider's knowledge of what the boys were drinking in New York. The book provides, for instance, a recipe for the Amaranth Cocktail that tallies with the Cocktail attributed to the Amaranth Club (a Gotham theatrical club) in the *Galveston Daily News* in 1873 (see the Manhattan) and, more important, recipes for the Manhattan itself (tied for the first in print) and the Martinez (the first). All this is by way of lengthy preamble to suggesting that the most likely culprit for the Metropolitan Cocktail was probably Jerry Thomas's old stand, the bar at the Metropolitan Hotel.

The Metropolitan Hotel closed in 1895, only a few years after the Considine brothers opened up the Metropole Hotel, at the quiet corner of Forty-second Street and Broadway. The Metropolitan had been favored by actors and politicians. The Metropole drew actors and politicians, too—though where the Metropolitan's were touring thespians and congressmen, the Metropole's were burlesque stars and ward-heelers. And there were a lot of pugilists, cardsharps, workers of the short con, organized gamblers, chorus girls, you name it. Small wonder: George Considine was a bookmaker, John R. was an ex–theatrical manager, and James P., who ran the café, was an amateur painter on the lam from an armed robbery rap in Ohio. O. Henry hung out there, of course, until he pissed off Jimmy by telling him he didn't know how to paint cows (he was, after all, a Texan, and some things cannot pass unremarked).

The Metropole's house Cocktail is to the Metropolitan's as the one hotel was to the other: more or less the same ingredients, but stronger, spicier, and definitely flashier, yet not without style.

Two dashes gum-syrup [½ tsp], **two dashes Peyschaud** [sic] **bitters, one dash orange bitters, half a jigger** [1½ oz] **brandy, half a jigger** [1½ oz] **French vermouth, a mixing-glass half-full fine ice. Mix, strain into cocktail-glass, add a maraschino cherry.**

SOURCE: GEORGE J. KAPPELER, *MODERN AMERICAN DRINKS*, 1895

NOTES ON INGREDIENTS: Kappeler loved his Peychaud's bitters, but here they're a particularly good choice, as they blend beautifully with brandy—which, to be true to the old Metropole, should be a nice cognac, VSOP or better. Paul E. Lowe, "whose locks have been whitened by the shaved ice and powdered sugar of many a sweltering summer," as he boasted in his 1904 *Drinks as They Are Mixed*, suggests using 2 parts brandy to 1 vermouth. This is a fine suggestion. For a Metropolitan, replace both bitters with 3 dashes of Angostura, cut the cognac by half and add 1 barspoon of gum. It's worth noting that Kappeler finished his Metropolitan with the more elegant twist of lemon peel rather than the cherry, but what chorus girl would want to nibble on that?

NOTES ON EXECUTION: "Mix" means "stir."

ROB ROY COCKTAIL

In 1897, the *New York Herald* noted that "the Fifth-Avenue hotel has two new drinks this winter, the Star cocktail and the Rob Roy cocktail. . . ." We'll get to the Star in a moment. As for the Rob Roy, which was probably already a couple of years old when the Fifth Avenue got to it, seeing as the Reginald

DeKoven musical after which it was most likely named opened in 1895: "Of course, the Rob Roy is made of Scotch whisky. It is completed by vermouth and orange bitters."

In the 1900s and '10s, Scotch whiskey was all the rage. In the past, it had been imported in smallish quantities in its pure malt form and generally consumed hot (see the Hot Toddy, page 137). With the introduction of golf into America in the 1890s, there was a new interest in things Scottish. The whisky salesmen, real pioneers in the black arts of marketing, did not let this slip by them, and before you knew it Tommy Dewar and his ilk were sluicing the American provinces with liberal amounts of the new blended whiskies. Result: By 1900, the Scotch Highball was the most fashionable drink in America. Yet of the hundreds of Cocktails in Jaques Straub's *Drinks* and Hugo Ensslin's *Recipes for Mixed Drinks*—the two most comprehensive Cocktail books of the age—only a wee thirteen use Scotch, and the only one of them to gain any traction was the Rob Roy, which was the first of them all.

The fact is, Scotch is just plain tricky to mix with, and Italian vermouth happens to be one of the very few things with which it does get along. The Rob Roy was probably the result of sheer luck, of plugging Scotch into a now-standard formula and seeing what happened, but there's nothing wrong with being lucky.

A little stronger than the vermouth [i.e., Cocktail] **is this one, which is made warmer by half a jigger** [1½ oz] **of Scotch whiskey and the same amount of vermouth (Italian), with lemon peel and two dashes of bitters.**

SOURCE: *THE BANQUET BOOK*, 1902

NOTES ON INGREDIENTS: Although the early recipes all agree that the Rob Roy contains Scotch and vermouth, after that they're about as harmonious as a Glasgow pub at last call on a Saturday night. Proportions, brand of bitters, garnish, and kind of vermouth are all very much in play. Personally, I find French vermouth and Scotch to be a nasty combination, so I chose a recipe (which seems to have the additional advantage of being the very earliest for this drink) that agrees with me. If the proportions began at fifty-fifty, as was usual with vermouth drinks, before long they had gravitated to two-to-one. With the lower-proof liquors we get today, I prefer the latter. Of the various bitters suggested, I find orange bitters—and particularly Regans' Orange Bitters No. 6, with their complex bite—to work the best. And while you're at it, a twist of orange peel is particularly nice here.

NOTES ON EXECUTION: Stir. Strain. Twist.

STAR COCKTAIL

A further variation on the theme of brown liquor plus vermouth, the Star Cocktail enjoyed rather a vogue in the last years before Prohibition. It appears to have been a New York creation; at least, it was first attested to by George Kappeler, of the Holland House Hotel, in 1895 and soon after was being served at the Fifth Avenue Hotel. In its official history, the Manhattan Club claimed it as one of its own; it may be. Beyond that, and a brief mention in the *Philadelphia Inquirer* from early 1897, the archives are silent. Why was it called the Star? I don't know. It is nonetheless an entirely palatable tipple.

Fill a mixing-glass half-full fine ice, add two dashes [1/2 tsp] gum-syrup, three dashes Peyschaud [sic] or Angostura bitters, one-half jigger [1 1/2 oz] apple brandy, one-half jigger [1 1/2 oz] Italian vermouth. Mix, strain into cocktail-glass, twist small piece lemon-peel on top.

SOURCE: GEORGE J. KAPPELER, *MODERN AMERICAN DRINKS*, 1895

NOTES ON INGREDIENTS: The gum is strictly optional. I prefer Angostura in this, but Peychaud's bitters will work fine, too. (It's worth noting that the Fifth Avenue Hotel, noted for the quality of its bar, preferred orange bitters.) For the applejack, see the Jack

Rose (page 225). Harry Johnson suggested adding a dash of curaçao, which is also a nice touch.

The Manhattan Club blandly asserted that the drink was made with applejack, vermouth, yellow Chartreuse, and cherry bounce. I'm just impressed that anyone in electric-age New York had even heard of cherry bounce, a drink last seen in the city when Martha Washington hosted dinners for her husband at their house on Cherry Street—in a neighborhood that, by the time the Manhattan Club was founded, had been a vicious slum for fifty years. One could, I suppose, cautiously essay the effects of ½ teaspoon of the Chartreuse and a dash or two of cherry brandy on the drink. I await your correspondence.

SARATOGA COCKTAIL

This isn't the place for a history of Saratoga Springs, nineteenth-century New York's northern equivalent of the Hamptons, only with gambling. How pleasant it must have been to catch the morning steamboat and spend the day sipping cooling drinks from the bar and enjoying the breeze as the still largely agricultural Hudson Valley unspooled its vistas before you. A night on the water, and next morning you were there. Somehow, eighteen hours on a steamboat seems infinitely preferable to four hours on the Long Island Expressway.

Once there, the sport ran pretty high, especially later in the century. High-stakes table games courtesy of Jerry Thomas's pal John Morrissey and Richard Canfield, two of the greatest gamblers America has ever known; horseracing on a first-class track; beautiful women; roguish men; mediocre dinners (you can't have everything); ice cream; and potato chips—which were invented there. And, for them what wanted, there were Cocktails. As early as 1839, people were remarking on the "keen blades" who slept in in the mornings, antifogmatized immediately with a snort of cognac, smoked and lounged, lounged and smoked, emptied tumblers and popped corks. "At 6, four bottles of wine. Supper at 9. At 10, mint-julaps . . . At 11, cards and cocktails till 1." Then things got ugly.

By the 1880s, the Cocktail class had more or less taken over the resort. As if to acknowledge this, there were two different Saratoga Cocktails in general circulation. One was basically a Fancy Brandy Cocktail with a squirt of champagne (alias a Chicago Cocktail). Then there's this one, which splits the difference between a Manhattan and a Metropolitan. The fact that it could hold its own against the other—a Fancy Brandy Cocktail with a squirt of champagne being one of the most irresistible drinks going—is really saying something.

(U S E   S M A L L   B A R - G L A S S .)

TAKE 2 DASHES ANGOSTURA BITTERS

1 PONY [1 OZ] OF BRANDY

1 PONY [1 OZ] OF WHISKEY

1 PONY [1 OZ] OF VERMOUTH

Shake up well with two small lumps of ice; strain into a claret glass, and serve with a quarter of a slice of lemon.

SOURCE: *JERRY THOMAS'S BAR-TENDER'S GUIDE*, 1887

NOTES ON INGREDIENTS: The whiskey should be rye and the vermouth red. And definitely use more ice.

Replace the vermouth with absinthe and you have what the Hoffman House called a "Morning Cocktail." If that's what you need to get going in the A.M., God help you.

NOTES ON EXECUTION: This one is better stirred. For the glass, see the Vermouth Cocktail (page 235).

BIJOU COCKTAIL

If you take Harry Johnson's word for it, he was the greatest bartender of his time. His book, the *Modern Bartender's Manual*, does nothing to contradict that impression, and not just because it went to a respectable three editions between 1882 and 1900 (Johnson claimed there was also an 1860 San Francisco edition). The last two editions are also full of detailed and thoroughly professional information on restaurant and bar management and toothsome, if wretchedly organized, recipes—and they're illustrated! Unfortunately for Herr Johnson (he was yet another of the Germans who so distinguished themselves behind the bar), unlike our modern mixologists, to whom he is a cult figure (copies of his books bring up to four figures), his contemporaries didn't seem to think he was such hot stuff, if they thought about him at all. True, he had made the papers in 1885 as one who was "noted among New York . . . drinkers as a mixer of complicated beverages" to the point that various millionaires were hiring him to train their valets in the art.

But beyond that, if the bar he opened in Chicago in 1868 was indeed "recognized as the largest and finest establishment of the kind in this country," as he claimed, he must've used another name. And if in 1869 he was "challenged by five of the most popular and scientific bartenders of the day to engage in a tourney of skill, at New Orleans," thereby winning the "championship in the United States," the event seems to have gone unremarked by the national press. And that San Francisco book from 1860, the one that should be the first bartender's guide on record? No earthly trace of its publication or of any of the "ten thousand (10,000) copies" he said were printed and sold "within the brief period of six weeks" has either turned up or is likely to. In other words, there are grounds for taking the things that came out of his mouth with a grain of salt. Yet another example: In 1910, he told a reporter from the *New York Herald* that when he was at the Little Jumbo, the bar at 119 Bowery, which he ran from the late 1870s until 1887, "mixed drinks were unknown in New York then" and while there he "first made the gin sour, the mint julep and the cocktails." Indeed. (He also claimed that he served Horace Greeley his first Cocktail; if so, it was probably his last— Greeley was a notorious teetotaler.)

Although fondly remembered for its Cocktails and other Epicurean beverages, the Little Jumbo was hardly one of New York's showplaces. It's difficult to imagine one of the Hoffman House's patrons pulling out a roll of bills to pay for a disputed check and having three men jump him and run off with the boodle. (When young William Randolph Hearst met his father, the senator, at the Hoffman House bar and asked him for some money, Hearst Senior sent someone to get his coat from the check room and, according to Berry Wall, who was there, "drew thirty thousand dollars from the pocket, his winnings that day at the races, peeled off two thousand, and gave them to his son, saying 'Is that enough, Willie?' " Willie hoped it was.) Nor does one hear of one of Jerry Thomas's waiters shooting his bouncer five times in an after-hours joint, thus expediting his demise.

To be fair, both of those events took place in 1902, by which point Johnson was long off the scene, but the Bowery hadn't changed all that much in the meanwhile and they do give an impression of the tone that prevailed on the street. It's unclear where he went after his stint at the Little Jumbo, but wherever it was nobody paid him much attention. The self-published 1900 edition of his *Bartender's Manual* gives his address as 1 and 2 Hanover Square, in the Financial District, but that may have just been a mail drop. In any case, in 1902 or 1903 he gave up on New York entirely and retired to Europe, ending up in Berlin (his book had already been published in German). The *New York Herald* caught up with him when he came back for a visit.

Blowhard he might have been, but at least he knew how to mix drinks, if his version of the Bijou is any indication (another version, published by Cincinnati bartender Chris Lawlor in 1895, uses Grand Marnier rather than Chartreuse; nice, but not nearly so interesting).

(U S E   L A R G E   B A R - G L A S S .)

½ GLASS FILLED WITH FINE SHAVED ICE

⅓ WINE GLASS [1 OZ] CHARTREUSE (GREEN)

⅓ WINE GLASS [1 OZ] VERMOUTH (ITALIAN)

⅓ WINE GLASS [1 OZ] OF PLYMOUTH GIN

1 DASH OF ORANGE BITTERS

Mix well with a spoon, strain into a cocktail glass; add a cherry or medium-size olive, squeeze a piece of lemon peel on top and serve.

SOURCE: HARRY JOHNSON, *BARTENDER'S MANUAL*, 1900

NOTES ON INGREDIENTS: I strongly suggest you use the cherry and not the olive.

WEEPER'S JOY

William Schmidt. The Only William. In later years, Julian Street—then one of America's leading culinary authorities, but once a cub reporter in New York—would recall his encounter with greatness:

The newspapers were published downtown, so of course there were many downtown restaurants and bars that catered to newspapermen. A favorite bar was that of "The Only William," off lower Broadway, and it was a great moment in the life of the young reporter when a bearded elder of the craft escorted him to William's pleasant place, bought him a Weeper's Joy . . . and over it introduced him to the celebrity behind the bar, a short round-headed man with an amiable eye and an immense mustache.

Street's turn came in 1899, and I envy him for it. William Schmidt was an unlikely candidate to succeed Jerry Thomas as America's official Number One Mixer of Drinks, but succeed him he did. He was everything that Thomas was not—fussy, precise, vain, pedantic, even faintly ridiculous—but he was also a wildly creative and talented mixologist (he used to boast that he invented an entirely new drink every day). As proof, I offer that selfsame Weeper's Joy, a drink that looks like a train wreck on the page but tastes like an angel's tears. For at least a decade before his death in 1905 (of senile dementia, according to the papers, although he had been mixing drinks almost to the last), he was the newspapers' go-to guy for mixology, and this drink proves that it wasn't just because he was right around the corner.

A GOBLET ⅔ FULL OF FINE ICE

3 DASHES [½ TSP] **OF GUM**

½ PONY [1 OZ] **OF ABSINTHE**

½ PONY [1 OZ] **OF VINO VERMOUTH**

½ PONY [1 OZ] **OF KÜMMEL**

1 DASH [2 DASHES] **OF CURAÇAO**

Stir very well, and strain into a cocktail glass.

SOURCE: WILLIAM SCHMIDT, *THE FLOWING BOWL*, 1892

NOTES ON INGREDIENTS: This one's pretty straightforward. If you want to eliminate the gum, go ahead; the drink's sufficiently sweet without it. But I'd think twice: The extra sweetness gives the drink a thick mouthfeel and helps round that final edge off of the absinthe.

In 1890, a group of American naval officers stationed in Yokohama assumed part interest in the newly expanded Grand Hotel, which offered the best accommodations in town. Soon after, the hotel reached across the Pacific and hired a West Coast saloonman by the name of Louis Eppinger. A German-born contemporary of Jerry Thomas's, Eppinger had run bars in San Francisco and perhaps New Orleans, hotels in Portland, and God knows what else. "Fussy little Louis" was a wise choice. Under his stewardship, the massive five-acre pile of a hotel became "a far-famed rendezvous for round-the-world travelers," one of those cardinal outposts of Western culture around which the amorphous, cosmopolitan mass of steamship-borne moneyed vagabonds bent their endless paths. For almost two decades, Eppinger greeted guests, "haunt[ed] the markets for delicacies," planned menus (the Grand was known for its cuisine, and even served a couple of Japanese dishes every day), arranged entertainments, and bustled around the premises until, "grown grey and almost blind in the service of catering to the public" and so rheumatic that he needed a couple of boys to carry him up and down the stairs, he finally retired. That was in 1907; before the year was out, he'd be dead and buried. His remains still lie in the Jewish section of the Yokohama Foreigner's Cemetery.

Although Eppinger, in his old age, was particularly concerned with the Grand Hotel's kitchen, he didn't neglect the bar; it was widely known as a congenial place to "play billiards and drink Japanese Martini cocktails," as one visitor noted and through its doors passed many a celebrity, including Rudyard Kipling and humorist George Ade. Not only that, at some point during his first decade there, he took up the glass and spoon and mixed up a new Cocktail. The "Bamboo," as he christened it, was a simple, light, and thoroughly delightful aperitif that rapidly spread across the Pacific. By 1901, anyway, it was being advertised by West Coast saloons, and soon after it was sold widely in bottle form.

None of this explains how the drink—recipe and all—turned up in the "uptown Broadway hotels and cafes" in 1893 with the moniker "Boston Bamboo," unless that "Boston" was merely a misheard "Yokohama." (I seem to recall hearing somewhere that, taken in large quantities, vermouth does strange things to the eustachian tubes; it's the quinine.)

Originated and named by Mr. Louis Eppinger, Yokohama, Japan. Into a mixing-glass of cracked ice place half a jiggerful [1½ oz] of French vermouth, half a jiggerful [1½ oz] of sherry, two dashes of Orange bitters and two drops of Angostura bitters; stir thoroughly and strain into a stem cocktail glass; squeeze and twist a piece of lemon peel over the top and serve with a pimola or an olive.

SOURCE: WILLIAM T. "COCKTAIL" BOOTHBY'S *WORLD DRINKS AND HOW TO MIX THEM* (1908)

NOTES ON INGREDIENTS: For the sherry, use a fino or an amontillado, but not a particularly expensive one. The two drops of Angostura can be generated by lightly tipping the bottle over the glass without actually dashing it. A pimola is simply a pimiento-stuffed olive, which makes a nice touch. On the other hand, if there's a Japanese specialty foods store in your area, it might be worthwhile to pop in and see if anything suggests itself as an alternate garnish.

If you make this with Italian vermouth instead of French, omitting the drops of Angostura, not only will you have a plusher, if less elegant, drink, you'll have an **Adonis**, named after what has been called the first Broadway musical. *Adonis*, starring Henry E. Dixey, opened in 1884 at the Bijou—in Jerry Thomas's old space at 1239 Broadway—and ran for more than six hundred performances.

PRINCETON COCKTAIL

As mixing spirits with fortified, aromatized wines went from novelty to orthodoxy, mixologists began experimenting with things beyond vermouth, leading to drinks like the **Zaza**, which combined equal parts of dry gin and Dubonnet (see under the Bronx Cocktail, page 222), and the Calisaya Cocktail, which mixed a Spanish aromatized wine with whiskey. The deep thinkers behind the bar soon realized that the fortified wine didn't have to be aromatized to make a fine Cocktail. Case in point, the **Tuxedo**, which combined gin, dry sherry, and orange bitters to excellent effect (proportions: two to one with a dash). Or the Princeton. This is another of George Kappeler's; his book also offered the Harvard and the Yale, which gives you some indication of the sort of folks who propped up the bar at the old Holland House. All three are fine drinks, but for some reason this one's the most artistic. Interestingly enough, a simplified version of this—as "Top and Bottom"—became a staple of Harlem rent-parties during the 1920s. Go figure.

A mixing-glass half-full fine ice, three dashes orange bitters, one and a half pony [2 oz] Tom gin. Mix, strain into cocktail-glass; add half a pony [¾ oz] port wine carefully and let it settle in the bottom of the cocktail before serving.

SOURCE: GEORGE J. KAPPELER, *MODERN AMERICAN DRINKS*, 1895

NOTES ON INGREDIENTS: For the Tom gin, use Plymouth and add ½ teaspoon of gum, to round the edge off and add texture. You don't want to add too much sugar, though, or the layering effect will get messed up (it depends on the relative densities of the port and the gin). Charlie Mahoney of the Hoffman House suggests a lemon twist on this one; I prefer orange, but whichever you use, don't drop it in the drink or you'll mess up the visuals.

NOTES ON EXECUTION: To get the top-and-bottom effect, the port has to be slowly slid down the side of the glass. The drink will taste better if the port has been chilled in advance.

VI. THE STINGER

Properly considered, the Stinger shouldn't be here. Not only is it made without vermouth or any other kind of fortified wine, but according to many of its devotees it isn't even a real Cocktail. Joyce Kilmer (the author of the oft-quoted poem "Trees"), for one: "white mint and brandy shaken up together with cracked ice," he wrote his mother in 1914, "make a good substitute for a cocktail." And indeed, the bartender's guides of the time always list this combination among the after-dinner drinks; the sticky, multilayered Pousse-Cafés; the Champerelles (a simpler Pousse-Café); the Sam Wards (this last is a surprisingly tasty device named after the great lobbyist and gourmet; simply invert the skin of half a lemon and fill the resulting cup with shaved ice and yellow Chartreuse). But unlike the others, the Stinger was produced like a Cocktail and served like a Cocktail, and eventually it was drunk like a Cocktail, which is to say before dinner, or in the morning, or in the afternoon, or any time at all, even including after dinner.

As for its origins. Despite its name, which in the vernacular meant a quick shot to the head, whether liquid or fistical, the Stinger has always been considered a Society drink. As Hermione—the ultradumb young socialite that Don Marquis created for a series of columns in the *New York Sun* lampooning the dim-bulb civic and spiritual pretensions of the rich—notes while supporting Prohibition for the working classes, "Of course, a cocktail or two and an occasional stinger is something no one can well avoid taking, if one is dining out or having supper after the theater with one's own particular crowd." And in point of fact, New York folklore has always associated the drink with Reginald Vanderbilt (Gloria's father). This, it turns out, is no coincidence: according to a gossipy 1923 syndicated piece on this worthy, back in the Roosevelt years "Reggie" was highly devoted to the ritual of Cocktail hour, which "was observed in all its pomp and glory in the bar of [his] home, and he himself was the high priest, the host, the mixer." From four to seven every day, Reggie would stand behind the bar—which was modeled on the one in the William the Conqueror tavern in Normandy—and shake up Stingers, "his favorite cocktail." In fact, "the 'Stinger' was his own invention, a short drink with a long reach, a subtle blending of ardent nectars, a boon to friendship, a dispeller of care." Well, okay; properly concocted, the Stinger is all of those things.

a la J. C. O'Connor proprietor of the handsomest café for gentlemen in the world, corner Eddy and Market Sts. S.F. Calif.

¼ [¾ oz] **white crème de menthe and** ¾ [2¼ oz] **cognac. Shake well and serve cold in sherry glass.**

SOURCE: UNDATED TYPED SUPPLEMENT TO WILLIAM T. "COCKTAIL" BOOTHBY'S *AMERICAN BAR-TENDER* (1900); THE SUPPLEMENT MOST LIKELY DATES TO AROUND 1905

NOTES ON INGREDIENTS: Other recipes call for two parts or even one part cognac (and don't skimp on the quality!) to one part liqueur. This way's better. In any case, the only crème de menthe to use for a top-flight Stinger is the French "Get" brand; well worth tracking down. And whatever you use, it must always be white, not green. Report has it that Reggie liked a dash of absinthe in his. He would, wouldn't he?

NOTES ON EXECUTION: Even though it has only spirits in it, this drink is always shaken. That bolsters the Vanderbilt story: If you were a millionaire making drinks for show behind your replica Norman bar in your Fifth Avenue mansion, wouldn't you want to shake them? As for the glass: Use a Cocktail glass, on the small side.

CHAPTER 8

CHANNELING THE PROFESSOR—NEW DRINKS FROM SIXTEEN OF THE TOP MIXOLOGISTS OF OUR TIME

For someone who has been dead for 120 years, Jerry Thomas is doing pretty well. His book is in print, his name flits through the mouths of men, his drinks are mixed and dissected and even enjoyed. In contemporary cocktail culture, he is frequently evoked as an arbiter and a benchmark, one of the (pathetically few) authorities every serious drink-mixer has to know.

But the Professor's work is more than a point of academic reference; it also serves as a source of inspiration, a jumping-off point in the creation of new drinks. And rather than merely asserting this, I can prove it. When assembling this book, I asked a bar full of the world's best mixologists if they would be kind enough to contribute any original recipes they might have that were inspired in some way by Jerry Thomas and his drinks. Their responses, which you will find below, should put to rest any thoughts that the Professor's work is a mere historical curiosity.

Not that they all agree exactly how his legacy should be used; like all artists, mixologists are a diverse-thinking bunch. Between them, they manage to box the compass of inspiration, so to speak, from taking one of his recipes, brushing off its shoulders, straightening its seams, and sending it on out there, to filling in the blanks in one of his categories (even some blanks he would never have thought existed, like the one in the Sour category that calls out for horseradish), to bringing different classes together, to . . . well, to the Regans. The incorrigible Regans. The thing about Gary and Mardee, they just won't—can't—follow the rules, color between the lines, stay on the reservation. You ask them for a drink inspired by Jerry Thomas and they send you something sweet and dangerous that (almost) swipes the name of a highly toxic Australian gold-miner's drink employing controlled substances (it's not the rum, not the cayenne, but the opium you've got to watch out for) and claim that somehow it fits with Thomas's life and character. And, come to think of it, somehow it does. So they get off the hook—this time.

The only way I can justify insinuating a drink of my own in this august company is because it uses one final way of honoring the master, which is robbing him blind. The alert—or even not-so-alert—reader will immediately recognize my so-called Tombstone Cocktail as nothing more than a plain old Whiskey Cocktail, fitted out with new identity papers. But I will plead in my own defense that it nonetheless deserves a name of its own. Not because of any slight originality in conception or execution (the only way it differs from the Professor's drink is in its use of Demerara sugar syrup instead of white), but because of the occasion its name commemorates: It was first served on October 3, 2004, when a group of New York writers and bartenders—including Audrey Saunders, Julie Reiner, Toby Cecchini, Del Pedro, and John Hodgman—accompanied me to Woodlawn Cemetery in the Bronx to help me look for Thomas's grave. Upon finding it we broke out the enormous shaker we had brought with us, unpacked the freezer bag full of ice and the Cocktail glasses (no plastic for the Professor), assembled this Cocktail, passed the shaker around so we all had a jiggle, and had a drink with the Professor.

I'll close this discussion with some of the words Eben Klemm and Francesco Lafraconi sent in along with their recipes. Mr. Klemm, I believe, correctly assesses the continued relevance of Jerry Thomas and his great contemporaries to the modern art of mixing drinks mixographer when he notes that

> Even with all the flim-flam shaken up these days (some of which I myself indeed produce), most mixology past the 1890s I believe is but a footnote. For the most part, the sense of what we want and what works has been determined long before we were born. The contrapuntality of sour, savory, bitter and sweet found in the best of cocktails is now a centuries-old motif, and one not found in only the most suspect of current drinks.

But the Professor's legacy extends beyond the nuts and bolts of combining liquors, sugars, and acids. As Mr. Lafranconi notes, "although he was an incredibly committed and creative individual behind the bar, full of ingenuity and know-how, his personality wasn't only related to mixing drinks; he also had that savoir-faire; that elegance and class behind the bar. Above all, he was a man of trust. God bless JT!" I heartily concur.

(ALMOST) BLOW MY SKULL OFF

BY GARY REGAN AND MARDEE HAIDIN REGAN

www.ardentspirits.com

2 OUNCES COGNAC

½ OUNCE PEACH SCHNAPPS

½ OUNCE JÄGERMEISTER

Stir and strain into a chilled cocktail glass.

BAKEWELL PUNCH

BY BEN REED

Author and IP Bartender

1 LIME WEDGE (SQUEEZED TIGHTLY AND DROPPED INTO SHAKER)

5 RASPBERRIES

35 ML [1¼ OZ] WRAY AND NEPHEW WHITE OVERPROOF RUM

35 ML [1¼ OZ] FRESH PINK GRAPEFRUIT JUICE

10 ML [2 TSP] CANE SYRUP

10 ML [2 TSP] ORGEAT SYRUP

Gently muddle the lime and the raspberries to extract essential oils from the lime skin. Shake all the ingredients sharply over cubed ice, strain (through a fine strainer) into a small bar-glass filled with cracked ice, and garnish with two raspberries and a lime zest (edge the glass). Serve with two straws.

BERRY INTERESTING

BY FRANCESCO LAFRANCONI

Director of Mixology, Southern Wine & Spirits, Inc.

1½ OUNCES PLYMOUTH OR TANQUERAY NO. TEN GIN

¾ OUNCE COINTREAU

2 DASHES FEE BROTHERS PEACH BITTERS

3–4 WHOLE FRESH RASPBERRIES

1 OUNCE FRESH SWEET & SOUR (PASTEURIZED EGG WHITE—OPTIONAL FOR A FOAMY LOOK)

Shake all ingredients with ice. Strain into a chilled cocktail glass or serve over crushed ice in a tumbler glass.

Garnish with lemon twist and fresh raspberries on a cocktail stick.

CALVINO

BY EBEN KLEMM

Director of Cocktail Development, B. R. Guest Restaurant Group

2 ½ OUNCES PLYMOUTH GIN

TINY SPLASH MYRTLEBERRY AMARO

½ OUNCE GRAPEFRUIT JUICE

Shake all ingredients over ice and strain into cocktail glass that has approximately 2 tablespoons Campari-rose foam* in the bottom. Garnish with a petal of yellow rose or Chicago peace rose.

*CAMPARI-ROSE FOAM (FOR HALF LITER):

Soak two sheets gelatin in ice water.

In a saucepan over medium heat, stir ¼ liter rosehip jam into ¼ liter Campari until it dissolves. Bring to 60 degrees Celsius, to a light simmer at most.

Remove from heat.

Remove gelatin from water, gently squeeze out excess water, and whisk into Campari mix until completely dissolved. Strain.

When mixture is cool (you may keep for a couple of days in refrigerator beforehand or accelerate by putting in ice bath) add to whipped cream canister following the instructions of the manufacturer.

Charge with two nitrogen canisters, shaking gently each time. Store in cooler. I recommend storing the canister upside down for 1 hour just before the first use.

CHERRY SMASH

BY JULIE REINER

Co-owner and Mixologist, Flatiron Lounge, New York

1½ OUNCES COURVOSIER VS COGNAC

¾ OUNCE ORANGE CURAÇAO

¾ OUNCE FRESH LEMON JUICE

½ OUNCE CHERRY HEERING

Muddle 4 brandied cherries in a mixing glass.

Add all other ingredients and shake well with ice.

Strain into a cocktail glass and garnish with 2 brandied cherries.

HORSERADISH EGG SOUR

BY RYAN MAGARIAN

Mixologist at large

1½ OUNCES HORSERADISH-INFUSED VODKA*

¼ OUNCE NOILLY PRAT SWEET VERMOUTH

¾ OUNCE FRESH LEMON JUICE

½ OUNCE SIMPLE SYRUP

½ OUNCE FRESH ORANGE JUICE

1 DASH ANGOSTURA BITTERS

1 WHITE OF AN ORGANIC BROWN EGG

Combine ingredients in a pint shaker glass.

Fill glass with ice, shake vigorously for 10 seconds, and strain into a 7½-ounce cocktail glass. Garnish with flamed orange peel.

*Horseradish-Infused Vodka:

1 750 ML BOTTLE OF VODKA (I GENERALLY USE FRÏS, BUT MOST MID-RANGE WHEAT-BASED VODKAS WILL BE FINE.)

½ CUP CLEANED, PEELED AND THINLY SLICED HORSERADISH

Let sit for one turn of the earth and strain through cheesecloth into a sealable glass container.

LULU COCKTAIL

BY TED "DR. COCKTAIL" HAIGH

Author, Vintage Spirits & Forgotten Cocktails *(2004)*

2 OUNCES ST. CROIX RUM

3 DASHES OF PEYCHAUD BITTERS

2 BARSPOONS OF PORT

1 DASH OF CRÈME DE NOYEAU

1 PINCH OF NUTMEG

1 BROAD SWATCH OF FRESH ORANGE PEEL, TWISTED SMARTLY ATOP THE COCKTAIL SHAKER AND DROPPED IN.

Combine ingredients in a well-iced cocktail shaker. Shake well and strain into a 3½-ounce stemmed cocktail glass. Garnish with an orange twist.

"MISTER" COLLINS

BY WAYNE COLLINS

Brands Mixology Senior Manager, Maxxium Worldwide

1 OUNCE FRESHLY SQUEEZED LEMON JUICE

2 DASHES ANGOSTURA BITTERS

2 BARSPOONS LYCHEE SYRUP*

1½ OUNCES PLYMOUTH GIN

Shake ingredients well with ice. Strain into a chilled sour glass and charge with American dry ginger ale.

*TO MAKE LYCHEE SYRUP SIMPLY ADD THE SWEET JUICE FROM TIN OF LYCHEES (OR RAMBUTANS) IN SYRUP AND MIX WITH A LITTLE PLAIN SUGAR SYRUP OR, ALTERNATIVELY, USE A GOOD-QUALITY LYCHEE LIQUEUR IF YOU HAVE IT.

MODERN TEA PUNCH

BY FERNANDO CASTELLON

Author, Larousse des cocktails *(2004)*

(O L D - F A S H I O N E D [R O C K S] G L A S S .)

METHOD: SHAKER

TYPE OF ICE: CUBES

½ OUNCE SUGAR CANE SYRUP

½ OUNCE FRESH LIME JUICE

3 OUNCE COGNAC (HENNESSY VSOP)

2 BARSPOONS OF RAW GREEN TEA (SENCHA TYPE)

GARNISH: LONG LIME TWIST

Pour the ingredients in the glass part of the shaker (except the lime twist) and add 4 to 5 ice cubes. Fit the stainless steel part of the shaker and shake vigorously until the shaker is very cold. Strain into an Old-Fashioned glass full of ice using a cocktail strainer and a tea strainer (fine-mesh strainer). Twist the long lime peel over the glass and drop it in the drink. Serve immediately.

ROCHESTER COCKTAIL

BY ROBERT HESS
www.drinkboy.com

2 OUNCES RYE WHISKEY

1 OUNCE DUBONNET

½ OUNCE LICOR 43

¼ OUNCE ABSINTHE

2 DASHES ANGOSTURA BITTERS

Stir, up, garnish with a lemon twist.

SIERRA COBBLER

BY DANIEL ESTREMADOYRO
Head Bartender, Pucara Bar, Cordoba, Argentina

Fill a large bar-glass with cracked ice and add:

1 TABLESPOON SIMPLE SYRUP

2 OUNCES PERUVIAN PISCO ITALIA

A FEW DROPS OF FERNET BRANCA

Fill to the top with *Cedron* (Lemon verbena) cold infusion.*

Finally, place several strips of lemon and orange peel on top.

Shake well, garnish with berries and fresh *cedron* leaves. Serve with straws.

*CEDRON COLD INFUSION: PLACE 5 OR 6 DRIED LEMON VERBENA LEAVES INTO A PINT OF BOILING WATER AND LET IT COOL AT LEAST FOR 1 HOUR, IN ORDER TO EXTRACT FULL COLOR AND FLAVOR.

SPICED CIDER TODDY

BY TONY ABOU GHANIM
www.modernmixologist.com

5 CINNAMON STICKS

30 WHOLE CLOVES

½ VANILLA BEAN

1 GALLON APPLE CIDER

½ CUP CLOVER HONEY

25 OUNCES HOMEMADE ROCK & RYE**

(SERVES 15)

Start by breaking the cinnamon sticks and cloves and bruising the vanilla bean. Next make a mirepoix bag with the spices. In a large saucepan combine cider, honey, and mirepoix bag; bring to a boil and let cool for at least 4 hours. Remove mirepoix bag and reheat cider when ready to serve, adding the Rock & Rye at the last moment. Serve in heated mugs with a cinnamon stick garnish.

**HOMEMADE ROCK & RYE (RECIPE FROM THE GENTLEMAN'S COMPANION, 1938, BY CHARLES H. BAKER, JR.):

RYE WHISKEY, ⅕ GALLON, NOT A FULL QUART

JAMAICA RUM, JIGGER

ROCK CANDY, ½ CUP, LEAVE IN LARGE LUMPS

WHOLE CLOVES, 1 DOZ.

QUARTERED SMALL CALIFORNIA ORANGE, PEEL LEFT ON

QUARTERED SEEDLESS LEMON, PEEL LEFT ON

1 STICK OF CINNAMON, OR 2

Put ingredients in a jar, cover with Rye, and stand for a fortnight. Strain out spices through fine cloth or filter paper. Put back on fruit until needed.

TOM & JERRY & AUDREY

BY AUDREY SAUNDERS
Co-owner and Mixologist, Pegu Club, New York

12 FRESH EGGS (YOLKS & WHITES SEPARATED)

2 POUNDS WHITE SUGAR

6 TABLE SPOON FINE MADAGASCAR VANILLA EXTRACT

1½ TEASPOONS GROUND CINNAMON

¼ TEASPOON GROUND CLOVES

6 OUNCES BOILING MILK

½ TEASPOON GROUND ALLSPICE

2 OUNCES BACARDI 8 ANEJO RUM

1 OUNCE COURVOISIER VS COGNAC

½ TEASPOON GROUND NUTMEG

4 DASHES ANGOSTURA BITTERS

Prepare the batter: Beat egg yolks until they are thin as water. Add sugar, spices, rum, and vanilla to egg yolks (while beating). Beat egg whites until stiff and fold them into the egg yolk mixture. Refrigerate.

To serve: Place 2 ounces of batter in an Irish coffee mug.Add 1 ounce of Bacardi Anejo rum, and 1 ounce of Courvoisier VS Cognac. Fill with 6 ounces boiling milk. Dust with freshly grated nutmeg.

TOMBSTONE

BY DAVID WONDRICH

SHAKE WELL WITH CRACKED ICE:

2 OZ 100- OR 101-PROOF STRAIGHT RYE WHISKEY

1 TEASPOON RICH SIMPLE SYRUP*

2 DASHES ANGOSTURA BITTERS

Strain into chilled cocktail glass and twist a thin-cut swatch of lemon peel over the top.

*TO MAKE RICH SIMPLE SYRUP, STIR 4 CUPS DEMERARA SUGAR AND 2 CUPS WATER OVER LOW HEAT UNTIL ALL SUGAR HAS DISSOLVED. LET COOL, BOTTLE, AND ADD ½-OUNCE GRAIN ALCOHOL OR 151-PROOF RUM TO RETARD SPOILAGE.

VELVET WILLIAMS

BY ANISTATIA MILLER AND JARED BROWN
Authors of Shaken Not Stirred: A Celebration of the Martini *(1997)*

2 OUNCES FRESH GREEN COCONUT WATER

2 OUNCES FRESH PINEAPPLE JUICE

1½ OUNCES PLYMOUTH GIN

1 SPLASH COINTREAU

1 DASH ANGOSTURA BITTERS

½ FRESH ORGANIC EGG WHITE

Mix all ingredients in a shaker filled with ice. Shake vigorously until icy cold. Strain into a large, chilled cocktail glass. Cut an orange twist with a vegetable peeler to reduce the amount of pith. Flame the twist over the top and add to the drink.

WHISKEY PEACH SMASH

BY DALE DEGROFF

Author, Craft of the Cocktail *(2002)*

5 MINT LEAVES AND 1 MINT SPRIG

3 PEACH SLICES

½ LEMON, QUARTERED

1 OUNCE ORANGE CURAÇAO (NOTHING LESS THAN MARIE BRIZARD, BOLS, OR HIRAM WALKER)

2 OUNCES BONDED BOURBON WHISKEY

Muddle the mint leaves, 2 peach slices, lemon pieces, and the orange curaçao together in the bottom of a bar-glass. Add the bourbon and ice and shake well. Strain into an iced rocks glass. Garnish with mint sprig and remaining peach slice.

CHAPTER 9

BITTERS AND SYRUPS

Most nineteenth-century bartender's guides closed with a section on compounding bitters and syrups and producing cheap booze out of raw whiskey and various natural, if dodgy, and artificial flavorings. Since this book is devoted to the best traditions of the bar, I'll ignore that last part entirely. As for the bitters and syrups, were these to receive the attention they deserve, they would easily fill another volume the size of this one. But I shall confine myself to offering formulae for three kinds of bitters (including Jerry Thomas's own, for historical purposes) and a handful of essential syrups.

I have not indicated individual sources for botanicals and other ingredients. In general, they are relatively easy to source online, but I am reluctant to give websites for each as these have a distressing habit of disappearing as soon as they appear in print. But I will say that two I have found to be stable and reliable are www.baldwins.co.uk and www.frontiercoop.com.

BITTERS

Fortunately, the return of the Cocktail has brought in its wake a renewed interest in bitters, and every year brings more varieties on the market. Orange bitters, for a long time a rarity, are now much easier to find (both Fee's West Indian Orange Bitters and Regans' Orange Bitters #6 can easily be located online). Here, however, are three kinds that cannot yet be purchased.

JERRY THOMAS'S OWN DECANTER BITTERS

This is one recipe in Jerry Thomas's book that we can be absolutely sure is his own. Evidently, it was successful enough for Thomas to keep making it, or something like it, since the 1871 *Bonfort's Wine & Liquor Circular* devoted to the Thomas brothers' cellar closes by mentioning that "Mr. Jerry Thomas makes a very wholesome kind of bitters, for the use of his bar, himself." Unfortunately, modern medical science begs to differ about their wholesome nature, since aristolochic acid, found in the Virginia snakeroot *(aristolochia serpentaria)* Thomas used to give the bitters their herbal punch, has been proven to cause liver failure, and snakeroot can no longer be purchased. Nor can it be adequately replaced: Having taken the trouble to grow some from cuttings, I can attest that this fragrant, spicy root imparts a bewitching I-know-not-what to the bitters that is unlike anything I know.

I offer the Professor's recipe—which was clearly sold as a tonic, by the glass—for its historical interest only and *do not recommend that it be reproduced or consumed.*

(BOTTLE AND SERVE IN PONY-GLASS.)

TAKE ¼ POUND OF RAISINS

2 OUNCES OF CINNAMON

1 OUNCE OF SNAKE-ROOT

1 LEMON AND 1 ORANGE CUT IN SLICES

1 OUNCE OF CLOVES

1 OUNCE OF ALLSPICE

Fill decanter with Santa Cruz rum.

As fast as the bitters is used fill up again with rum.

SOURCE: JERRY THOMAS, 1862

STOUGHTON'S BITTERS

There is a surfeit of old recipes for Stoughton's Bitters in existence, but unfortunately none of them can be traced to the good doctor himself (then again, I must confess that I have not yet searched through the British patent office records from 1712, if indeed they still exist). Most of the existing recipes contain snakeroot. Here is one that does not. It is a composite recipe from several sources, the earliest of which is Charles B. Campbell's 1867 *American Bartender*.

Macerate one-quarter ounce of chamomile flowers and one-half ounce each of gentian root, bitter orange peel, cassia bark, and calumba root in thirty ounces of brandy and ten ounces of grain alcohol. After two weeks, stir in one ounce by weight of burnt sugar, strain through filter paper and bottle.

SOURCE: COMPOSITE

NOTES ON INGREDIENTS: The burnt sugar can be purchased in some ethnic food stores, or you can make your own. Many recipes for Stoughton's Bitters call for them to be colored with cochineal; this can easily be replaced by a few drops of red food coloring, in which case the burnt sugar should be reduced by at least half (it is merely there for coloring).

NOTES ON EXECUTION: If you plan on making bitters frequently, it will be worthwhile to acquire a vacuum filtration rig (aka Büchner funnel/flask), which will make filtering your bitters quick and easy. Otherwise, you'll need a coffee filter and a lot of patience.

BOKER'S BITTERS

I won't delve deeply into the complex history of Boker's Bitters. The leading Cocktail bitters for much of the nineteenth century, they were produced by the L. J. Funke Company of New York City. By Prohibition, their heavy, Christmas-spiced nature made them quite old-fashioned. An adequate substitute is Fee Brothers' Old-Fashioned Aromatic Bitters (see www.feebrothers.com). Or you can make your own, as many a bartender did. This English formula for them hails from 1883, when there was still plenty of genuine Boker's around to test it against.

1½ OZ. QUASSIA

1½ OZ. CALAMUS

1½ OZ. CATECHU (POWDERED)

1 OZ. CARDAMOM

2 OZ. DRIED ORANGE PEEL

Macerate for 10 days in ½ gallon strong whiskey, and then filter and add 2 gal. water. Color with mallow or malva flowers.
SOURCE: ROBERT HALDAYNE, *WORKSHOP RECEIPTS (SECOND SERIES)*, 1883

NOTES ON INGREDIENTS: For the whiskey, which would have been the young, rectified kind, not the old, wood-mellowed kind, you can substitute 151-proof rum or even Everclear. The water is added in this quantity to make these decanter-type bitters, for drinking straight; to make them into Cocktail bitters, cut the amount of water in half. And there's no shame in making a half-sized recipe.

SYRUPS

In general, the recipes in this book call for a thicker syrup than the one-to-one formula that is in general use today, the glassware then being much smaller and hence easier to fill without "volumizing" the drinks.

GUM SYRUP (TRUE)

The gum Arabic, an emulsifier, gives this a silky texture that helps to soften the bite of drinks made with liquor and nothing else—plain Cocktails, in other words. But it works well in just about anything, and is worth the extra expense in time and money.

Dissolve 1 lb. of the best white gum Arabic in 1½ pints of water, nearly boiling; [take] 3 lbs. of white sugar or candy; melt and clarify it with half pint of cold water, add the gum solution and boil all together for two minutes. This gum is for cocktails.

SOURCE: E. RICKET AND C. THOMAS, *GENTLEMAN'S TABLE GUIDE*, 1871

NOTES ON INGREDIENTS: Make sure the gum Arabic is food-grade (you can get it from www.frontiercoop.com). Plain white sugar will work fine.

NOTES ON EXECUTION: It's easier to simply melt the sugar in the half-pint of water over a low flame, rather than melting the sugar first and then adding the water (our sugar needs less clarifying). The mixture should be kept refrigerated.

GUM SYRUP
(BARTENDER'S)

While the gum may be nice in drinks, bartenders rapidly discovered that few customers could tell the difference, and the vast majority of bartenders' recipes for gum syrup omit the gum altogether. Since the period ones are heavily concerned with clarifying the syrup, a step that is no longer needed, a modern recipe is provided here.

Over a low heat, dissolve two pounds of white sugar in one pint of water. Let cool, bottle and add one-half ounce grain alcohol or one ounce vodka to retard spoilage. Keep refrigerated or use quickly.

NOTES ON INGREDIENTS: To make what I call **Rich Simple Syrup**, replace the white sugar with Demerara sugar. The resulting syrup will be brown, which sometimes causes visual problems, but it adds a depth of sugar flavor that I find an improvement to most drinks.

PINEAPPLE, RASPBERRY,
AND OTHER FRUIT AND
BERRY SYRUPS

These are easy to make: Simply cube the large fruits and wash and pat dry the small ones, put them in a bowl, press them lightly, and add enough gum or rich simple syrup to cover. Leave them overnight, strain out the solids, and you're done.

APPENDIX I:
THE BON VIVANT'S
COMPANION

On June 23, 1859, the young New York trade-book publishing firm of Dick & Fitzgerald did something nobody had done before. That day, they registered a book with the copyright clerk of the Southern District of New York bearing the following title:

> *The Bar Tender's Guide, or Complete Encyclopaedia of Fancy Drinks, Containing Plain and reliable directions for making all the Fancy Drinks used in the United States, together with the most popular British, French, German and Spanish recipes. To which is appended a Manual for the Manufacturing of Cordials, Liqueurs, Fancy Syrups, etc etc, the same being adapted to the trade of the United States and Canadas.*

Before this, there had been a slew of assorted Innkeeper's, Cellarman's, Publican's, and Vintner's Guides published, mostly in London, going back at least to William Augustus Smyth's 1779 *Publican's Guide, or Key to the Distill House.* All contain much useful advice for the proprietor of a drinking establishment relating to the management of liquors and whatnot, but precious little about mixing drinks (unless you count adulterating gin as a branch of the mixological art)—a recipe or two for Punch, maybe a quick look at Purl and Flip, and that's about it.

Then there was *Oxford Night Caps*, a little booklet published in Oxford in 1827 (and frequently thereafter) by one Richard Cooke, presumably for the edification of the students of the university. This, the first known book devoted entirely to the art of mixing drinks, provided a goodly number of recipes with comments on their history and execution, but with its lapses into Latin and verse (and even Latin verse) and its focus on complicated social drinks, it was aimed strictly at the bibulous amateur. Until Dick & Fitzgerald's project, nobody had thought to fuse these; to produce a book of drink recipes for the use of the working bartender. (Cocktail history geeks will note that this copyright registration even predates the chimeric bartender's guide that Harry Johnson alleged he published in San Francisco in 1860.)

We'll never know exactly what prompted the firm's principals, William Brisbane Dick (1827–1901) and Lawrence Rees Fitzgerald (ca.1825–1881), to attempt this new sort of book, but here's how they explained it in the introduction to the volume as it finally appeared:

> *We very well remember seeing one day in London, in the rear of the Bank of England, a small drinking saloon that had been set up by a peripatetic American, at the door of which was placed a board covered with the unique titles of the American mixed drinks supposed to be prepared within that limited establishment. The "Connecticut eye-openers" and "Alabama fog-cutters," together with the "lightning-smashes" and the "thunderbolt-cocktails," created a profound sensation in the crowd assembled to peruse the Nectarian bill of fare, if they did not produce custom. It struck us, then, that a list of all the social drinks—the composite beverages, if we may call them so—of America, would really be one of the curiosities of jovial literature; and that if it was combined with a catalogue of the mixtures common to other nations, and made practically useful by the addition of a concise description of the various processes for "brewing" each, it would be a "blessing to mankind."* *

History has proved that William Dick, to whom we must probably assign the authorship of this (he was the artistic half of the duo and wrote or compiled

---

* This incident must have occurred before November 1857, when Jacob Martin Van Winkle, the American who had set himself up as a "dealer in the American drinks, described as cock-tails, tiger's-milk, bull's-milk, brandy smashes & c." in part of the King's Head tavern in the Poultry (right around the corner from the Bank of England's Threadneedle Street headquarters) was declared bankrupt; evidently those perusers never did screw their courage up enough to actually liquorate.

many of the firm's books himself) was correct in his instincts. There must have been some doubt at the time, though, since as far as we can tell this 1859 book never actually appeared: It was announced twice that summer in the *American Publisher's Circular and Literary Gazette*, and then nothing. Not an advertisement, notice, casual reference, or, more important, a single surviving copy.

I won't speculate as to why the book didn't come out, but I think it's indicative that neither the copyright notice nor the notices in the *American Publisher's Circular* mention Jerry Thomas or indeed any other bartender. If the two young publishers recognized that the old craft of "brewing" drinks had developed to the point that it could use a guidebook, they apparently had not yet realized that it had also developed to the point that its arcana were beyond the amateur's grasp. Perhaps that point was made to them, causing them to shelve the book.

Sometime during the next couple of years, one or both of the partners crossed paths with Jerry Thomas. This could have happened any one of a number of ways. Dick, in particular, was a likely vector of contact: Not only was he interested in art and specifically in prints (he, too, was a collector), his booklist reveals a professional interest in minstrelsy (Dick and Fitzgerald published several different volumes devoted to blackface songs and jokes) and games of chance (as "Trumps," he edited for many years the standard American edition of Hoyle). However it happened, it seemed to have galvanized the firm into action and in June 1862 *Harper's Weekly* carried an ad for their new book:

> *How to Mix Drinks. Containing Recipes for mixing American, English, French, German, Italian, Spanish, and Russian Drinks. . . .* By Jerry Thomas, Late Bartender at the Metropolitan hotel, New York, and Planters' House, St. Louis.

Not only did it now have an actual name attached (this was far from the norm for how-to books of the day, which usually carried the publisher's name but not the author's), but the actual book itself—of which hundreds of copies survive—adds another change, in the form of a sporty subtitle: "The Bon-Vivant's Companion." In one form or another, this book would remain in print for some thirty-five years—and a lot more after that if you count the dozens of bartender's guides that plagiarized it wholesale. As the *New York World* observed upon the Professor's death, "the editions sold were very large. Unfortunately, though, "of this his family [and, we must assume, Thomas himself] got no percentage." Not only was his book the first bartender's guide, it was also the first of many successful ones that were written as work-for-hire, whereby the hard shaking and stirring of the poor author served to promote a book that only put money in another's pocket. But I digress.

In keeping with Dick & Fitzgerald's original 1859 conception of the book, this one was two books in one: the drinks guide published over Thomas's name, which took up eighty-seven pages, and a translation of the far less revolutionary guide to the manufacture of obscure cordials (*Escubac d'Irelande*, anyone? Creme de Nymphe?), bitters, and so forth penned by Professor Christian Schmidt of Basle, Switzerland, which took up another 153 pages. Clearly, Dick & Fitzgerald were double-shotting their guns here: If bartenders—as is their wont now and probably was then, too—didn't want to acknowledge that they had anything to learn about mixing drinks from some damn book, they might be convinced to pony up the rather hefty $1.50 the book cost (as much as twelve drinks) by Schultz's clear and detailed instructions for making the fancy European syrups and liqueurs that were just coming into vogue. At least, that's what they could tell the other bartenders.

But even in the part of the volume we're concerned with, the one bearing Thomas's name, Dick & Fitzgerald hedged their bets, as that sporty subtitle suggests. Though it contains far too many drinks and far too little fancy writing and pleasant digression to make it a true work of convivial literature as the contemporary reader would have understood it (the genre, a popular one in Victorian literature, stretched roughly from *Oxford Night Caps* on the utilitarian side to *The Pickwick Papers* on the ornamental), between the book's subtitle and its invocations of "jovial literature" and the "amenities of *bon vivant* existence" in the preface, *How to Mix Drinks, or the Bon Vivant's Companion* takes a stab at it, anyway. But it was not until 1928, when Herbert Asbury tacked a hasty edition of the book onto the biographical essay he had published the year before in Mencken's *American Mercury* and put it out as *The Bon Vivant's Companion*, that Jerry Thomas's guide would find a place in the home. By then, almost a decade into Prohibition, Americans had grown used to taking mixology into their own hands. Before that, in America at least, they were content to leave it in the highly skilled ones of the white-coated professional—a fact that Dick & Fitzgerald effectively acknowledged by blazoning the book's cover not with the actual title, but with their original one, "*Bar Tender's Guide*" (thus occasioning a century and a half's confusion about what to call it).

Whatever the book is called, as one reads through it, it rapidly becomes clear that more than one voice is speaking here. Mixed in with the terse, practical recipes for drinks whose production was the preponderance of the American bartender's daily work; with the Juleps and Smashes, Cobblers, Cocktails, and glasses of Punch, there are an ungodly number of complicated foreign concoctions that would drive any bartender I've ever met into howling conniptions if ordered. But without further information, it's difficult to say precisely which parts are Jeremiah P. Thomas and which are William

B. Dick. For years, I considered the book's breezy, informal recipe for Arrack Punch as an instance where the Professor's voice spoke loudest, only to discover, while researching this book, that it was pinched from an earlier work of convivial literature. There are, however, some things in the book that reek of the sporting life. The instruction appended to the recipe for the Brandy Crusta, for instance: "Then smile," it says. In sporting lingo, a drink was a "smile," and to "smile" was to take one. The double entendre here is redolent of barroom wit.

If the book's lack of a strong unitary voice is its weakness, it's also its strength. Unlike the straight bartender's guides that followed it, which were all function and American efficiency, this one encompasses both wings of the sporting life; the aristocratic English one and the egalitarian American one; it's Tattersall's and the Astor bar, Willard and the Prince Regent. It works for amateurs—indeed, the introduction claims as one of the motives for its creation that "there would be no excuse for imbibing, with such a book at hand, the 'villainous compounds' of bar-keeping Goths and Vandals, who know no more of the amenities of *bon vivant* existence than a Hottentot can know of the bouquet of champagne."

But it also has a feature that, above and beyond its recipes, means that it works for professionals, and here, if anywhere, is the true greatness of the *Bar Tender's Guide*, or whatever it is to be called: It's divided into distinct, explicit categories. Punches are with Punches, Juleps with Juleps, Fixes with Fixes. This is the sign of a true bartender at work. Mixology works by pattern and variation, and with the drinks explicitly arranged like this, it's easy to quickly grasp the essential features of each class. This seems obvious today, but none of the book's antecedents did it, and neither did many of the guides that followed it, including influential ones like O. H. Byron's and Harry Johnson's. In this, Jerry Thomas—and it had to be Thomas who was responsible for the classification—was truly the father of mixology, of the rational study of the mixed drink.

While the reviewers didn't exactly fall over themselves in their haste to evaluate Dick & Fitzgerald's new book, the *Philadelphia Inquirer*, at least, recognized its worth: "There is something new under the sun, and something good to be shown," it opined in July 1862. "Many drinks have been mixed since stimulants first came into vogue . . . but an elaborate treatise containing recipes for every nectar ever brewed is a good thing. . . . To anyone who wants to know how to prepare *any* summer drink, and Jerry's number is literally *legion*, we can recommend this book as unique, carefully prepared and perfect of its kind." The public seems to have agreed: Judging by the number of surviving copies, and by the fact that Dick & Fitzgerald raised the price to $2 and then $2.50, demand must have been quite strong.

After Thomas, for a few years there was silence from the other mixologists. Then, in 1867, Charles B. Campbell, an Englishman working in San Francisco, published his *American Bartender*. There's only one known copy in existence now, which is a fair indicator of its success. Two years later, Jesse Haney & Co of New York, publisher of a series of how-to-books, put out a thoroughly workmanlike *Steward & Barkeeper's Manual*. This one, sadly anonymous, seems to have done a little better anyway. In any case, both of these can be read as commentaries and corrections of Thomas's book. Each contains a few drinks not found in his, but the bulk of their content shows how astute he was at collecting drinks. A handful of other guides followed in the 1870s, prompting Dick & Fitzgerald, with a clearer sense of the market, to publish a revised edition of their guide in 1876. Unburdened by Schultz's work, this one was handier and cheaper (it was 75 cents, 50 cents in paperback), and it had a supplement containing a selection of the new drinks of the day, including the first appearance of the Fizz (or "Fiz") and the Daisy. The cover was different, too: no longer was it the "Bon Vivant's Companion"; now, it was simply "Jerry Thomas's Bar-Tenders Guide."

The next ten years saw a lot more competition, including the first bartender's guides to offer the Manhattan and the Martinez. In 1887, two years after the Professor's death, Dick & Fitzgerald responded with their final version of his book. Gone was the witty convivial and biographical preface, replaced by a piece of pabulum about it being an age of progress and there being no end to the making of drinks, and a lengthy set of "Hints and Rules for Bartenders"—precisely the sort of thing Jerry Thomas would have hated. How can you teach somebody to arc flaming whiskey over his head with a book? Bartenders are gentlemen, not servants. But whoever revised the book, it must be conceded that he did a thoroughly workmanlike job. The old recipes were dried out and tightened up; new, up-to-date ones were added; and many of the ornamental English things were banished to a section at the end of the book with the comment,

We give the following group of English drinks for the benefit of the curious in such matters. Many of them are rather troublesome to prepare, and some of them, which we have tried, have not yielded the satisfaction expected or desired.

All true, and all good sense. But thus the old order passeth. By the turn of the century, Thomas's guide appears to have been out of print, although there were scads of cheap bartender's bibles that pirated his recipes in circulation.

APPENDIX II:
SOME ADDITIONAL CONSIDERATIONS ON THE ORIGIN AND NAMING OF THE COCKTAIL

Generally, it's been assumed that the Cocktail's origins lie in the hard-liquoring South. But people have been investigating the origin of the Cocktail since the 1880s without turning up a single firm reference to its consumption in the region before the late 1820s. On the other hand, every single one of the drink's early mentions fits neatly into the triangle between New York, Albany, and Boston (where they were still talking about "bitter sling" as late as 1836). If we follow the available evidence, then the Cocktail originated somewhere in the Hudson Valley, Connecticut, or western Massachusetts. At least, odds are it was a Northern drink, not a Southern one. But then again, the South had fewer newspapers and publishing houses to record people's doings, so certainty once again eludes us. (We must discount anything contained in the extraordinarily detailed article on "The Origin of the Cocktail" published by the *Baltimore Sun* in 1908, which claims that it was invented in Maryland; the piece is one of H. L. Mencken's insidious hoaxes.)

Given its distribution in 1803 to 1806, it's also likely that the Cocktail had been known for some time. In fact, there may be a grain of truth in Cooper's story in *The Spy* that it was invented during the Revolution at Four Corners, north of New York City on the Albany Post Road—which also, not coincidentally, runs through Hudson (where its first definition was published in 1806).

As pioneer food writer Julian Street established in the 1940s, Cooper's "Betty Flanagan," whom he credits with the invention, was in fact based on one Catherine "Kitty" Hustler, who had kept an inn at Four Corners during the war. In 1809, she and her husband moved west and opened an inn at Lewiston, near Buffalo, where Cooper boarded while writing *The Spy*. (Lewiston still maintains a local tradition that it's the birthplace of the Cocktail.)

This still doesn't solve the conundrum of How the Cocktail Got Its Name. In truth, we may never be able to solve it; that's not unusual for slang, and especially barroom slang. Why do we call it a "Martini"? People will argue that one until the last trumpet. In the absence of certainty, bullshit blooms. This b.s. can basically be shoveled into four different piles, or schools of thought.

There's the Imported Word school—"cocktail" is an Americanization of *coquetel*, supposedly an ancient Bordeaux drink; *coquetier*, French for "egg cup" (which it is claimed the drinks was originally served in); or "Xochitl," who was either the Aztec goddess of Agave or a Mexican princess named after her (don't ask). None of these have ever been supported by any contemporary evidence and are highly unlikely, and I shall trouble them no more.

Then there's the Rooster Tail school, which derives the name either from the practice of garnishing the drink with a tail feather or from the way the interplay of the drink's polychromatic ingredients reminds the observer of the interplay of colors on said avian's tail. This last, a pretty theory, is completely sunk by the fact that Colonial-era liquors were white, tan, or brown; no fancy Technicolor liqueurs for the first Greatest Generation. So a Pigeon Tail, perhaps even a Chicken Tail, sure—but not a Cock Tail. As for the feather in the drink: In all the hundreds, even thousands of contemporary descriptions of mixed drinks I've read, not a single one has ever mentioned such a garnish. You'd think something like that would stick out, especially to the many fault-finding British travelers poking around the Republic in its early days, all poised to pounce on any eccentricity or rusticity of manner they found their American cousins practicing. But no, not until the first generation of Cocktail-tipplers was long dead did anyone mention the practice, and then it's always set comfortably in the old days. It's funny how we're willing to kick common sense out the door when it comes to thinking about the past. How would you react if someone stuck a feather yoinked from a bird's ass in your drink? Precisely.

The Tail Is Ale school, which holds that the name comes from "cock tailings," the dregs in the bottom of an ale cask, or "cock ale," ale mixed with a whole lot of God-knows-what and fed to fighting cocks, is not only without proof, but it works on the mistaken root assumption that the Cocktail was a sort of leftovers-hash kind of a drink, that you could put just about anything in it. You couldn't, at least not until the 1890s (which helps us date that theory).

This leaves the Cut-Tail school. Again, there are two branches, both rooted in the prevalent eighteenth- and nineteenth-century practice of docking draft horses' tails to prevent them getting caught in the harness. When cut short like this, they tend to stick up like a cock's tail, which lead to such beasts being called "cock-tailed" horses (this usage is found as early as 1769). This has spawned the conjecture that (as the reader's letter to the *Balance* implied) the Cocktail was so named because it would cock your tail up in the morning. Possible, but I prefer one based on a secondary usage of the term. Because thoroughbred horses were too "well-blooded" (i.e., valuable) to be used to pull things around, that job fell to ones that were of mixed breed. This led to mixed-breed horses in general being known as "cock-tails," particularly in the sporting world, where it was applied to a racehorse that was part thoroughbred and part not. This usage doesn't appear widely in print until the second or third decade of the nineteenth century, but it does turn up in John Lawrence's popular *A Treatise on Horses*, published in London in 1796 and frequently reprinted (including excerpts in the *New York Magazine* in 1797), where he talks about the difficulty of controlling a "huge cock-tail half-bred."

It's safe to say the majority of American loungers, dram-drinkers, "Slingers" (as morning drinkers were called), "eleveners" (as late-morning drinkers were called), and other votaries of the bar would have been intimately acquainted with the ins and outs of racing and its slang, both domestic and imported: Early American newspapers carried an inordinate amount of British turf news. It would have been the work of a moment to transfer the nickname for a fast mixed-breed horse to a fast mixed-breed drink— "Make me a 'cock-tail' of Sling and Bitters, if you please" (think of how a "jazz," a bit of San Francisco baseball slang meaning "vigor" was transferred to a new and conspicuously vigorous kind of music). I can't say that this is the ultimate truth about the drink's name, but it's certainly the simplest explanation that fits the available evidence.

APPENDIX III:
THE ORIGIN OF
THE MARTINI

We may never know the true origin of the King of all Cocktails. It's possible that a definitive answer lies entombed in the crumbling pages of an old newspaper somewhere, waiting for some lucky researcher to stumble upon it, but it's equally possible that the first meeting of gin and vermouth was one of those momentous occasions that don't seem all that momentous at the time; that everybody involved took their drinks, smacked their lips, and toddled on home without further remarking the occasion.

What early evidence we have is hazy and contradictory, and as always, that has allowed a number of theories to bloom. Discarding the purely fictional ones regarding Dr. Johnson and Mr. Boswell or eighteenth-century Squires journeying from Boston to Dartmouth, these generally fall into two groups, one centered around San Francisco (we can call these the "Martinez" theories) and the other around New York (the "Martine/Martini" theories); we'll deal with them both in some detail.

Early on, the drink also appears under a couple of names that suggest another provenance entirely, but alas the "Martigny" Cocktail and the "Martineau" Cocktail both turn out to be dry wells for further research. Then there's the claim advanced in the *Chicago Times-Herald* in 1900, that the "martinez" was invented by the Maverick financier Joe Leiter. The drink first appeared in print when he was sixteen, so that's unlikely, but you never know. Ultimately, though, writing history is the art of balancing evidence and probability, and there are really only four theories that make it to round two of the judging.

THE JERRY THOMAS THEORY

THE CLAIM: Jerry Thomas made the first drink with gin and vermouth when he was working in San Francisco in the early 1860s, for a traveler heading for the East Bay town of Martinez who asked for something new. To commemorate the occasion, Thomas named it the "Martinez" and published the recipe in his bartender's guide.

ORIGINS OF THE CLAIM: First fully stated in a Beefeater's gin advertisement of the 1960s.

PRO: Thomas certainly worked in San Francisco in the early 1860s and the Martinez does appear in an edition of his *Bar-Tenders Guide*. The first Cocktail book to mention the drink, O. H. Byron's 1884 *Modern Bartender's Guide*, also calls it the Martinez. Vermouth and Old Tom gin were available in California in the 1860s.

CON: The Martinez appears only in the 1887 edition of Thomas's book, which of course came out two years after his death.

Furthermore, by the time the Professor died, the Martini was a fashionable and popular drink, yet not a single one of the numerous obituaries devoted to him mentions it. Nor did Thomas himself mention it to any of the many reporters who interviewed him or wrote about him, and he was not the type to hide his light under a bushel. If he had invented it, it is almost inconceivable that nobody at the time would have known it or mentioned it.

Finally, aside from in Byron's, Thomas's, and a few other bartender's guides that plagiarized them, only two other contemporary mentions of the "Martinez" have been found, the one from 1900 claiming it for Joe Leiter and a 1914 menu for a banquet held by the Bartenders' International League of Fort Wayne, Indiana. Against this, there are hundreds, even thousands of references to the Martini (or "Martina," as they spelled it in Georgia; I love phonetic English).

VERDICT: Extremely unlikely.

THE JULIO RICHELIEU THEORY

THE CLAIM: Julio Richelieu, who kept a bar on Ferry Street in Martinez invented the drink one day in the mid-1870s as change for a gold nugget a miner gave him in return for a bottle of Jesse Moore whiskey. The drink became popular when he moved his saloon to Market Street in San Francisco, across from the landmark Lotta Fountain.

ORIGINS OF THE CLAIM: John "Toddy" Briones, Julio Richelieu's brother-in-law, as cited in a 1965 article in the *Oakland Tribune*.

PRO: Since the 1950s, Martinez has claimed the drink as a local product. Briones's account is quite detailed, and some of the details are verifiable. There was a Richelieu Café in San Francisco, across from Lotta's Fountain. In the late nineteenth century, Jesse Moore was a popular brand of whiskey on the West Coast. Gin and vermouth were available in California in the 1870s. There was a Gold Rush in California.

CON: To begin with, the whole claim falls under a certain pall of suspicion when we learn, from a 1975 article in the *Oakland Tribune*, that it was first advanced publicly in 1950, in a banquet speech to various California civic leaders by the president of Martinez's chamber of commerce, Claude Patrick Greety. Under those circumstances, a person will say anything. Although Greety stuck to his guns when later questioned about his story, a reporter who nosed about town in 1950 couldn't find any evidence to corroborate the claim and only a couple of people who had even heard of it. "The city of Martinez," as he wrote, "has ignored its role in history. There is no Spring Martini festival, complete with martini queen. There is no Old Original Martini house, of the kind New Orleans could prefabricate in a week's time, complete with candles in bottles." Given the American propensity to ballyhoo, this made him highly suspicious, and it does me as well.

In any case, if the town of Martinez, which continues to defend this theory to the death (and has even added the Martini festivals), has any actual evidence that Julio Richelieu lived there, or even existed at all, it has not made it public. What is certain is that he does not appear in California census records (and yes, I looked under "Jules" as well, and any other possible spelling). Furthermore, by the 1870s, the Gold Rush had essentially been over for a decade, and it is unlikely that anyone would have still been trying to buy things with gold nuggets or that there would still be a weigh-in scale on the bar, as Briones claimed. Of course, since Briones was ninety-one at the time he was interviewed, and his information was secondhand (he was born in 1874, which many cite as the year of Richelieu's discovery), he may have been a bit confused.

Judging by the history of the Richelieu Café, that is the case. For one thing, it didn't open until 1893 at the earliest, nine years after the drink first saw print. Furthermore, although the Richelieu went through three sets of proprietors until it closed in 1917, no Julio Richelieu was ever listed as being among them—indeed, he doesn't appear in San Francisco city directories at all. "Richelieu" was a popular name for swank cafes at the time, and Café Richelieus appear all over the country, so there need not have been an actual person of that name on the premises to give it its name. And of the dozen-odd newspaper articles I've been able to find touching on the place, not one makes any mention of its Martinis—or Martinezes.

Finally, there is the possibility that the drink was in some way connected with the man who ran New York's second-most expensive restaurant, the Maison Doree on Union Square, in the 1860s: His name, too, was Martinez.

Verdict: Unlikely, and will remain so until Martinez documents its claim.

THE JUDGE MARTINE THEORY

THE CLAIM: The Martini was invented at New York's Manhattan Club by a certain Judge Martine.

ORIGINS OF THE CLAIM: Advanced as a passing comment in the *New York Times*'s "About Clubs and Clubmen" column, July 24, 1904.

PRO: Randolph B. Martine (1844–1895), a New York judge and former district attorney, definitely existed, and he was (it so appears) a member of the Manhattan Club. He also liked a drink now and then, going by his public and outspoken opposition to the puritanical Dr. Parkhurst's attempt to enforce the Sunday closing of saloons—and, more important, by his status as a regular at Phil Milligan's Tenderloin District saloon, where "high-class sportsmen, the gambling fraternity and the 'sporty' elements of the Legislature and the Judiciary" congregated. This is not proof, to be sure, but it certainly does nothing to rule the judge out, either.

Beyond mere personal proclivity, there's some other confirming evidence. One of the earliest printed mentions of the Martini is in Harry Johnson's 1888 *New and Improved Illustrated Bartender's Manual*. In his book,

Johnson prints a recipe for the "Martini Cocktail"—yet, as Lowell Edmunds points out in his groundbreaking *Martini, Straight Up*, in the illustration of the drink it is labeled a "Martine Cocktail." Indeed, the Martine continues to appear as such in the occasional recipe book for another twenty years or so, including Charles Ranhofer's magisterial gastronomical compendium, *The Epicurean*, from 1893 (Ranhofer, as head chef at Delmonico's, was well placed to observe what the swells were drinking, and to page through his book is to gain the impression he was not given to making mistakes). And when the International Association of Bartenders met in Chicago that same year, it was the Martine that was among the items of their agenda, not the Martini (if the *Chicago Tribune* is to be believed).

CON: In 1884, Martine was reportedly "proud of the fact that nothing but champagne, in the way of alcoholic beverage, [had] crossed his lips for five years." Thus the *Albany Journal*, anyway, for what it's worth. The invention of the Martine Cocktail is not listed among the judge's accomplishments in his obituaries (on the other hand, to mention such a thing might have been considered a breach of judicial dignity) nor has my research turned up any other reference to this story. By the mid-1880s, vermouth and gin—or something, anyway—was traveling under the Martini moniker, as evidenced by an 1887 reference in the *Brooklyn Daily Eagle* to the "bewildering depths of the 'Martini cocktail,' " and this is certainly the name that ultimately prevailed. On the other hand, the drink's name could have been affected by its being compounded with Martini vermouth, available in New York since 1867 (in 1891, quite early in the drink's history, we find the *Washington Post* insisting that the drink had to be made with "the Martini vermouth")—or even by the widespread fame of the British Martini-Henry rifle. Hence the joke current in the 1890s about the visiting Brit who orders a "Winchester" when he wants a Martini ("I knew it was some sort of a demmed gun," he explains).

VERDICT: Possible, but not proven.

THE "TOUGH CLUB" THEORY

THE CLAIM: Gin and vermouth were first mixed at New York's Turf Club, a rather rowdy organization (hence the above nickname) for socially prominent gamblers that, from 1880 to 1883, occupied the Leonard Jerome mansion on the corner of Twenty-sixth Street and Madison Avenue (the same building that later housed the Manhattan Club and gave rise to the myth about Jennie Jerome having a hand in the Manhattan's creation). "Gambling was high there," later recalled "King of the Dudes" Evander Berry Wall, "so extravagant that after a few years the club went out of existence. But during its reign all other clubs in New York were deserted."

ORIGINS OF THE CLAIM: A Turf Club Cocktail made of gin and vermouth appears in the anonymous *How To Mix Drinks—Bar-Keeper's Handbook* published by the G. Winter Co in 1884—the same year the first reference to a Martinez appears.

PRO: The evaluation of this one relies on the existence of a certain amount of confusion between the Martini/Martinez (combining gin and vermouth) and the Manhattan (combining whiskey and vermouth) at the time those drinks were first coming to public notice.*

Case in point: The first known mention of the Manhattan (a September 1882 article from the Olean, New York, *Sunday Morning Herald*) notes that "It is but a short time ago that a mixture of whiskey, vermouth and bitters came into vogue" and that "It went under various names—Manhattan cocktail, Turf Club cocktail, and Jockey Club cocktail." On the other hand, there's the bartender interviewed some fifteen months later by the *Chicago Tribune*, who said, "Manhattan cocktails are in demand, too . . . I introduced them some time ago, and they have become quite popular. They are made of vermouth and gin." Therefore, whiskey + vermouth = gin + vermouth; a Manhattan = a Martini/Martinez; and a Martini/Martinez = a Turf Club. Got it? (As you may have noticed, I'm ignoring the Jockey Club. Why add to the madness? In any case, the Turf Club and the Jockey Club were in the same building.)

CON: Gin and vermouth went into the annals of mixology as a Martini, not a Turf Club. Also, as the drink's popularity grew, nobody ever stepped forward to claim the drink for the Turf Club. (On the other hand, the use of Martini vermouth might have affected the name; see the Judge Martine Theory. Also, the early dissolution of the Turf Club would've helped to take the name out of circulation. And if Thomas Burnett, the club's head bartender, was responsible for the invention he was in no position to take credit, seeing as he was killed in a train wreck in 1883, a couple of years before the drink really caught on.)

VERDICT: In a muddle like this, anything is possible.

---

*It may seem impossible to confuse gin and whiskey, but bear in mind that these drinks were mixed with a good deal of vermouth and bitters, which would help mask both color and flavor, and the malty, full-bodied gins in use in the 1880s were much closer to a young whiskey than the London dry gins in use now.

BIBLIOGRAPHICAL NOTE

A list of every book, pamphlet, article, item, blog, post, or squib I have consulted in the assembly of the present work would swell what is already a bulky text beyond any reasonable limits. To some degree, it would also be redundant: I have included sources for each of the recipes, and attempted to give enough information elsewhere to allow quotations to be tracked down by those determined to further pursue them. I will therefore not even attempt to list all the pre-Prohibition books and periodicals I have consulted in the two years I've spent writing this book, or the secondary sources I have turned to to corroborate what I found there.

There is, however, a clutch of modern books—by which I mean ones written after the close of the Saloon Age—that have very much helped me to form my views on Jerry Thomas and the drinks of his age (at least, the parts of those views that make sense), and I would be remiss in not citing them. William Grimes's *Straight Up or On the Rocks* (2001) is still the best connected narrative of the history of mixed drinking in America, followed by Gary Regan's introduction to *The Joy of Mixology* (2003). Lowell Edmunds's *Martini, Straight Up* (1998), Richard Barksdale Harwell's *The Mint Julep* (1975), and Guillermo Toro-Lira's *Alas de los querubines* (2006) are all invaluable monographs on essential drinks (the last is a history of Pisco Punch). Ted "Dr.

Cocktail" Haigh's *Vintage Spirits & Forgotten Cocktails* (2005) is an essential aide to exploring some of the byways of booze. Byron and Sharon Peregrine Johnson's pioneering *Wild West Bartenders' Bible* (1986) is still the best modern look at how you ran an old-time saloon. Henry Crowgey's *Kentucky Bourbon: The Early Years of Whiskeymaking* (1971) is thorough, accurate, and uninfected by bourbon jingoism. Stanley Clisby Arthur's 1937 *Famous New Orleans Drinks and How to Mix 'Em* is one of the first attempts to uncover the history of American drinks and still of great value. For any questions of technique, I have made a beeline to Dale DeGroff's *Craft of the Cocktail* (2002). If Dale can't do it, it can't be done.

The things that have made this possible though, are the computerized databases of nineteenth-century books and periodicals. As I noted in the Introduction, Cocktails, Punches, Fizzes, and the like were not considered worthy of headlines or historical attention, and their traces in the press of the day are well buried, if omnipresent. To dig them up the old-fashioned way, by scrolling through reel after reel of microfilm, is a lifetime's work. Thankfully, such a thing as Optical Character Recognition software exists, imperfect as it is. But with its help, this buried culture of the bar can be unearthed and examined. This is truly a revolution in the study of popular culture (if it can uncover something as trivial as the history of the Florodora Cooler, think what it can do with things that are *really* important, like the origins of jazz). In general, though, it should be noted that this technology is all very new and making it yield useful results requires persistence and often more ingenuity than I am able to command.

Two of the most useful and best-designed of these databases are also entirely free. The *Brooklyn Daily Eagle* was a beautifully written paper, and the Brooklyn Public Library has every issue from 1841 to 1902 (http://brooklynpubliclibrary.org/eagle) available online. Google Books is also easy to use, and the sheer number of obscure volumes available to search—and view in full text!—is staggering (http://books.google.com); and when you're done there, check out their patent search (www.google.com/patents); lots of cool barware. Equally useful and well-designed are the databases supplied by ProQuest for the *New York Times*, the *Chicago Tribune*, the *Washington Post*, and a handful of other urban dailies as well as a goodly collection of other old periodicals, including the indispensable *Police Gazette*. Unfortunately, some of these (the newspapers; check the individual papers' websites) are quite expensive, charging several dollars for articles that may or may not have what you are looking for and others (the American Periodical Series) cannot be accessed at home at all. As long as you're trooping off to a major research library, it's also worth having a look in the America's Historical Newspapers database. While ProQuest is better on the latter part of our period, this one is better on the earlier part.

Then there's NewspaperArchive (www.newspaperarchive.com). This one you can access at home, as much as you want for a quite reasonable yearly fee. Millions and millions of pages of American (and a few foreign) newspapers, all scanned and searchable. But the scanning is atrocious, frequently yielding gobbledygook (to be fair, their source microfilm is often illegible) and your results cannot be displayed in chronological order. In short, it requires the temperament of Buddha and the patience of a rock to wring meaningful results out of this resource, but there is more gold there for the collecting than anywhere else. (NewspaperArchive has few of the big urban papers and many, many small-town ones, but then as now these tended to run items from their city cousins.)

Finally, I must mention the Library of Congress's invaluable American Memory Collection, a massive pile of digital stuff that includes hundreds of travel books, newspapers, magazines, and other writings of precisely the sorts in which the history of mixology lurks (http://memory.loc.gov). Without these, and a number of others besides—the archives of the *Times* of London, the fantastic Internet Library of Early Journals (free at www.bodley.ox .ac.uk/ilej)—this would have been a far poorer, and thinner, book.

ACKNOWLEDGMENTS

I could not have done this by myself. Well, parts of it I could have—the
jumping to conclusions, the unsubstantiated opinionizing, the throwing my
hands up in the air and saying "Who the hell knows," all that stuff I can do
without any help whatsoever. But wherever I've managed to avoid that and
actually offer something substantial that makes sense, I've had help. I can't
thank everyone who pitched in here—hell, so may people have rallied around
this project that I can't even *remember* everyone (it doesn't help that a significant part of the road-testing was conducted in bars). In other words, if your
name is not on this list and should be, you have my sincere apologies and it's
my round.

There are some people without whom there would be no book at all. The
divine Ms. Theodora Sutcliffe, although contemplating a book on the Professor herself, was generous enough to share her research with me at a very early
stage, which infected me with the bug. Throughout this project, Dale De-
Groff has been my model of the perfect saloonkeeper, a wise and convivial
presence who can meet any challenge with confident good humor and compe-
tence; he and the Professor would have got along famously. My editor, Marian
Lizzi, has been patient beyond belief with a project that stretched far beyond
its appointed bounds; no author could hope for better. My agent, Janis

Donnaud, stuck with this celebration of the life and works of somebody few people have ever heard of until it found its perfect home. My fellow partners in Beverage Alcohol Resource, Dale (again), Doug Frost, Steve Olson, and Paul Pacult, displayed remarkable forbearance as my writing drew me away from our collective enterprise. Brendan Vaughan, Tara Q. Thomas, and David Mahoney, my editors at *Esquire*, *Wine & Spirits*, and *Drinks*, respectively, were similarly tolerant.

There are many, many other people who assisted in the research. Some—William Grimes, Angus Winchester, John C. Burton, and John Myers—lent or even outright gave me rare old bartender's guides, the essential building blocks of this book. Many others were kind enough to answer my queries, look things up for me or even send me items of interest even without my asking, among them Brian Rea, Gary Regan, Phil Greene (whose brother Ed procured me a copy of Dick & Fitzgerald's original 1859 copyright), Ted "Dr. Cocktail" Haigh (who provided lots of good advice and a few rare illustrations), Lowell Edmunds, George Thompson, Guillermo Toro-Lira, Robert Hess, Anistatia Miller & Jared Brown, Philip Duff of Bols (who generously sent me enough *corenwyn* to test the gin drinks), Chris McMillan, Paul Erickson, Jeff Pogash, John Burton (who graciously allowed me to use the business card of Jerry Thomas in his collection), Mauro Mahjoub, Jorg Meier, George Sinclair, Michael Waterhouse, Barry Popik, and David A. Smith of the New York Public Library.

Besides taking some wonderful photographs of vintage barware that we ultimately couldn't find space for, Nick Noyes has provided me with venues and support to test some many of the larger recipes herein, as have Melissa Clark and Sherwin Dunner. Audrey Saunders and her crew at Pegu Club and Julie Reiner and hers at the Flatiron Lounge have made many an old drink to my specifications and acted as sounding boards for my half-mixed theories, and it is at their establishments you will find me—there, or online with Robert Hess at his DrinkBoy board or with the cocktail geeks who loiter on www.egullet.com.

Finally, my wife, Karen, and my daughter, Marina. Thanks, guys (and Karen, now you can have the dining room back). Without you, the book would mean nothing.

A FEW
RECOLLECTIONS
OF THE DISTANT
PAST

The double Bronxes at the Holland House . . . the stingers at the Belmont . . . the silver fizzes at the Manhattan . . . the ginger-ale highballs at the bar of the Buckingham . . . the Benedictine at the Lafayette . . . the seidels of Münchner at Lüchows . . . the Navy Rainbows at Maxim's . . . the Château Yquem at Mouquin's . . . the Manhattan Cocktails at the Hotel Knickerbocker . . . the gin daisies at the Astor . . . the yellow chartreuse at the Brevoort . . . the Infuriators at the Beaux Arts . . . the pousse-cafés at Rector's . . . the Stone Fences at Churchill's . . . the milk punches at the Savoy . . . the Martinis at Sherry's . . . the champagne cocktails at Delmonico's . . . the Central Park Souths at the Plaza . . . the sherry flips at the Cadillac . . . the Clover Clubs at Bustanoby's . . . the Jack Roses at Eberlin's . . . the beakers of stout at Dinty Moore's . . . the Louis Röderer at Martin's . . . the mint juleps at the Casino . . . the kummel, with a dash of tabasco, at the Fifth Avenue . . . the Tom & Jerry at Shanley's . . . the Pilsener with scrambled eggs and Irish bacon at 5 a.m. at Jack's. . . .

—*Life* magazine, 1925

INDEX